FOR DUMMIES™

COMPUTER
BOOK SERIES
FROM IDG

AutoCAD For

D1429861

Cheat Sheet

The Standard Toolbar

Icon	Tool Tip	Purpose
	New	Creates a new file and opens it.
	Open	Opens an existing file.
	Save	Saves the current file.
	Print	Prints the current file.
	Spelling	Spell-checks.
	Cut	Cuts selected object(s) to the Clipboard.
	Copy	Copies selected object(s) to the Clipboard.
	Paste	Pastes previously cut or copied object(s).
	Undo	Undoes previous action.
	Redo	Redoes previous undo.
	Tool Windows	Turns aerial view, toolbars on/off.
	Select Object	Starts different object selection methods.
	Object Group	Creates an object grouping.
	Object Snap	Uses an object snap mode.
	Point Filters	Uses a point filter.
	UCS	Changes User Coordinate System.
	View	Creates or switches to a view.
	Redraw	Redraws the current view or all views.
	Pan	Pans the drawing in the current view.
	Zoom In	Zooms closer in.
	Zoom Out	Zooms farther out.
	Zoom Window	Zooms to a window.
	Zoom	Zooms to show all objects, limits.
	Space	Changes from model to paper space.
	Help	Starts AutoCAD Help.

AutoCAD For Dummies

Cheat Sheet

The Object Properties Toolbar

Icon	Tool Tip	Purpose
	Layers	Opens Layer Control dialog box.
	Layer Control	Icon-based control of layer options.
	Color Control	Opens Select Color dialog box.
	Linetype	Opens Select Linetype dialog box.
BYLAYER	Linetype Control	Directs choice of linetype.
	Object Creation	Opens Object Creation Modes dialog box.
	Multiline Style	Opens Multiline Styles dialog box.
	Properties	Selects objects; opens Modify dialog box.
	Inquiry	Selects objects; performs inquiry.

Ten AutoCAD Commands

Command	Purpose
NEW	Creates a new file and opens it.
QSAVE	Saves current file to current name; no options.
UNDO	Undoes last step or number of steps.
REDRAW	Redraws current viewport from display list.
REGEN	Recreates display list; redraws current viewport.
ZOOM	Zooms in or out; Dynamic option pans, too.
PAN	Pans left, right, up, down; draws line to indicate direction and distance.
LINE/PLINE	Draws line segments as separate objects/single object.
ARC	Creates an arc.
CIRCLE	Creates a circle.

Six AutoCAD Dialog Boxes

Command	Dialog Box Name	Purpose
DDIM	Dimension Styles	Sets options for dimensioning.
DDLMODES	Layer Control	Creates, sets options for layers.
DDMODIFY	Modify <object type>	Sets options such as color, layer, linetype, thickness for objects; additional options depend on the type of object selected.
DDOSNAP	Running Object Snap	Turns object snaps on and off.
DDRMODES	Drawing Aids	Sets modes for current drawing such as Blips, Groups; controls Snap and Grid.
DDVPOINT	Viewpoint Presets	Changes the viewing angle; best used for 3D objects.

IDG BOOKS

. . . For Dummies: #1 Computer Book Series for Beginners

References for the Rest of Us

COMPUTER BOOK SERIES FROM IDG

Are you intimidated and confused by computers? Do you find that traditional manuals are overloaded with technical details you'll never use? Do your friends and family always call you to fix simple problems on their PCs? Then the . . . *For Dummies*™ computer book series from IDG is for you.

. . . *For Dummies* books are written for those frustrated computer users who know they aren't really dumb but find that PC hardware, software, and indeed the unique vocabulary of computing make them feel helpless. . . . *For Dummies* books use a lighthearted approach, a down-to-earth style, and even cartoons and humorous icons to diffuse computer novices' fears and build their confidence. Lighthearted but not lightweight, these books are a perfect survival guide for anyone forced to use a computer.

> *"I like my copy so much I told friends; now they bought copies."*
>
> **Irene C., Orwell, Ohio**

> *"Quick, concise, nontechnical, and humorous."*
>
> **Jay A., Elburn, Illinois**

> *"Thanks, I needed this book. Now I can sleep at night."*
>
> **Robin F., British Columbia, Canada**

Already, hundreds of thousands of satisfied readers agree. They have made . . . *For Dummies* books the #1 introductory level computer book series and have written asking for more. So if you're looking for the most fun and easy way to learn about computers, look to . . . *For Dummies* books to give you a helping hand.

AutoCAD
FOR
DUMMIES™

AutoCAD FOR DUMMIES™

by Bud Smith

IDG BOOKS

IDG Books Worldwide, Inc.
An International Data Group Company

Foster City, CA♦ Chicago, IL ♦ Indianapolis, IN ♦ Braintree, MA ♦ Dallas, TX

AutoCAD For Dummies™

Published by
IDG Books Worldwide, Inc.
An International Data Group Company
919 E. Hillsdale Blvd.,
Suite 400
Foster City, CA 94404

Library of Congress Catalog Card No.: 94-79312

ISBN: 1-56884-191-4

Printed in the United States of America

10 9 8 7 6 5 4 3 2 1

1A/RY/QR/ZV

Distributed in the United States by IDG Books Worldwide, Inc.

Distributed by Macmillan Canada for Canada; by Computer and Technical Books for the Caribbean Basin; by Contemporanea de Ediciones for Venezuela; by Distribuidora Cuspide for Argentina; by CITEC for Brazil; by Ediciones ZETA S.C.R. Ltda. for Peru; by Editorial Limusa SA for Mexico; by Transworld Publishers Limited in the United Kingdom and Europe; by Al-Maiman Publishers & Distributors for Saudi Arabia; by Simron Pty. Ltd. for South Africa; by IDG Communications (HK) Ltd. for Hong Kong; by Toppan Company Ltd. for Japan; by Addison Wesley Publishing Company for Korea; by Longman Singapore Publishers Ltd. for Singapore, Malaysia, Thailand and Indonesia; by Unalis Corporation for Taiwan; by WS Computer Publishing Company, Inc. for the Philippines; by WoodsLane Pty. Ltd. for Australia; by WoodsLane Enterprises Ltd. for New Zealand.

For general information on IDG Books in the U.S., including information on discounts and premiums, contact IDG Books at 800-434-3422 or 415-655-3000.

For information on where to purchase IDG Books outside the U.S., contact IDG Books International at 415-655-3021 or fax 415-655-3295.

For information on translations, contact Marc Jeffrey Mikulich, Director, Foreign & Subsidiary Rights, at IDG Books Worldwide, 415-655-3018 or fax 415-655-3295.

For sales inquiries and special prices for bulk quantities, write to the address above or call IDG Books Worldwide at 415-655-3000.

For information on using IDG Books in the classroom, or ordering examination copies, contact Jim Kelly at 800-434-2086.

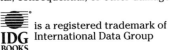

About the Author

Bud Smith

A long-time computer user whose initial experience as a data-entry clerk led to work as a programmer, technical writer, computer journalist, and market analyst, Bud Smith is quite at home around computers — even those loaded with programs as complex as AutoCAD. *AutoCAD For Dummies* is his seventh book about AutoCAD and computers in general.

Welcome to the world of IDG Books Worldwide.

IDG Books Worldwide, Inc. is a subsidiary of International Data Group, the world's largest publisher of computer-related information and the leading global provider of information services on information technology. IDG was founded more than 25 years ago and now employs more than 7,000 people worldwide. IDG publishes more than 220 computer publications in 65 countries (see listing below). More than fifty million people read one or more IDG publications each month.

Launched in 1990, IDG Books Worldwide is today the #1 publisher of best-selling computer books in the United States. We are proud to have received 3 awards from the Computer Press Association in recognition of editorial excellence, and our best-selling *...For Dummies*™ series has more than 12 million copies in print with translations in 25 languages. IDG Books, through a recent joint venture with IDG's Hi-Tech Beijing, became the first U.S. publisher to publish a computer book in the People's Republic of China. In record time, IDG Books has become the first choice for millions of readers around the world who want to learn how to better manage their businesses.

Our mission is simple: Every IDG book is designed to bring extra value and skill-building instructions to the reader. Our books are written by experts who understand and care about our readers. The knowledge base of our editorial staff comes from years of experience in publishing, education, and journalism — experience which we use to produce books for the '90s. In short, we care about books, so we attract the best people. We devote special attention to details such as audience, interior design, use of icons, and illustrations. And because we use an efficient process of authoring, editing, and desktop publishing our books electronically, we can spend more time ensuring superior content and spend less time on the technicalities of making books.

You can count on our commitment to deliver high-quality books at competitive prices on topics consumers want to read about. At IDG, we value quality, and we have been delivering quality for more than 25 years. You'll find no better book on a subject than an IDG book.

John J. Kilcullen

John Kilcullen
President and CEO
IDG Books Worldwide, Inc.

Acknowledgments

The staff at IDG Books, especially Janna Custer up front and Bill Barton at the end, has been extraordinarily patient, supportive, and flexible in getting a solid book out of a sometimes recalcitrant author. Thanks, everyone.

This book could not have been written without the benefit of my previous AutoCAD writing experience with Mark Middlebrook of Daedalus Consulting and Jake Richter of Panacea, Inc. I'd buy these guys a beer, but Mark brews his own, and Jake mostly drinks cranberry juice and saki, so I'll just say thank you.

Thanks also go to Ellen Finkelstein for her called-in-at-the-last-minute emergency review of the second half of the manuscript while this author was away in Japan. Good job!

(The Publisher would like to give special thanks to Patrick J. McGovern, without whom this book would not have been possible.)

Dedication

This book is for my loving wife, Jacyn, and the kids, James and Veronica. It's been said that it takes a whole village to raise a child. It also takes a whole family to write a book, and never more so than on this one. Thanks, you guys.

Credits

**Executive Vice President,
Strategic Planning
and Research**
David Solomon

Editorial Director
Diane Graves Steele

Acquisitions Editor
Megg Bonar

Brand Manager
Judith A. Taylor

Editorial Managers
Tracy L. Barr
Sandra Blackthorn

Editorial Assistants
Tamara S. Castleman
Stacey Holden Prince
Kevin Spencer

Acquisitions Assistant
Suki Gear

Production Director
Beth Jenkins

Project Coordinator
Valery Bourke

Pre-Press Coordinators
Tony Augsburger
Steve Peake

Project Editor
William A. Barton

Editor
Mike Kelly

Technical Reviewer
Randy Bush, Autodesk Training

Production Staff
Paul Belcastro
Cameron Booker
Sherry Gomoll
Barry C. Jorden
Mark Owens
Carla Radzikinas
Dwight Ramsey
Patricia R. Reynolds
Theresa Sanchez-Baker
Gina Scott

Proofreader
Jennifer Kaufeld

Indexer
Anne Leach

Cover Design
Kavish + Kavish

Contents at a Glance

Cartoons at a Glance

By Rich Tennant

Page 9

Page 121

Page 205

Page 263

Page 305

Page 321

Page 100

Page 190

Page 234

Page 314

Table of Contents

Introduction

 A utoCAD is kind of an amazing thing. It was dreamed up at a time when most people thought that personal computers weren't all that big a deal and when even someone who liked PCs would hardly dream of pushing them to do something as hard as CAD (*Computer-Aided Design*, that is). But AutoCAD, to the surprise of many, was a hit from its first day and has grown to define a whole new way of creating architectural, mechanical, geographical, and other kinds of drawings.

In its evolution, however, AutoCAD has also grown complex and somewhat difficult to use. Recent versions of AutoCAD attempt to fix this problem. This book attempts to bridge some of the remaining gap that still exists between AutoCAD and the rest of the world of PC software. This book won't tell you how to become an AutoCAD maven, but it will show you where some of the bones are buried from AutoCAD's difficult-to-use past — and, more important, how to step around them. With this book, you actually have a chance of creating an attractive, usable, and printable drawing without putting a T-square through your computer screen in frustration.

About This Book

This book is not designed to be read straight through, from cover to cover. It's designed as a reference book so that you can dip in and out of it as you run into new topics. Look for the part that contains the information you want, narrow your search down to a specific chapter, find out what you need to know, and then get back to work. This book is not designed to be comprehensive either. Thousands of pages of documentation are required to describe completely how to use AutoCAD, and the resulting proliferation of weighty manuals and third-party books just leaves most people confused.

You don't need to memorize anything or correlate scads of information from dozens of separate chapters, books, and manuals either. Just look up what you need to know in these handy pages and get right back to work. (Did I already say that? Well, it bears repeating!)

How to Use This Book

AutoCAD is bound to leave you confused at some point. If you're new to the program, the first time you click an icon and only a prompt shows up on a command line, you may wonder whether something's wrong with your computer. Slightly more experienced users are likely to trip up on the intricate relationship between setup, drawing, and printing. And sometimes even experts may stumble over the details of paper space or making things work well in 3D.

Use the table of contents and the index in this book to find the topic that stumps you. Go to that section and read up on the topic. Usually, you'll find a set of steps, a picture, or a description of how to do the task that's troubling you — and often, you'll find all three. (How's that for service?) Use that section to get yourself back on track and then close the book and go on.

What's Not in This Book

Unlike many other ...*For Dummies* books, this one *does* tell you to consult the manuals sometimes. AutoCAD is just too big and complicated for a single book to attempt to describe it completely (though a few of the 1,000-page-plus tomes some companies put out on AutoCAD certainly try). Make no mistake about it: AutoCAD is a beast, a huge program/environment that is an entire world of computing unto itself. So occasionally, this book points you off to the manuals for more detailed or advanced information.

This book is also carefully restricted as to which versions of AutoCAD it covers. This book does not talk about AutoCAD's less-capable, lower-cost sibling, AutoCAD LT, except for some general discussion in Chapters 1 and 19. Among AutoCAD's many releases, this book focuses primarily on Release 13, the newest and easiest-to-use version of the program. This book does cover Release 13 versions of both AutoCAD for DOS and AutoCAD for Windows, because many readers have both versions — or start out with one and move to the other — but it doesn't cover the higher-end features such as customization, add-on programs that make new features available, and other complicated areas.

Please Don't Read This!

Sprinkled through the book are icons labeled *Technical Stuff.* These icons alert you to discussions of minute detail that are unlikely to concern you unless you're a confirmed AutoCAD techno-nerd. As you slowly advance to expert status, however, you may find yourself going back through the book to read all that technical stuff. (At that point, you may also want to ask your boss for a vacation, because you just may be working a little *too* hard.)

Who Are—and Aren't—You?

AutoCAD has a large, loyal, and dedicated group of long-time users. For the most part, this book is *not* for these long-time members of the AutoCAD faithful. This book is probably not for you if . . .

✔ You were using AutoCAD when it still had versions instead of releases.

✔ You have lectured at AutoCAD University.

✔ You are a registered AutoCAD developer.

✔ You read all those 1,000-page-plus technical tomes about AutoCAD for pleasure.

✔ You have made suggestions for AutoCAD changes in the Wish List and had them incorporated in a subsequent release.

✔ After your suggestion was incorporated into the program, you sent e-mail to Autodesk explaining how they did it wrong.

If you *don't* fall into any of these categories, well, this is *definitely* the book for you.

Whether you use the DOS or Windows version of AutoCAD, however, you do need to have *some* idea of how to use your computer system before tackling AutoCAD—and this book. (*Total* novices need not apply.) You need already to know how to copy and delete files, create a subdirectory, and find a file. You need to know how to use a mouse to select (highlight) or to choose (activate) commands and other items. If a Windows user, you should also know how to use the mouse to close a window and to minimize and maximize windows. If not, run—don't walk—to your nearest bookstore and pick up IDG Books' *DOS For Dummies, 2nd Edition,* and *Windows 3.1 For Dummies, 2nd Edition,* and try to learn some basics before you start with AutoCAD. (At least have those books handy as you start using this book.)

How This Book Is Organized

This book is really well-organized. Well, at least it's organized. Well, okay, I drew some circles on the floor, threw up scraps of paper with different ideas and topics on them, and organized the book by which scrap landed in which circle.

Seriously, its organization into Parts is one of the most important, well, *parts* of this book. You really *can* learn AutoCAD one piece at a time, and each Part represents a group of closely related topics. The order of Parts also says something about priority; yes, you have my permission to ignore the stuff in later Parts until you've learned most of the stuff in the early ones. This kind of building-block approach can be especially valuable in a program as complex as AutoCAD.

The book breaks down into the following parts:

Part I: AutoCAD 101

Need to know your way around the AutoCAD screen, whether you use AutoCAD for DOS or AutoCAD for Windows? Why does AutoCAD even exist anyway? Which version should I use? Is everything so *slooow* just because it's supposed to be slow, or do I have too wimpy a machine to truly use this wonder of modern-day computing? And why am I doing this in the first place?

Part I answers all those questions — and more. This Part also includes what may seem like a great deal of excruciating detail about setting up your drawing. But what's even more excruciating is to do your setup work incorrectly and then have the printer laugh at you as you attempt to print that final version of the drawings due the next day at 9 a.m. (And let me tell you, a Hewlett-Packard pen plotter can click its pen advance mechanism in a rhythm eerily reminiscent of an evil chuckle.) Read this stuff.

Part II: Let There Be Lines

This is "real" AutoCAD — drawing two-dimensional lines, circles, rectangles, and so on, all of which become a CAD drawing that represents a real-world design. After you get these lines and circles, also known as *geometry,* down, you'll undoubtedly want to learn to edit and view your drawing. Or someone else's drawing. Or something. This Part has you covered.

Part III: Make Your Drawing Beautiful

AutoCAD has more ways to gussy up a drawing than you can ever think of. And maybe more than you need. Text, dimensions, and hatch patterns all contribute to the appearance of your drawings. This Part helps you find your way through the maze of possibilities to a good solution. It then tells you how to get the drawing off your screen, out through a plotter, and onto paper where it belongs.

Part IV: Having It Your Way

All right, I admit it: This Part is less than perfectly organized. The main relationship between paper space, blocks and external references to data, and 3D is that they're all things you can probably wait to learn until after you've mastered the basics of making AutoCAD work. They're also powerful features that would be nearly inconceivable in old-style, pencil-and-paper design and drafting. Dip in and out of this Part to experiment and do even more neat things with AutoCAD.

Part V: Part of Tens

Everyone loves lists, unless it's the overdue list at the local library. This Part contains several lists of things relating to AutoCAD. Is that tightly related or loosely related? You be the judge.

Icons Used in This Book

Icons, once confined to computer screens, have escaped and are now running amok in the pages of this book. (Yeah, I know icons started out in print in the first place, but computer people stole them fair and square. Now the publishers are getting even.) These icons are like the ones in AutoCAD for Windows, except that they're fewer, simpler, and used more consistently. (Who, me, an attitude problem?) The icons used in this book are as follows:

This icon points out places where you may find more data than information. Unless you're *really* ready to learn more about AutoCAD — a *lot* more—steer clear of these.

This icon tells you that a pointed insight lies ahead that can save you time and trouble as you use AutoCAD. For example, maybe learning how to type with your nose would help increase your speed in entering commands and moving the mouse at the same time. (And maybe not . . .)

This icon tells you how to stay out of trouble when living a little close to the edge. Failure to heed its message could have disastrous consequences for you, your drawing, your computer — and maybe even all three.

Remember when Spock put his hand over McCoy's face and implanted a suggestion in his brain that later saved his (Spock's) life? This is like that. Helpful reminders of things you've already learned but that may not be right at the tip of your brain . . . or whatever.

"Not DOS" means, quite simply, that the topic of that paragraph applies only to AutoCAD for Windows. AutoCAD is adding more and more features that work only with AutoCAD for Windows, and this icon warns you when one of those features is about to be described.

This icon tells you how to do things from the keyboard instead of by using menus, toolbars, or whatever. The keyboard stuff is usually hard to remember, but quicker to use.

This icon points to new stuff in AutoCAD Release 13. It's mostly designed for scanners who know AutoCAD pretty well already and just want to find out what's new in this release, but other people may find this interesting, too.

A Few Conventions — Just in Case

You probably already know all the information I'm about to impart in this section, but just in case you don't, here it is.

Text you type into the program, at the command line, in a dialog box text box, and so on, appears in **boldface type**. Actions for you to take that are listed on the AutoCAD command line, such as using the mouse to select something on-screen, appear in *italics type* (usually surrounded by angle brackets) in the examples of AutoCAD commands and prompts. I should also mention that these examples appear in a `special typeface`, as does any other text in the book that echoes a message, a word, or one or more lines of text that actually appear on-screen. (Longer segments also have a shaded background.)

Sidebars also are set off in their own typeface, with a fancy head all their own, and are surrounded by a shaded box, much like this:

This is a sidebar head

And this is how the text in a sidebar appears. Neat, huh? Well, different at least. Hey, two-column text can be pretty nifty all on its own, even without peripheral AutoCAD material to occupy its space! What? You don't buy that? Oh, well, back to our main event then.

Regarding menus and menu items or commands, if you're told to *open* a menu or *choose* a command, you can use any number of methods to do so — pressing a shortcut key combination on the keyboard, clicking the menu or command name with the mouse, highlighting the name by moving over it with the cursor arrow keys and pressing Enter — whatever way you're most comfortable with. Sometimes I'll tell you to do it a certain way, because that's how I, as the AutoCAD expert (ahem), think it's done best. But if you know what I'm talking about, feel free to do it your way instead. (And if it doesn't work, of course, you didn't hear this from me.) Oh, and often in this book you'll see phrases such as "choose Data⇨ Layers from the menu bar." The funny little arrow (⇨) separates the main menu name from the specific command on that menu. Here you would open the Data menu and choose the Layers command. The underlined letters (in Windows only) are the *hotkeys*—keys you can press in combination with the Alt key to open menus and activate commands. (See Chapter 17 for more information.)

Well, that should cover the basics. The details, ah, those are yet to come. And believe me when I tell you with the utmost sincerity that you have *much* to look forward to . . . (Cue lightning, thunder, and a low moan from the nether regions of your computer.)

Where to Go from Here?

If you've read this Introduction, you're probably at least a little bit like me: You like to read. (People who don't like to read usually skip this front matter stuff and use the table of contents and index to get to exactly, and only, the part they need.) So take a few more minutes to page through and look for interesting stuff. And pick up a pen and some sticky notes; the icons and headings in this book are only a start. You should personalize your book by circling vital tips, drawing a smiley face if you like a joke, even X-ing out stuff that you disagree with. (And I've hidden lots of my own opinions in this book, so get those Xs ready.)

Part I
AutoCAD 101

In this part...

AutoCAD is more than just another application program — it's a complete environment for design and drafting. So if you're new to AutoCAD, or just new to Release 13, you need to learn a few things to get off to a good start. Even the experienced user can benefit from taking another look at AutoCAD's different versions and the basics of setting up and configuring the program — all neatly separated from the actual mechanics of drawing and other things that seem more like real work.

Chapter 1
The AutoCAD Family Tree

The first thing you need to know about AutoCAD is that it's not just another software program. AutoCAD is, in fact, a complete drawing environment that engages in a sometimes friendly, sometimes antagonistic relationship with you, with the hardware on which it runs, and with all the other software installed on your computer.

On a good day, you may agree that AutoCAD is simply a *wonderful* tool — one of the more important extensions of the human intellect yet committed to software. On a bad day, however, you may decide that AutoCAD is in truth the world's largest computer virus — and start looking for ways to terminate it with extreme prejudice.

Autodesk, the company that makes AutoCAD, sells several different versions of the product. The multiple versions exist partly for historical reasons, partly to offer a range of price and performance alternatives, and partly, as is true of any successful business, as a way to extract money from as many people's pockets as possible. To get a good start with AutoCAD, however, you need to understand the differences between the versions available and the capabilities of each version. (This way, when you hurl curses at the program, you can at least know that you're cursing the right version.)

DOS and Don'ts

MS-DOS is, of course, the original operating system for all IBM-compatible computers. DOS, in fact, is the culprit directly responsible for the C : \> prompt that we all know and love so much — not! AutoCAD for DOS is the first and most successful version of AutoCAD, with a current installed base of more than a million users.

Because DOS doesn't do much—compared, that is, to graphical environments such as Windows—AutoCAD for DOS must provide its own support for additional hardware devices such as graphics accelerator boards, printers and plotters, mouses and digitizer tablets, and just about anything else you may want to add to your basic, unadorned PC. (But don't worry. You get tips on installation, which tells AutoCAD how to talk to those pesky devices, in Appendix A.) AutoCAD for DOS also features a unique semigraphical display, (which looks a little like Windows with a hangover), as shown in Figure 1-1.

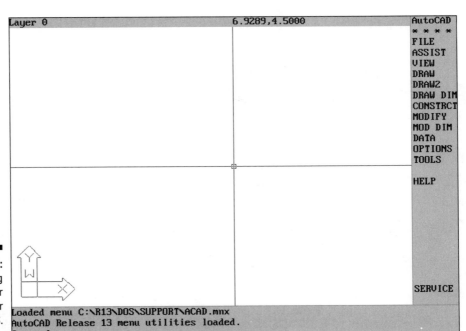

Figure 1-1:
The starting
screen for
AutoCAD for
DOS.

The problems involved in coaxing all the hardware and software to work together has kept hundreds of AutoCAD dealers in business for more than ten years now. (The difficulty of making AutoCAD work right may, in fact, be why the program isn't pirated even more than it already is.) But more and more, users shop around for the lowest prices on AutoCAD and then configure the program themselves. (This task, of course, is about as easy — and as painless — as, say, removing a loose tooth with a rusty wrench. Ouch!)

The good news about AutoCAD for DOS

AutoCAD currently is the world's leading PC *computer-aided design* (or *CAD*) program. (And here you thought a CAD program was something that taught people to be rude.) Its status as world champ rests almost entirely on the laurels of AutoCAD for DOS. This version of the program still retains its main selling points, which include the following features:

- **Speed:** Many CAD models are extremely complex, so speed is crucial. Starting with Release 13, AutoCAD for DOS includes a built-in graphics accelerator program, called a *display list processor*. (In Release 12, only AutoCAD for Windows did.) With its display list processor — and freed from the memory-eating overhead imposed by Windows — AutoCAD for DOS is the fastest version of AutoCAD available for IBM-compatibles.

- **Lower hardware requirements:** AutoCAD for DOS requires less hardware support than does AutoCAD for Windows. You can, in fact, grit your teeth and run it at glacial speeds on an old-style 386 microprocessor with a 387 math coprocessor and only 8MB of memory — if you *really* want to — but a 486DX with 12MB of memory works *much* better.

- **Extensive hardware support:** You have available right at your fingertips a huge range of hardware that works directly with AutoCAD for DOS. In many cases, graphics boards, digitizers, plotters, and other such hardware devices come with their own software *drivers* — small software programs that can make hardware really sing — that are specially tuned just for AutoCAD.

- **An abundance of third-party applications:** Of all the existing CAD programs on the market today, AutoCAD for DOS claims the greatest number of available *third-party applications* — add-on software programs that help AutoCAD work even more efficiently for specific usages such as architectural work, mechanical design, or even genetic reengineering.

- **A highly customizable interface:** AutoCAD for DOS supports all of AutoCAD's customization interfaces, including the built-in AutoLISP programming language and support for programs written in the popular C language. (AutoLISP is the original programming language for customizing AutoCAD.) Many shareware programs are available for the DOS version, as well as a huge number of commercial add-ons.

✔ **A mammoth infrastructure:** Most available help resources, including books, training centers, videotaped training courses, and consulting expertise, still focus primarily on AutoCAD for DOS. Although AutoCAD for Windows is catching up in this area, obtaining expert help for the DOS version is easier by far.

Hey, what's a third-party application?

A *third-party application,* in case I lost you with the term, is an add-on program that runs on top of AutoCAD. The add-on provides AutoCAD with additional capabilities or features, such as drawing management, setup routines, layer management, and custom features for use in architecture, mechanical design, geographic information systems, and other disciplines.

Because AutoCAD is somewhat naked without such programs, AutoCAD by itself is often called *bare* AutoCAD. This is appropriate because, for many users, running AutoCAD without any third-party application is about as comforting as going to work without your clothes on.

If you run a third-party application on AutoCAD, most of the information you find in this book still applies, but additional functions also may be available to you. But sorry — you'll still need to read the documentation that comes with your third-party application. As a bonus, however, that third-party application may even smooth over a few of AutoCAD's rougher edges.

The bad news about AutoCAD for DOS

In spite of its strengths, AutoCAD for DOS does have some major problems. These problems help explain why Autodesk is moving to Windows as its major AutoCAD platform for the future. Count the following liabilities among the DOS version's negatives:

✔ **Configuration nightmares:** Trying to entice DOS, AutoCAD, various third-party applications, different pieces of hardware, and any custom drivers you need all to work together while sidestepping the DOS 640K memory limit, using AutoCAD's built-in memory extenders, is a task that ranges anywhere from hard to impossible. (You can somewhat reduce this configuration problem by using hardware components that are specifically recommended for use with AutoCAD, but — hey! — PCs are supposed to be *flexible,* right?)

Note: AutoCAD requires a very specific memory setup that can be hard to make work right. The program also uses custom device drivers that may conflict with other drivers in your computer system. Most people who really, really hate AutoCAD have lost a significant part of their sanity attempting to coax AutoCAD for DOS into working with troublesome hardware and software combinations.

✔ **Harder to use:** No version of AutoCAD is truly easy to use, but the DOS version is especially difficult. Even after you fumble through all the configuration difficulties that often occur, using AutoCAD for DOS is both hard to learn and easy to forget, especially without regular use.

✔ **No multitasking capabilities:** AutoCAD for DOS limits you to working only in AutoCAD and only on one drawing at a time. You probably want to do other tasks, too, such as reading your e-mail, looking at another drawing, reconfiguring your hardware, playing a quick game of Doom, or even editing a database. The impossibility of performing other work without leaving AutoCAD is a big drawback of the DOS version of the program.

✔ **Poor interaction with other programs:** AutoCAD for DOS must have morning breath; it doesn't interact well with other programs. In fact, AutoCAD for DOS doesn't even support the simple task of cutting and pasting between programs, let alone the other, more advanced features possible under Windows.

The bottom line on DOS

Much of the personal computing world is rapidly moving to Windows and leaving DOS behind— much like a political candidate who buys a plane ticket when an unpopular president comes to town to campaign. AutoCAD is doing the same thing. AutoCAD for DOS already trails the Windows version in overall usability; it soon will trail Windows in available features, third-party support, and all other important categories, except higher speed and lower hardware requirements.

If you're using AutoCAD for DOS, your best bet for continuing viability is to plan now to upgrade to AutoCAD for Windows sometime in the next couple years — if not sooner. Planning on buying a new computer or changing to a new release of AutoCAD in the very near future? Take my advice: Switch to the Windows version then. (You'll be glad you did.)

Windows Wins?

Windows is Microsoft's wildly successful add-on to DOS. Windows enhances an IBM-compatible PC with many of the graphical, easy-to-use features familiar to Macintosh users. Although it's still the "new kid on the block" compared to the DOS version, AutoCAD for Windows is off to a fast start and, in fact, is now the second-most popular version of AutoCAD, boasting more than 100,000 users.

Autodesk now reports that Windows is its number-one strategic platform for the future of AutoCAD, and the company seems to be trying to make the move as desirable as possible for users. Third-party application support for the Windows version is catching up reasonably well, too, although DOS is likely to enjoy the lead in such support for a while yet.

AutoCAD for Windows features a nifty interface that initially gives the program an appearance similar to that of any other well-behaved, albeit complex, Windows application. Figure 1-2 shows the initial AutoCAD for Windows screen; compare it to the AutoCAD for DOS screen to see how much nicer this one looks.

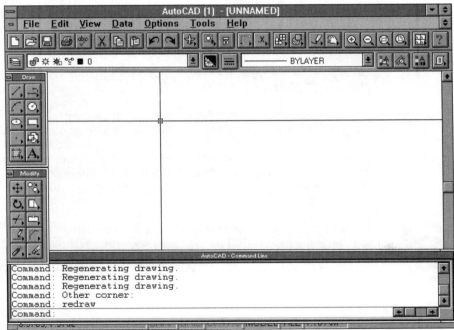

Figure 1-2:
The starting screen for AutoCAD for Windows.

The good news about AutoCAD for Windows

Experienced and new users alike are switching to AutoCAD for Windows by the tens of thousands. The reasons for this migration include the program's following advantages:

✔ **It's Windows, stupid:** Windows is the success story of the '90s, and all the reasons that users are moving to Windows and Windows applications apply to AutoCAD as well. Easier hardware configuration and support, ease of use, multitasking capabilities with other programs, and the removal of the DOS 640K memory barrier are only a few of the reasons AutoCAD for Windows is a good idea.

✔ **Additional features:** With AutoCAD for Windows, you can perform several tasks that the DOS version can't even attempt, such as keeping open several drawings at once, displaying an aerial view of a drawing, and running a built-in tutorial.

✔ **Interoperability:** Windows adds more and more support for operating between programs, and AutoCAD benefits greatly from this support. By using a Windows feature called *object linking and embedding* (*OLE*), for example, you can open an AutoCAD drawing from within a Word document — but only if you own AutoCAD for Windows, of course! (As the company that makes AutoCAD, Autodesk simply *loves* this kind of stuff.)

✔ **Even more highly customizable:** AutoCAD for Windows supports all the ridiculously large numbers of DOS customization interfaces. And Windows-specific features such as OLE give you even more control over your PC environment.

The bad news about AutoCAD for Windows

Yes, despite how wonderful Windows is, AutoCAD for Windows hasn't quite solved all the problems inherent in AutoCAD — and even loses some of the pluses of the DOS version:

✔ **It's still somewhat clumsy:** Some features of even this version—how you select multiple items for example—function more like those of AutoCAD for DOS than of any other Windows program ever written. These differences make moving back and fourth smoothly between AutoCAD for DOS and other programs difficult.

✔ **It's bigger and slower:** As is the case with any Windows program, AutoCAD for Windows is a virtual glutton for hard disk space, megabytes of memory, and processing power, even compared to the DOS version. Autodesk, however, has tried hard, with at least moderate success, to minimize the differences between the two versions.

✔ **Less third-party hardware and software available:** Writers of hardware device drivers and add-on software applications have been slow to jump onto the Windows bandwagon. You can still find more drivers and add-on applications for AutoCAD for DOS than for its Windows-based cousin.

> ✔ **Less technical support:** Available help resources, such as trainers, book writers, and other Autodesk hangers-on, are still largely stuck back in the DOS world. And that grizzled AutoCAD veteran down the hall from you is likely to know far more about the DOS version of AutoCAD than he does the Windows version.

The bottom line on Windows

AutoCAD for Windows is unquestionably where the action is. Whether you're running under "regular" Windows or the newer, souped up Windows NT (described in the following section), you're on the leading edge of the CAD crowd. Life with AutoCAD is certain to get better from here on. If you're already in Windows-land, stick with it; if not, now is high time to hop on the bus. (So what are you waiting for . . . ?)

Windows NT: Nearly Time? (Or "NoT"?)

Windows NT is the more powerful younger sibling of Windows. Although few people currently use Windows NT, it has long been expected to become a rousing success in the near future. (Unfortunately, the near future has continued to elude us so far.) The upcoming Windows 95, however, may be the *real* long-term success story.

On the surface, AutoCAD for Windows NT is virtually indistinguishable from AutoCAD for Windows. The plusses and minuses of the program largely mirror those of Windows NT itself. NT also supports the use of multiple microprocessors on a single machine, greatly aiding performance. It offers security features that "regular" Windows lacks and is less likely to crash. But NT uses a *lot* of memory and is incompatible with some hardware devices and third-party add-on programs.

AutoCAD for Windows NT is not a good choice for most users. In the long term, AutoCAD's future may very well depend on Windows NT, or other versions of AutoCAD may use it less centrally as a processing server. But unless you're an expert who knows exactly what NT can do for you, you're best off sticking to the plain-vanilla version of Windows.

LT: Lower-Tech, but LighT on the Wallet

AutoCAD LT for Windows is a "light" (or "lite," depending on your preference) version of AutoCAD for Windows. With a street price of less than $400 — compared to $3,000 or so for "full" AutoCAD for DOS or Windows — and fewer hardware requirements, LT is in many ways a real bargain. LT is also the only CAD program costing less than $3,000 that offers full native support for the DWG file format used by regular AutoCAD to store drawings.

So what's missing? Some three-dimensional features, the capability to open multiple drawings, a few other minor features, and almost every single programming interface that exists in full AutoCAD. Its lack of programming interfaces means no shareware, no third-party applications, and no customizing capabilities for AutoCAD LT.

Just as significant is the fact that Autodesk seems to update LT more slowly than it does most of its other AutoCAD products. So AutoCAD LT users often must wait to get many improvements available in the other versions. AutoCAD LT users can expect to be stuck with a Release 12-style interface, for example, for quite a while after the much easier-to-use Release 13 has hit the markets. Also missing from the AutoCAD LT package is most of the documentation, which is a *real* problem if you're one of those users who try to push program features close to their limits.

LT is mostly identical to AutoCAD for Windows. And using LT can be a great way to get started in the sometimes perplexing world of AutoCAD — as well as the perfect solution for occasional users who must share drawings with other AutoCAD users. But if you require the power of third-party applications in your work, you quickly need to bite the bullet and buy the full-blown, higher-priced AutoCAD for Windows.

Mac and UNIX: Not on the Fast Track

Earlier versions of AutoCAD are also available for the Macintosh and for UNIX platforms. Release 13, however, is unlikely to appear for these non-IBM-compatible platforms anytime soon.

The new Power Macintosh line offers a price and performance advantage for *native applications* (that is, applications created especially for the Power Macintosh), but a native version of AutoCAD for Power Macintosh does not yet exist. And AutoCAD is continuing to "evaluate" Macintosh and the Power Macintosh as target platforms for Release 13, so go very carefully if you're considering migrating to one of these environments. Be aware, too, that few third-party applications currently exist for AutoCAD on the Macintosh; this is unlikely to change anytime soon.

AutoCAD for UNIX, if run on a fast workstation, may offer a performance advantage over the program's IBM-compatible versions. A few third-party applications have been made available for UNIX platforms. The stable and powerful networking environment of UNIX is a draw for many users. But Windows NT may soon match that environment. And, again, Autodesk offers no promises as to the availability of Release 13 for UNIX.

If you already own Macintosh or UNIX hardware and software, you may have little choice except to purchase the AutoCAD version for your platform. Getting the most out of AutoCAD, however, probably means moving to AutoCAD for DOS or AutoCAD for Windows.

A release, by any other name...

Once upon a time, AutoCAD named its versions like other normal programs, such as Version 1.0, Version 2.1, and so on. But after Autodesk realized how popular AutoCAD may become — and wanted to justify charging ever-higher prices — the company came up with the more grandiose-sounding Release naming scheme. Every new version of AutoCAD is now called a Release, as in Release 12 (or the subject of this book — ta *daaaah* — Release 13).

Typically, a new release is made available for the most popular platforms first. Release 12 came out on DOS first, followed by Windows, UNIX, and finally Macintosh. Now, with Release 13, Autodesk is releasing AutoCAD simultaneously for DOS and Windows; versions for other platforms, however, may come quite a bit behind these.

New releases generally come out about two years apart. Releases that fix program bugs (as opposed to completely new versions) are indicated by a *c,* followed by the number of the fix. The first bug fix to Release 12, for example, was called R12c1. Many users are content to wait three months or so after a new release before upgrading so that others can debug it for them. R12, for example, experienced significant printing problems that were fixed by the c1 version. If you buy a new version of AutoCAD when it first is released, check back with your dealer after a few months for a possible update.

You can tell how important your hardware platform (DOS, Windows, and so on) is to Autodesk by how quickly the company offers a new release. Platforms popular with significant numbers of users get updated frequently; other platforms don't. Expect Windows to be at the top of the AutoCAD food chain for years to come; UNIX and Macintosh bottom-feeders, on the other hand, can expect their upgrades when Autodesk gets darn good and ready to accommodate them.

Which Way Do I Go, Which Way . . . ?

Choosing the version of AutoCAD that's right for you can be a big decision. (Many users even buy a specific kind of computer to go with their AutoCAD version, further magnifying the decision.) Choosing the wrong version can mean thousands of dollars in misspent software and hardware costs. Multiply your choice by the size of your workgroup, department, or company and you can understand why picking the right version is a big deal.

In first starting out with AutoCAD, you can do worse than buying AutoCAD LT for Windows. It's a great choice for learning the program, for occasional use, and for viewing and editing drawings created by others. LT just doesn't offer much in the way of documentation, programmability, or third-party applications. At this writing, too, it's compatible only with Release 12, not Release 13 of regular AutoCAD. And, unfortunately, Autodesk doesn't give you any credit for the cost of LT if you later upgrade to another version of AutoCAD. If you find yourself stuck with a copy, use it to work at home or to train new users.

Additional features, additional programmability, and support for third-party applications—not to mention being fully up to date—are the main reasons to buy "full" AutoCAD. Coverage in this book is yet another bonus; LT isn't covered, except briefly here and in Chapter 19. AutoCAD for Windows is the better choice because of its key additional features: easier setup, multiple open drawings, and better rendering support. (It's also easier to use, but many hardcore AutoCAD users claim to be above that sort of thing.)

Note: Rendering in AutoCAD by the way, has nothing to do with meat preparation. It refers to using advanced 3D features to produce a realistic-looking image.

The programming capabilities of AutoCAD for Windows are better by far than those of the DOS version. AutoCAD for Windows still lacks some hardware drivers and some third-party applications that are available for AutoCAD for DOS, but then again, you may not want to buy an application from such a behind-the-times vendor.

AutoCAD for DOS is speedier and offers more third-party application and device support than does the Windows version. The best and most popular of such add-ons, however, are now available for Windows, too. And the laggards in this area must catch up shortly or be left behind in the silicon dust. DOS's hardware requirements, especially for RAM, are somewhat less than those of AutoCAD for Windows, but the savings in hardware costs may be canceled out by the many hassles you experience in the program's installation and use.

A future version of AutoCAD Release 13 for the Power Macintosh may be very fast indeed, and the absolute fastest speed may be available on one of the forthcoming UNIX versions of AutoCAD. Expect third-party application and device support for these platforms, however, to remain poor. Consider Mac or UNIX versions only if you truly need the highest speed possible and are absolutely sure that the add-ons you need are available.

Table 1-1 summarizes the differences between the LT, DOS, Windows, and Windows NT versions of AutoCAD. (My own recommended processor and memory configurations, displayed here, are real-world figures that are actually higher than what Autodesk recommends.) Start out on LT if you want to save money, Windows if you need full AutoCAD, and DOS only if your hardware isn't up to Windows specs or you need a driver or third-party application that's still available only for DOS.

Table 1-1	AutoCAD Versions for IBM-Compatibles				
Version	**List Price**	**Processor Needed**	**Memory Needed (RAM)**	**Swap File Size Needed**	**Benefits**
AutoCAD LT for Windows	$495	386/387 or 486DX	4MB or more	2–4x RAM	Easiest to install and use; cheap.
AutoCAD Release 13 for DOS	$3,750	486DX or Pentium	12MB or more	4x RAM	Most device drivers and third-party applications.
AutoCAD Release 13 for Windows	$3,750	Pentium	16MB or more	4x RAM	Easier to install and use; greater programmability; more features.
AutoCAD Release 13 for Windows NT	$3,750	Pentium or multiple processors	16MB or more	4x RAM	More robust.

Okay, got all that committed to memory? Great. Of course, you don't need it all—just what applies to the version you currently own. (Unless you're thinking, of course, of switching to another version or platform.) This book primarily covers the DOS and Windows versions of AutoCAD Release 13, which are nearly identical in functionality, though different in appearance. The NT version is so similar to the "regular" Windows version that you can learn it from this book, too. The book doesn't cover the other versions directly, but after they are upgraded to Release 13 capabilities, they're pretty sure to be much like AutoCAD for Windows; so nearly everything in the book should be at least indirectly applicable to all those other versions as well. (What a bargain, huh?)

Chapter 2
Le Tour de AutoCAD for DOS

In This Chapter

▶ The AutoCAD for DOS screen

▶ The status line and menu bar

▶ The drawing area

▶ The command line

▶ The side-screen menu

▶ Setting system variables and using dialog boxes

▶ Getting Help

*F*or now — and undoubtedly for some time to come — the DOS version of AutoCAD still makes up most of AutoCAD's installed base of users. Autodesk, however, has declared that the future of AutoCAD lies with Windows — though they're a little vague about which version that will be — and, in fact, many of the new features in Release 13 exist only in the Windows version.

If you're a longtime AutoCAD for DOS user, this headlong move toward Windows leaves you kind of stuck. Where once you were a master of the AutoCAD universe, eagerly courted by Autodesk and vendors of add-on hardware devices and software programs, you may now feel a bit like a newly transplanted Californian who's just received an earthquake warning. Should you move immediately or try to ride out the shock?

You still can count on several good reasons to stick with AutoCAD for DOS. If you own a carefully tuned hardware/software setup that works well for you, for example, changing to Windows — and starting over again from scratch — may not be worth all the trouble. And the lack of new features in Release 13 of AutoCAD for DOS may actually be a blessing in disguise. You have less to learn, so you can get right back to work as soon as you upgrade.

If you're a new user, AutoCAD for DOS may not be your best bet, but it may be your only choice. That is, to accomplish what you need to do with the program, you may require a third-party add-on program for AutoCAD or a hardware device driver that's available only for the DOS version. Or perhaps your hardware configuration isn't powerful enough to run AutoCAD for Windows well. Or, then again, you may just be a speed demon who wants the highest possible performance, and, well, the DOS version *is* faster than the Windows or NT versions on equivalent hardware.

In any case, I suggest that you consider moving to AutoCAD for Windows as soon as you can; the Windows version is easier to learn and use, and, as I've already stated several times (so maybe now you'll believe me), it's the future of AutoCAD. Chapter 3, in fact, shows you exactly what's in store for you in AutoCAD for Windows — although you may want to skip that chapter if you're still stuck in DOS; it just may leave you feeling more than a bit left out. But, I say again, the DOS version still has several good years left in it, as you discover in this chapter-long tour.

Note: This tour of AutoCAD for DOS is similar in structure and content to the tour of AutoCAD for Windows in the following chapter. The two versions of the program are similar, yet different in important ways. If you are moving from the DOS to the Windows version or using each version at least part of the time, comparing the similarities and dissimilarities should be as easy as flipping back and forth between these two chapters. The remainder of the book combines DOS and Windows coverage and does not display such a similar similarity . . . er, dissimilar dissimilarity . . . between adjacent chapters.

DOS Are the Breaks

If you're a new user, learning your way around AutoCAD for DOS can be a strange experience. The initial appearance of the screen, described in the following section, is different from that of any other program. And "driving" the program is different, too, because of the several ways you can enter the commands that tell the program what to do next. Imagine a car with three different steering wheels, each of which works somewhat differently, and you start to get the picture. The experienced driver can perhaps make this complicated car to do some neat stuff; the new driver, however, is sure to crash the first few times out. Luckily, AutoCAD for DOS is only software, so all you lose if you do crash it is time, perhaps some drawing data — and maybe a bit of sanity in the bargain.

To get started with AutoCAD for DOS, focus on learning how to use the menus at the top of the screen. These menus offer access to most of AutoCAD's functions and are always available to you; you don't need to remember much to use them. In fact, you can safely delay learning the other ways of "driving" AutoCAD until after you master the menu basics. (But wait! You say you don't see any menus at the top of your screen, where most programs stash them? Not to worry. Just check the following section "Five Easy Pieces," to discover the trick to locating those pesky little devils.)

You got the look

AutoCAD's on-screen appearance is often different for different people's AutoCAD setups. AutoCAD, in all its versions, is very easy to *configure* — that is, to modify, change, add to, rebuild, or whatever else you want to do to it. (The word *configure* sometimes seems to refer to the idea that you're a genius if only you *configure* it out! Sorry.)

The screen shots and descriptions offered in this chapter refer only to the *default* version of AutoCAD — that is, how the screen looks if you haven't changed anything about your AutoCAD setup and haven't added any third-party programs that further change its appearance.

If someone has already changed your configuration or added a third-party program, your screen probably looks somewhat different from the figures in this chapter. But most of what's written here still applies, and by reading this chapter, you should be able to understand what's different about your setup — and why.

An almost saving grace of the program, AutoCAD for DOS's extensive Help system really *is* a big Help (pun intended, of course). You'll probably come to know it intimately, especially if you hate rummaging around through printed documentation. But if you really intend to do much with AutoCAD, don't worry; you'll spend enough time with its printed documents, too.

Five Easy Pieces

The initial screen for AutoCAD Release 13 for DOS consists of five parts. Oddly enough, however, the AutoCAD screen seems at first glance to be missing the most important part of most modern programs: the menu bar at the top. But don't sweat it; the menu bar is merely hidden behind the status line at the top of the screen, as shown in Figure 2-1. (See, I told you all would be explained.)

For now, you can ignore the command line (that box down at the bottom of the screen) and the side-screen menu. The menu bar, status line, and drawing area — the big, nearly empty area in the middle — are the most important parts of the screen you need to learn about to get started. All five pieces of the screen make perfect sense, however, after you learn how to use them, and this chapter gets you well on your way to understanding what they do.

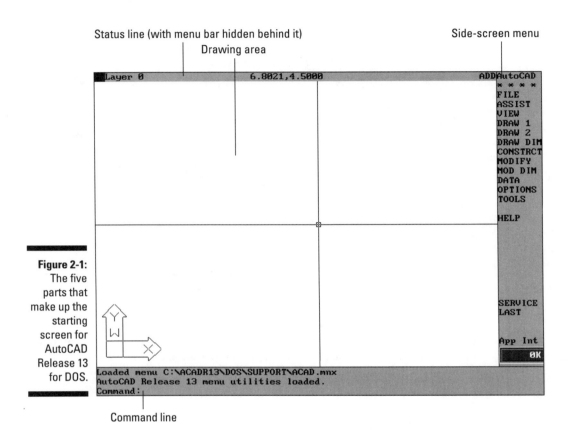

Status line (with menu bar hidden behind it)   Side-screen menu

Drawing area

Figure 2-1:
The five
parts that
make up the
starting
screen for
AutoCAD
Release 13
for DOS.

Command line

For status seekers only

The *status line* tells you several important things about the drawing you're currently working on. Its key function, however, is to hide the menu bar. Having the status line cover the menu bar is an apparent holdover from the old idea that menus are for weenies. *Real* AutoCAD users, or so they say, use the *command line* (see the section "Taking command of the command line," later in this chapter) or a *digitizer*, which is a kind of electronic drawing pad that is another strange story entirely.

Ah, but you *can* bring the menu bar out of its hibernation; you need only move the cursor onto the status line at the top of the screen and — voila! (as Harry Houdini would say) — the menu bar suddenly appears. Move the pointer off the thin strip at the top of the screen and the menu bar disappears while the status line makes an astounding comeback. Hey — some of us can have hours of fun simply moving the mouse up and down, watching the top strip change from status line to menu bar to status line to menu bar . . . .

Besides hiding the menu bar, the status line tells you three more bits of information: the *layer name*, the current *coordinates* of the cursor in the drawing area, and the odd notation *ADD*, which, of course, means "AutoCAD for Dummies, DOS" . . . or something . . . ? If you're new to the program, these items require some explanation (especially that last one):

- ✔ **Layer name:** In AutoCAD, one or more *layers* make up a drawing. Layers are similar to clear sheets of plastic that you *lay* on top of one another (hence the name!) to build up a complete drawing. (You may have noticed something similar in a student's textbook on human anatomy, for example, with the skeleton on one sheet, the muscles on the next sheet laid over the skeleton, and so on until you built up a complete picture. That is, if your mom didn't remove all the interesting parts.) Layers are the most important organizational tool for your drawing, and knowing which layer you're currently working in is vitally important; otherwise, objects get mixed up on different layers, and the whole point of having layers is lost.

- ✔ **Coordinates of the cursor:** The current coordinates of the cursor are extremely important in CAD (computer-aided design, remember?), because they actually relate the drawing to the real-world object or scene the drawing represents. In a CAD drawing of a soft drink can, for example, the top of the can should be about 5 inches, or 12.5 centimeters, from the bottom of the can. After you set up AutoCAD correctly for your drawing, the cursor coordinates reflect the real-life dimensions of the object or scene you're working on.

- ✔ **ADD:** Actually, this denotes the AutoCAD device driver used to generate the screen image and update it quickly.

Figure 2-2 shows the status line for AutoCAD for DOS.

The status line on your own AutoCAD setup may feature some additional elements. The status line is fairly easy to customize by using a custom programming language called *DIESEL*. A number of programs exist that can customize the status line, including neat little utilities that put the current drawing name in the status line and more complex programs that enable you to manage layers from the status line. So if your status line looks different from those in the figures in this chapter, you'll just have to figure out on your own what those added elements mean — or ask the AutoCAD guru who customized your setup (if you have one handy to talk to).

Figure 2-2:
The status
line in
AutoCAD
for DOS.

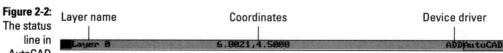

Layer name   Coordinates   Device driver

Layer 0   6.8021,4.5000   ADDAutoCAD

Raiders of the lost menu bar

Hidden underneath the status line is the *menu bar*. The menu bar appears after you move the cursor onto the status line. After you move the cursor back down off the menu bar, the status line replaces it again. Neat trick, huh?

Even if it isn't visible, however, you can usually determine what appears on the menu bar by looking at the *side-screen menu* (described in detail in the section "Ordering off the side-screen menu," later in this chapter). The side-screen menu's top-level labels (that is, the menu names) are very similar to the labels on the menu bar.

The menu bar enables you to access all the menus and their various commands in AutoCAD. You can, in fact, access nearly all the functions of AutoCAD by using these menus. A few functions, however, do require you to use the command line or even (urk!) the side-screen menu. Add-on programs, for example, sometimes use only the side-screen menu.

Shameless plug alert! You can find a complete reference to all the menus in all the versions of AutoCAD in the forthcoming *AutoCAD For Dummies Quick Reference*, the companion to the volume you're now reading. Of course, you *could* just pull down all the menus and make a note of them instead, but why make things cheap and easy?

Figure 2-3 shows the menu bar for AutoCAD for DOS with the Draw menu open. (It looks kind of weird just hanging there on-screen, all by itself, doesn't it?) Notice that the side-screen menu displays almost exactly the same titles as the menu bar.

So go ahead now and spend a few minutes in AutoCAD touring these menus and locating commands that look as though they may be fun to play with. The most important menu to fool around with initially is probably the Draw menu, because it enables you to draw different kinds of shapes in the drawing area. Pay close attention to the other menus that appear after you choose a menu item displaying an arrowhead next to it. These other menus enable you to specify, for example, different ways to draw a circle — far more, in fact, than you ever dreamed possible.

If you're connected to a network, in fact, try playing with these commands on *other people's* drawings first. After you make your beginner's mistakes there, you can then use the same commands correctly on your own drawings. What fun! (***Important Note:*** The IDG legal eagles compel me to make it perfectly clear that the last suggestion is a joke. Really. It is. Uh-huh.)

Menu bar —
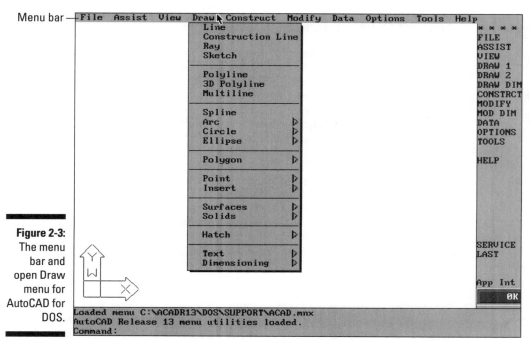

Figure 2-3:
The menu
bar and
open Draw
menu for
AutoCAD for
DOS.

Adding icons to AutoCAD for DOS

Many improvements in AutoCAD over the years started out life as third-party add-on programs. Autodesk often takes the best ideas from these add-on programs and incorporates them into the product itself. One of the best improvements for AutoCAD is the *icon menu,* a floating menu of icons, or pictures, that you can click to initiate a command.

Pulling down a menu every time you want to draw a circle can be a pain; and so can letting go of the mouse to type a command on the keyboard. By using an icon menu, you need only to click an icon with a circle marked on it whenever you want to draw a circle, and AutoCAD launches the circle command for you. This handy little convenience can greatly speed up your drawing work. (Of course, it can also leave you a little confused if you need to do a task for which you have no icon, but that's life, I guess.)

AutoCAD for Windows has its own icon menus, which are referred to as *floating tool palettes.* (Chapter 3 contains more info on this and other AutoCAD for Windows features.) AutoCAD for DOS, however, also has several good third-party icon menus that you can buy and install. (None come with the program itself, though. Maybe Release 14...?) You can find advertisements for — and, occasionally, reviews of — good icon menus in one of the magazines listed in Chapter 19, "Ten Great AutoCAD Resources."

The drawing room

In a house, the drawing room is an elegantly laid-out part of the living quarters in which you are expected to act civilized — at least that's what it's designed for. The AutoCAD *drawing area*, on the other hand, is an expanse of empty space on the AutoCAD screen on which you, by the act of drawing, create civilized designs. The drawing area, however, is more than just a blank space in which you can draw. With the correct configuration settings, the drawing area almost magically takes on the dimensions and other characteristics you need to help you create the exact drawing you want.

Two critical configuration settings help determine the drawing area's effectiveness: the *limits* and *snap* settings. The *limits* setting for the drawing area defines, of course, the *limits* of the drawing you're working on. To draw a football stadium, for example, the limits may be set at about 500 units (say, yards or meters) in the horizontal direction and 300 units (yards or meters again) in the vertical direction. After you set these limits, the drawing area acts as a 500- by 300-unit grid into which you can place various objects. (And, no, I don't mean football players; I mean lines, circles, and other shapes.)

Another important setting for the drawing area is the *snap* setting. The snap setting forces the mouse pointer to gravitate to certain points on-screen. If, for example, you're working on your football stadium and set the snap setting to ten units, drawing end lines and sidelines that fall on 10-yard intervals becomes child's play. To add in the seating areas of your stadium, you may want to set up an even finer snap setting, such as one unit, or turn off snap altogether so that you can start your line wherever you want. No matter what changes you make, however, the point is to make the drawing area help you do your work.

You can thus make the drawing area work wonders for your drawings, but *only* if you set up AutoCAD correctly in the first place. If you don't configure these settings correctly, however, the drawing area gets really, really mad at you and fights back — often with devastating results to your drawings. With the wrong settings, text can look fine on-screen, for example, but print out at only a millimeter high on paper. Good for an eye test, bad for real work. But don't freak out just yet: You can find valuable setup information in Chapters 4 and 5 of this book.

The drawing area looks pretty much the same in all versions of AutoCAD. (Hey, it's a big blank area on-screen. What do you expect?) Figure 2-4 shows the drawing area of AutoCAD for DOS with a drawing already created inside it.

Taking command of the command line

The *command line,* at the bottom of the screen, is probably the oddest-looking aspect of the AutoCAD screen and possibly the hardest to get used to as well. Figure 2-5 shows the command line as it appears after you first launch AutoCAD.

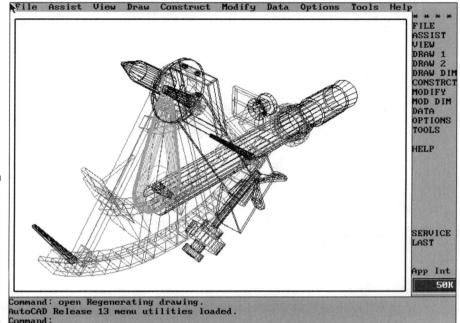

Figure 2-4:
The
AutoCAD
for DOS
drawing area,
containing a
sample
drawing of a
sextant.

The command line originated at a time long ago in the misty recesses of computer history, back when computer screens that used graphics were relatively new and mice were rodents, not peripheral devices. The idea behind the command line is that you use one main, text-only screen to communicate with the program; then, a second, graphics-only screen shows you the results of the commands you enter. The fairly recent adoption of graphical screens, *graphical user interfaces* (*GUI*s), and direct manipulation using a mouse has relegated the AutoCAD command line to its current status as something of a long-lost relic of computerdom's early days.

As a DOS user, however, you have one simple advantage over Windows users that can help put the AutoCAD command line to work for you: You're used to

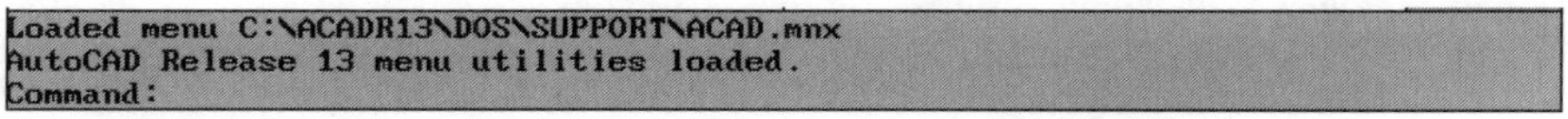

Figure 2-5:
The
AutoCAD
for DOS
command
line.

```
Loaded menu C:\ACADR13\DOS\SUPPORT\ACAD.mnx
AutoCAD Release 13 menu utilities loaded.
Command:
```

working with (and raging at) the good ol' DOS command line. The main difference between the DOS and the AutoCAD command lines is that you aren't forced to use the latter as your only method of interacting with AutoCAD. You can instead use the menu bar to find and enter most commands and then save the command line primarily for use as an accelerator to quickly enter the familiar commands you use most often.

You can thus use the command line to quickly instruct AutoCAD to perform tasks that otherwise require opening several menus and navigating through one or more dialog boxes. Unfortunately, you can carry out a number of AutoCAD tasks *only* from the command line — and not in any other way. (Sigh.) But if you treat it as a productivity tool and an adjunct to the menus whenever possible, the command line actually helps you more than it frustrates you. Really!

AutoCAD actually makes learning how to use the command line easy. After you choose any command from the menus, AutoCAD echoes that same command in DOS-speak down on the command line. (It precedes the command with an underscore character: _DDRMODES, for example, is how the AutoCAD command line displays the command to open the Drawing Aids dialog box.) As you use the menus and dialog boxes, just watch the command line and remember the commands that you use most often — or write them down if you're a bit faulty in the attention-span area. Then enter the command directly on the command line whenever you need that function.

Ordering from the menu vs. commanding from the command line

Some experienced AutoCAD users think that those sissy menus are strictly for wimps. New users, on the other hand, may want to get rid of that annoying command line completely. But each feature actually has a useful purpose.

While you're first learning AutoCAD, menus are great. You can just mouse around until you find the command or dialog box you need. To get fully up to speed in AutoCAD, however, you really do want to learn to use the keyboard to enter your most common commands. (Unless, of course, you're a terminally slooooowwww typist.) So memorize the commands that you use the most.

The command line is especially valuable in AutoCAD for DOS. In AutoCAD for Windows, floating tool palettes and keyboard shortcuts for menu items enable you to easily speed up your most frequently used commands, *sans* command line. In AutoCAD for DOS, however, the command line is the best tool you've got.

For occasionally used commands, though, such as those used in setting up AutoCAD, give your brain cells a break: *Don't* try to memorize these commands. You can always find them again by mousing around in the menus instead of typing half-remembered commands until you just happen to hit on the right one. (Although, if enough monkeys working on typewriters can pound out the works of Shakespeare, I have little doubt you'd chance on the right command eventually.)

You can even expand the command line to take over the entire screen. (You can also panic really inexperienced AutoCAD users by doing this when they're not looking! Ha!) Press F1 to inflate the command line box so that it fills up most of the screen, as shown in Figure 2-6. This feature enables you to review your last several commands as they appear on-screen within the now giant command line. Clicking the Go Text button in the upper left corner of this expanded command line area switches you to a text screen that displays nothing but commands. Press F1 again to return your screen to its normal appearance, with the command line once more consigned to a small area at the bottom of the screen.

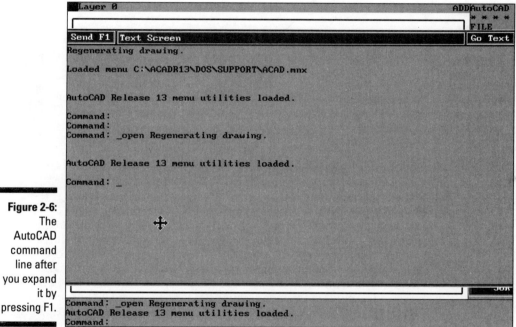

Figure 2-6:
The
AutoCAD
command
line after
you expand
it by
pressing F1.

Ordering off the side-screen menu

Figure 2-7 shows the *side-screen menu*, or *side menu* for short. (The question is whether the side menu is on *your* side; you may decide it's not worth the space it occupies and simply get rid of it instead of learning it.)

Side-screen menu

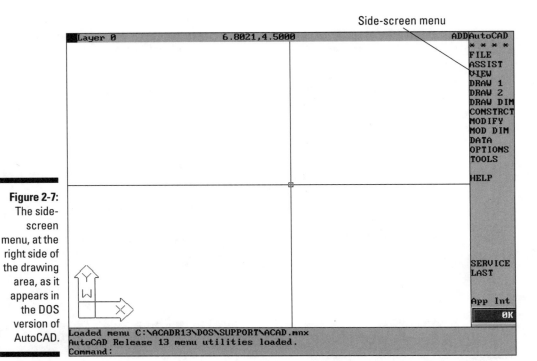

Figure 2-7:
The side-screen menu, at the right side of the drawing area, as it appears in the DOS version of AutoCAD.

Created and controlled by a program written in *AutoLISP*, a special programming language adapted specifically for AutoCAD, the side-screen menu first appeared several years ago as an evolutionary step between the pure, command-line approach found in earlier versions of AutoCAD and the "real," Macintosh-style menus that are now used in Windows, AutoCAD, and everywhere else. The side-screen menu, sadly, has largely served its purpose and is on its way out. It'll probably still hang on for quite some time, however, because many people are used to it and because so many third-party add-on programs still place their options in this menu.

In addition to AutoLISP programs, the side-screen menu is heavily used by *digitizers,* which are drawing tablets that you use to control AutoCAD as well as for drawing. Digitizers tend to incorporate drivers that use side-screen menus to control the program. A healthy debate continues between those who love and those who hate digitizers, but for most users, digitizers are on the way out, too. (Digitizers are great to use for tracing old paper drawings and for freehand sketching, but as a way to control AutoCAD itself, they're not worth the trouble to buy, hook up, learn, and use.)

The side-screen menu displays both a main menu, as shown in Figure 2-7, and secondary menus. Often after you choose a command from the main menu, a secondary menu appears. Choosing a command from a secondary menu may open yet another secondary menu (or tertiary menu at this point, I guess), and so on. One problem with all these secondary (*et al*) menus is that the last one you use stays on-screen until you choose the AutoCAD item up at the top of the side-screen menu. Choosing this item causes the side-screen menu to revert to its main menu.

You may want to use the side-screen menu as a menu accelerator, much the same as Windows users substitute keyboard shortcuts for choosing menu items. (In Windows, for example, pressing the keystroke combination Alt+F+S opens the File menu and then chooses the Save command.)

As you type on the command line, AutoCAD checks your keystrokes to determine whether they match anything in the side-screen menu. If the main side-screen menu is on-screen, for example, and you type **F** on the command line, the word FILE on the side-screen menu, which represents the File menu, is highlighted. Press the Insert key (marked Ins on some keyboards) to choose the highlighted item. The File menu then appears. Type **S** to highlight the first item that starts with an *S,* which is the Save command. Press the Insert key again to choose Save, and the Save dialog box appears.

This shortcut technique may help you, or it may prove more trouble than it's worth. If the latter, you can ditch the side-screen menu so that it doesn't take up valuable drawing space. You learn how to lose the side-screen menu in Chapter 4.

What Really Makes AutoCAD Tick?

In reading about and using AutoCAD, you encounter two topics with recurring frequency: *system variables,* which are very old, and *dialog boxes,* which in their current, highly usable form are relatively new. System variables and dialog boxes are actually closely related; understanding them and how they work together can dramatically speed your ascent to proficiency in AutoCAD.

Setting system variables

System variables are settings that AutoCAD checks before it decides how to do something. If you set the system variable SAVETIME to 10, for example, AutoCAD automatically saves your file every ten minutes (unless you don't do anything for a while, in which case it waits until you do). If you set SAVETIME to 60, the time interval between automatic saves is one hour.

Hundreds of system variables control AutoCAD's operations; more than 40 system variables control dimensioning alone. (*Dimensioning* is AutoCAD's automatic generation of labels that show the distance between two points. Different professions, and different professionals, have very different standards for how dimensions on their drawings should look. Chapter 11 describes dimensions in detail.)

AutoCAD, like most programs, has certain settings that you can change. AutoCAD is different from other programs, however, in that you can access and change its settings directly. (Most programs hide their variables behind dialog boxes, icons, and so on and do not permit you to change them directly.) Just type **SETVAR** on the AutoCAD command line, followed by the variable name, and then the new value you want for the variable. Then press Enter. Figure 2-8 shows the first 20 or so system variables in AutoCAD. (You can access this list by entering the command **SETVAR,** followed by **?** for the variable name, and then pressing Enter to specify a display list of all variables.)

The capability to change a system variable directly is a very powerful feature — and one well worth learning the names and appropriate range of settings for the system variables you use often. But expecting you to remember literally hundreds of variables, how they work, and how they interact with one another is really just too much — even for "power users." This is where dialog boxes come in.

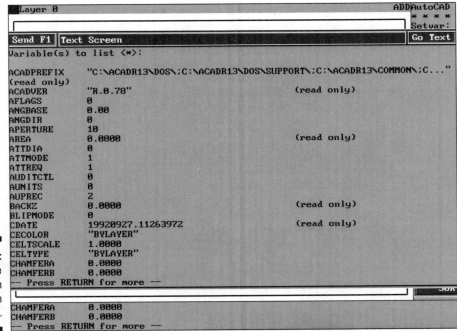

Figure 2-8:
Some of the system variables in AutoCAD.

Dancing with dialog boxes

AutoCAD's dialog boxes are an easy way to control collections of related system variables, much like the dashboard on a car enables you to see and control what's going on as you drive along the highway. By using dialog boxes, you can handle all the related settings that may otherwise be confusing if you changed them directly through system variables.

The best single example of the power inherent in using this technique is found in the set of dialog boxes you use to manage dimensions. Because you can specify so many different elements about each dimension, AutoCAD enables you to create *dimension styles* — named groups of dimension settings that you can choose via a single menu command. Dimension styles are controlled by using the Dimension Styles dialog box, as shown in Figure 2-9.

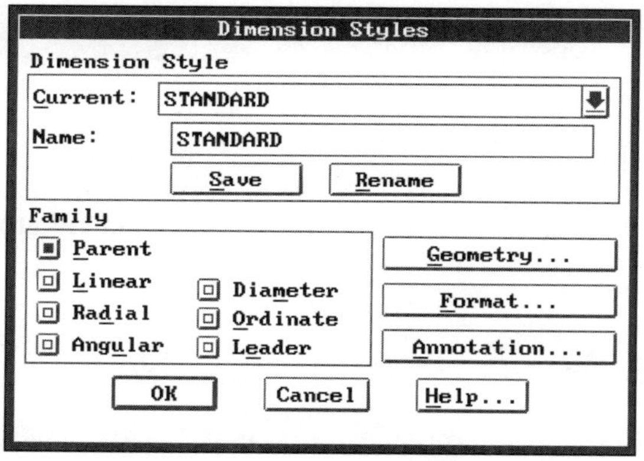

Figure 2-9:
The
Dimension
Styles
dialog box.

```
┌──────────────────────────────────────────────────────┐
│                   Dimension Styles                     │
│ Dimension Style                                        │
│ Current: │STANDARD                              │▼│    │
│                                                        │
│ Name:    │STANDARD                                │    │
│              │  Save  │    │  Rename  │                │
│ Family                                                 │
│  ■ Parent              ┌──────────────┐                │
│  □ Linear    □ Diameter│  Geometry... │                │
│  □ Radial    □ Ordinate│  Format...   │                │
│  □ Angular   □ Leader  │  Annotation..│                │
│       │  OK  │  │ Cancel │  │ Help... │               │
└──────────────────────────────────────────────────────┘
```

To open this dialog box, choose Data⇨Dimension Style from the menu bar or type **DDIM** on the command line. Each of the options in the right-hand corner of the Dimension Styles dialog box — Geometry, Format, and Annotation — opens another dialog box, each of which in turn controls several more system variables.

The Help option for each dialog box describes what that dialog box does as well as the system variables the dialog box controls. If you find yourself changing one setting often, you can use the Help option to find the name of the system variable that holds that setting and then change the value in the system variable quickly and directly from the command line. For complicated tasks such as creating new dimension styles, stick to using the dialog boxes.

Less Help but Not Helpless

Both the DOS and Windows versions of AutoCAD feature powerful Help systems. Each version includes a searchable topics database, information on how to use Help, and an overview of what's new in Release 13. Both versions are *context-sensitive*; in other words, if you request help in the middle of executing a command, a Help screen for that specific command appears first. (You can navigate from there to anyplace else in the Help system.) Figure 2-10 shows the Help menu from the menu bar.

Figure 2-10:
The Help
menu in
AutoCAD for
DOS.

The DOS version lacks some of the Help features of the Windows version, such as keyboard access to Help, graphics in the Help screens, an on-line overview of AutoCAD, and an interactive tutorial. But the Help system in AutoCAD for DOS is still pretty good and worth learning how to use.

Sensitive Help

No, *sensitive Help* isn't some new kind of psychotherapy; it's short for *context-sensitive Help,* probably the most useful kind of help you can get in AutoCAD. You access context-sensitive Help in AutoCAD in either of two ways: by choosing Help from the Help menu or by choosing the Help button in a dialog box.

If you're in the middle of entering a command, you can obtain help by choosing the Help option from the Help menu. Help appears for the command you're entering. This feature doesn't work, however, if you're choosing items from the menus, unless you've reached the point where the menu option finally appears on the command line.

If you open the Draw menu and just select (or highlight) the Circle command, for example, and then you choose Help, a series of choices appears. But if you highlight Circle, press Enter to choose it, and *then* choose an option from the Circle menu that appears, a command also appears on the command line. If you choose Help at this point, specific help for the Circle command appears. Figure 2-11 shows the Help screen for the Circle command, with the prompt for one type of circle displayed on the command line.

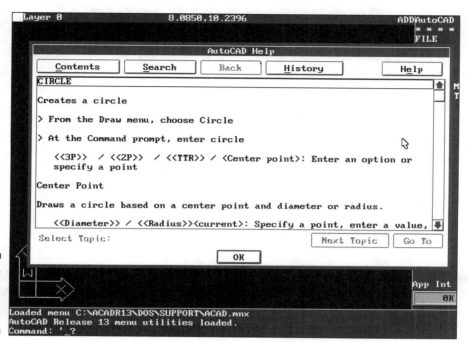

Figure 2-11:
Help for the
Circle
command.

You can also access context-sensitive Help from a dialog box. Every dialog box has a Help button, and you simply click that button to obtain help for that particular dialog box. Again, from this context-sensitive Help you can branch off to a Help screen for any other topic. Figure 2-12 shows the AutoCAD Help screen for Drawing Aids. The text in the Help screen describes what the Drawing Aids dialog box does and how to access it. This screen appears after you choose the Help option in the Drawing Aids dialog box.

Getting content with contents

You can access the same Help screens in a couple other ways: choosing Help from the Help menu if you're not in the middle of any specific command and choosing Contents from within an AutoCAD Help screen. Either choice opens a screen that enables you to access help for menu items, for commands, or for system variables. This screen is pretty useful, and just clicking around in it is a good way to learn some of the basics of AutoCAD. Figure 2-13 shows this Contents Help screen.

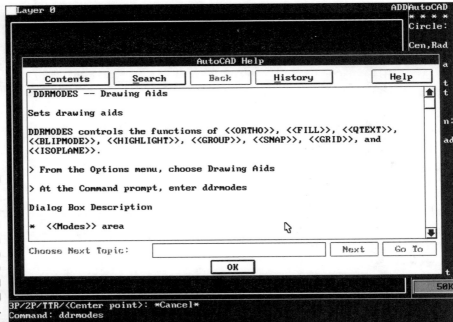

Figure 2-12:
This
AutoCAD
Help screen
offers help
for the
Drawing
Aids dialog
box.

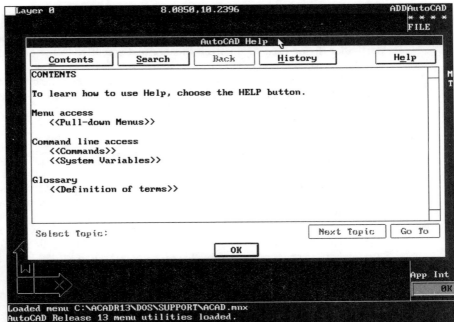

Figure 2-13:
The Help
Contents
screen.

The search is on

You can access a long, scrolling list of topics by opening the Help menu and choosing Search for Help On, or by choosing Search from within any AutoCAD Help screen. Figure 2-14 shows the AutoCAD Help Search dialog box that appears. Unfortunately, the list contains literally hundreds of topics, and finding just the one you need can be difficult unless you already know the command name, menu name, or system variable name you're looking for.

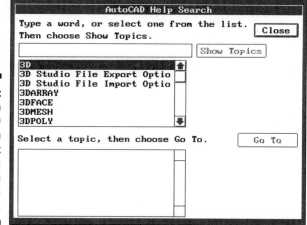

Figure 2-14:
The
AutoCAD
Help Search
dialog box
with a
search
already in
progress.

If you have only a vague idea of what you're looking for — different ways to print your drawing file, for example — you may have a whole heap of clicking ahead of you. As you learn more details about how AutoCAD works, however, the Help Search option becomes more valuable.

The mechanics of AutoCAD Help Search also are a little difficult to grasp. To find what you want in the scrolling list of search items, you must *scroll* by clicking the up or down arrow or *drag* the button in the list box scroll bar up and down (and up and down and . . .); sadly, typing the first few letters of a search item doesn't jump you directly to the item, as it does in many other programs. Then, after you do find the item and click it — still nothing happens! You must *double-click* it to get anywhere. Think you're done now? Think again. Even after you double-click an item in the list box, you don't immediately access Help for the topic; instead, a list of topics *related to* the double-clicked item appears in a separate scrolling box in the same dialog box. (Hmmmm . . .)

Unfortunately, only one item often appears in this second area, and moving the mouse down to this area just to double-click yet another item seems like more extra work than is necessary. (Even so, it's quicker than using the Show Topics and Go To buttons.) All this clicking is a minor quibble, though; you'll probably get used to it far more quickly than I did. And after you do double-click an item in this second area, the help you need quickly appears in a regular AutoCAD Help screen (finally!).

What's new in Release 13

If you're an experienced AutoCAD for DOS user, What's New in Release 13 is an especially valuable Help menu option. Just open the Help menu and choose What's New in Release 13 for an overview of all the new features and commands in this release. Herein you find instructions on using the What's New dialog box. Or just click the New Features option to discover what new functions are available in Release 13. Or click Command Summary to find out how to access a new function.

Figure 2-15 shows the New Features dialog box that appears after you choose the New Features option in the What's New in Release 13 dialog box. Recommended.

Figure 2-15:
The New
Features
dialog box,
which is
accessed
from the
What's New
in Release
13 dialog
box.

Chapter 3

Le Tour de AutoCAD for Windows

● ●

In This Chapter

▶ The AutoCAD for Windows screen

▶ The title bar, menu bar, and toolbars

▶ The drawing area

▶ The command line

▶ The status bar

▶ The aerial view

▶ The side-screen menu

▶ Setting system variables and using dialog boxes

▶ Getting Help

● ●

*W*ith this chapter, we take leave of the comfortable confines of AutoCAD's traditional DOS version and move to the somewhat sexier and more exciting world of Windows. Barring some truly unforeseen changes, the Windows and Windows NT versions of AutoCAD are the mainstream versions of the program going into the rest of this century. More than half of new sales of AutoCAD are for the Windows version, and that percentage is increasing daily.

More and more of the third-party add-on programs that make AutoCAD truly productive are becoming available for the Windows version. The current release of AutoCAD for Windows actually incorporates a number of functions provided in the DOS version only by such add-on utilities — icon menus and the aerial view, for example. Other utilities are now coming out in Windows versions, too.

If you're a new user of AutoCAD, the Windows or Windows NT versions are your best choice. The DOS version is too much work to learn and to use (unless, of course, you're a dyed-in-the-bit DOS fanatic), and the LT for Windows version still uses the Release 12 interface, which is noticeably more difficult to use than that of Release 13. The Windows version serves you well as you move up the learning curve. This does not mean, however, that AutoCAD for Windows is a simple program. This tour starts to unravel the program's mysteries.

Note: This tour of AutoCAD for Windows is similar in structure and content to the tour of AutoCAD for DOS in the preceding chapter. The two versions of the program are similar, yet different in important ways. If you are moving from the DOS to the Windows version or using each version at least part of the time, comparing the similarities and dissimilarities between the two versions should be as easy as flipping back and forth between these two chapters. The remainder of the book combines DOS and Windows coverage and does not display such a similar similarity . . . er, dissimilar dissimilarity . . . between adjacent chapters. (Wow! Déjá vu!)

Winning with Windows

Learning your way around AutoCAD for Windows can be an odd experience. You recognize from other Windows applications much of the appearance and workings of the program, such as its toolbars and pull-down menus, which you use for entering commands or changing system settings. But other aspects of the program's appearance — and some of the ways in which you work with it — are quite different from nearly any other program.

You can, for example, tell the program what to do in at least three ways, none of which is necessarily the best method to use for every task. The experience is much like that of having to act as several different characters in a play; you're likely to forget your lines (whichever "you" you are at the time) at least every now and then.

To get started with AutoCAD for Windows, focus on learning to use the menus at the top of the screen. These menus enable you to access most of the program's functions and are the easiest to remember of AutoCAD's three methods of issuing commands. You can safely delay committing to memory the other, faster ways of making AutoCAD do your bidding until after you learn to use these handy little menus.

The look of love?

AutoCAD's on-screen appearance is often different for different users' AutoCAD setups. AutoCAD for Windows, even more than other versions, is very easy to *configure*—that is, to modify, change, add to, rebuild, or whatever you want to do to it. (Hey! Maybe you're truly a genius if only you *configure* it out! Sorry — again.)

The screen shots and descriptions in this chapter refer to the *default* version of AutoCAD — that is, the way the screen looks if you haven't changed anything about your AutoCAD setup and haven't added any third-party programs that change its appearance.

If someone has already changed your configuration or added a third-party program to your setup, your screen may look somewhat different from those depicted in the figures in this chapter (and in others). But most of what's written herein still applies, and by reading this chapter, you should be able to figure out what's different about your setup — and why.

AutoCAD's extensive Help system is another saving grace; expect to spend a great deal of time using it — especially if you don't like referring to manuals. Because the AutoCAD Help system is based on Microsoft's widely used Help engine (varrooommm!), you may already know how to use it — provided, of course, you're proficient in other Microsoft programs. If not, what you learn in mastering the AutoCAD for Windows Help system can help you in grasping the fundamentals of the Help systems of similar programs for Windows.

Eight Is Enough

The starting screen for AutoCAD Release 13 for Windows has eight parts, as shown in Figure 3-1. The screen displays all the elements found in other modern Windows programs, plus a few more. Make no mistake about it — this screen is busy! It's simply bursting with activity — and that's even before you start using it!

But don't worry; for now, you can just ignore that pesky command line and most of those enigmatic icons. The most important elements you need to learn to get started are the *menu bar* at the top of the screen, the *status bar* at the bottom, the *drawing area* in the middle, and the *floating icons* in the drawing area. All the pieces of the screen make sense — really they do! — and this chapter gets you well on the way to understanding exactly *what* they all do.

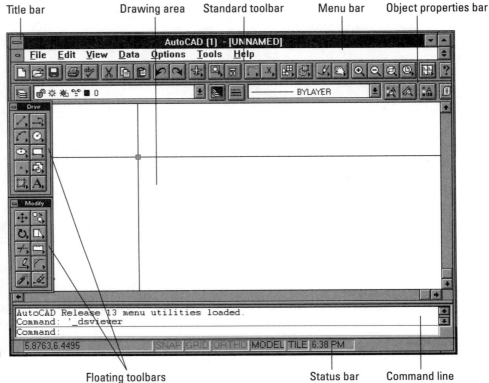

Title bar   Drawing area   Standard toolbar   Menu bar   Object properties bar

Floating toolbars   Status bar   Command line

Figure 3-1:
The starting
screen for
AutoCAD
Release 13
for Windows
contains
eight parts.

The title bar — where everyone knows your (drawing's) name

Okay, so is this where you go to order a royal coat of arms on the rocks, right?
No, nothing so esoteric, I'm afraid. The *title bar* is simply a little bar across the
top of the screen that shows you the name of the drawing you're currently
working on. If your system has sufficient memory, you can keep several drawings open at once, with more than one title bar visible on-screen. You can also
iconize your drawings — that is, minimize them to eensy-weensy *icons* (little
pictures) at the bottom of the screen — by clicking the little down-pointing
arrow in the upper right-hand corner of the screen. Iconizing turns your
AutoCAD session and current drawing into a typical Windows icon, confined to
the boundaries of the screen.

Bellying up to the menu bar

The *menu bar* contains the names of all the primary menus in your version of AutoCAD.

Shameless plug alert! You can find a complete reference to all the menus in both the DOS and Windows versions of AutoCAD in the forthcoming *AutoCAD For Dummies Quick Reference*, the companion to the volume you're now reading. Of course, you *could* just pull down all the menus and make a note of them instead, but why make things too cheap and easy?

Unlike AutoCAD for DOS, the Windows version does not hide its menu bar behind a status line — or anything else. The AutoCAD for Windows menu bar looks just like the menu bars in a number of other Windows programs and actually is less crowded than the menu bar in AutoCAD for DOS. That's because many of the functions provided by menu choices in AutoCAD for DOS are instead available as icons in AutoCAD for Windows.

Figure 3-2 shows the menu bar for AutoCAD for Windows with the Data menu open. If you spend a few minutes in AutoCAD for Windows touring the menus, opening dialog boxes, and so on, you quickly notice that AutoCAD makes considerable use of dialog boxes. You find more information about using dialog boxes in AutoCAD for Windows in the section "Dancing with dialog boxes," later in this chapter.

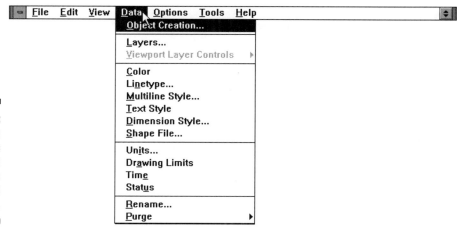

Figure 3-2:
The menu bar displays the open Data menu for AutoCAD for Windows.

Hot-wiring the menu bar

Some standard tips and tricks for DOS and Windows are especially useful in AutoCAD. Possibly the biggest single example of a generic tip that works well for AutoCAD for Windows is the use of *keyboard shortcuts* for menu choices. To fly around the menus, just press and hold the Alt key and then press the letters on your keyboard that correspond to the underlined letters on the menu bar and in the menu choices. To save your drawing, for example, press and hold the Alt key, press *F* for File, and then press *S* for Save. If all you learn from this book is to press Alt+F+S to save (and to do so *frequently*), you've learned more than all too many other users.

Better living with power toolbars

The most important elements in making AutoCAD for Windows do your bidding are the various toolbars that enable you to enter commands quickly and control how you draw, what you draw, and maybe even whether you're quick on the draw. The following three sections describe the three main kinds of toolbars — the *standard toolbar*, the *properties bar*, and the *floating toolbars*.

All the AutoCAD for Windows toolbars provide *tool tips*, an indispensable feature that identifies each icon by its function . . . if you lean on it a bit. Simply hold the mouse pointer over an icon — no need to click it — and, like magic, the name of the icon appears in a little yellow box below the icon. The tool tip feature incorporates yet another component that can be easy to miss: A longer description of the icon's function appears in the status bar, at the very bottom of the screen. (And if the identifying name and the description at the bottom of the screen aren't enough to tell you what the icon does, well, you can always bring in a little "out-of-town muscle" — in other words, look it up in the Help system, which is described in the section "Fun with F1," later in this chapter.)

Figure 3-3 shows the tool tip for the Undo icon on the standard toolbar. The tool tip identifies the icon and the line in the status bar describes the icon's function.

Setting the standard in toolbars

You can quickly access a number of file management, drawing management, and view functions in AutoCAD by using the *standard toolbar*. Using the standard toolbar enables you to change which drawing you're working on by clicking the Save and Open icons, fix a mistake by clicking the Undo or Redo icon, and move around in your drawing by clicking the Pan, Zoom In, and Zoom Out icons.

Tool tip

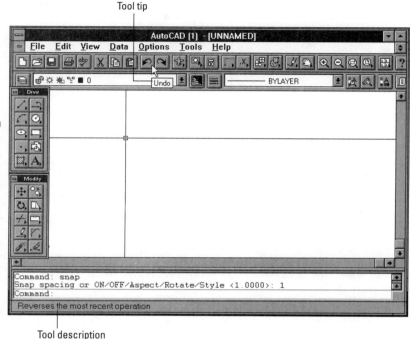

Figure 3-3:
Holding the
mouse
pointer on
the Undo
icon reveals
its tool tip
and the
longer tool
description
in the status
bar.

Tool description

Although you can move the standard toolbar around to different locations on-screen, leaving it right below the menu bar is probably your best bet. (Why? Well, for one thing, if you move the toolbar, a little title appears on top of it, which adds to the space it occupies on-screen, leaving you less room for your drawings.) You can also customize the standard toolbar to perform just about any function you want. Figure 3-4 shows the standard toolbar with its standard icons. (These icons are described on the Cheat Sheet at the front of this book.)

Objecting to the properties bar

The *properties bar,* also called the *object properties bar* (hence the title of this section), actually consists of several different elements lumped together. By using the drop-down lists that appear on the properties bar, you can change the current *layer* and modify its characteristics, change your drawing's colors, and change the linetype used to draw objects. You can use the buttons on the properties bar to view or change the properties that relate to text and to different objects in your drawing. Although all these capabilities are highly desirable, how their functions differ can be highly confusing. The capability to change layers quickly, however, is well worth the price of admission by itself. (See the following sidebar for a somewhat technical discussion about layers.)

Figure 3-4:
The
standard
toolbar in
AutoCAD for
Windows.

Looking at layers

In AutoCAD, a drawing consists of one or more *layers*. Layers are similar to those clear sheets of plastic that you place on top of one another to build up a complete drawing. (You may remember something like this from a student's book about human anatomy, with the skeleton on one sheet, the muscles on the next sheet that you laid over it, and so on until you built up a complete picture of the human body. That is, if your mom didn't re-

move some of the interesting parts.)

Layers are the most important organizational tool for your drawing, and knowing which layer you're currently working in is vitally important. The object properties bar lists the layer name following several icons that tell you things about the current layer. The layer in a drawing that hasn't yet had layers added to it is named *0* (zero).

You can also move the properties bar to a different location on-screen, as you can other toolbars, but it, too, is probably best left where it is. (By leaving it in its default position, just below the standard toolbar, you get used to it being in one location and can find it without looking or thinking too hard.) Figure 3-5 shows the properties bar. Notice the zero in the left-hand list box, which identifies the layer name. (In this case, no layers have yet been added to the drawing.)

Note: Moving the various toolbars around takes a little practice. They don't really have easy-to-grab borders, as do windows and dialog boxes — just little strips around the edges that you can grab with the mouse if you try hard. You may need a little practice to find just the right spot on the edge to click and drag.

Figure 3-5:
The object
properties
bar in
AutoCAD for
Windows.

Floating your toolbars

A *floating tool palette* (or *floating toolbar*), also often called an *icon menu,* is one of the most popular third-party utilities that people buy for AutoCAD for DOS. (By the way, I mostly call them just toolbars, and sometimes palettes, but "icon" call them either one if I want — and so can you.) AutoCAD for Windows, on the other hand, comes with its own floating toolbars. These built-in floating toolbars in AutoCAD for Windows are easy to customize and make AutoCAD's features more accessable.

You can move the floating toolbars around the screen easily enough as well. (This is undoubtedly why they're not called "stationary toolbars.") The default position for the two floating toolbars that normally appear on-screen, the Draw and Modify toolbars, is at the left edge of the screen, just outside the drawing area, but you can drag either or both to the top, right, or bottom of the screen, too. The palettes change shape to fit wherever you're dragging them.

Unlike with the standard toolbar and the object properties bar, dragging the floating toolbars around to different on-screen locations — so that they aren't in the way of what you're drawing — is usually a pretty good idea. You should also make a habit of opening and closing floating toolbars as you need them. (You close them by clicking their close boxes in the upper left corner and open them by choosing Tools⇨Toolbars from the menu bar.) AutoCAD's default configuration includes both the Draw and Modify toolbars, as shown in Figure 3-6. But you can also open — and close — toolbars for almost any other function.

Figure 3-6:
The Draw
and Modify
floating
toolbars in
AutoCAD for
Windows.

Drawing on the drawing area

Although it seems to just sit there, the AutoCAD *drawing area* is actually the program's most important and valuable piece of on-screen real estate. The drawing area is where the images you create in AutoCAD take shape. And the drawing area can actively help you do your work. With the correct configuration settings (to set the screen up the way you want), the drawing area can almost magically take on the dimensions and other characteristics you need to help you create the exact drawing you want.

Two important configuration settings help determine the drawing area's effectiveness. The first of these settings is the *limits* of the drawing you're working on. To draw a football stadium, for example, the limits may be set at about 500 units (yards or meters) in the horizontal direction and 300 units (yards or meters) in the vertical direction. After you set these limits, the drawing area acts as a 500- by 300-unit grid into which you can place objects. (Footballs, hot dog vendors, and rabid fans excepted, of course.)

The second important setting for the drawing area is the *snap* setting, which causes the mouse pointer to gravitate to certain points on-screen. If you are working on your football stadium and set the snap setting to ten units, for example, you can easily draw end lines and sidelines that fall on 10-yard intervals. To draw in the seating area, however, you may want to set snap to a finer setting, such as one unit, or turn off snap altogether so that you can start your line anywhere you want. No matter what changes you make, the point is to make the drawing area help you do your work.

You can make the drawing area work absolute wonders for your drawings — but *only* if you set up AutoCAD correctly in the first place. If you don't configure these settings correctly, however, the drawing area can become really, really mad at you and may even fight back — with potentially devastating results to your drawings. Wrong settings can, for example, turn perfectly acceptable on-screen text into microscopic — and unreadable — ant tracks on paper. But don't freak out just yet: Valuable setup information awaits your discovery in Chapters 4 and 5 of this book.

The drawing area appears essentially the same in all versions of AutoCAD. (Well, what do you expect from a big, blank area in the middle of the screen?) Figure 3-7 shows the drawing area in AutoCAD for Windows with a drawing already created inside it.

Commanding the command line

The *command line* is a unique feature of AutoCAD and is probably the hardest to get used to. Windows users, who thought they'd escaped the dreaded DOS command line, may be especially surprised to find yet a new command line lurking smack dab at the heart of AutoCAD. Yet the command line is actually a very handy tool for increasing speed and productivity in AutoCAD. Figure 3-8 shows the command line as it appears after you first open AutoCAD, skulking away down at the bottom of the screen, hoping you won't notice it below that big, open drawing area.

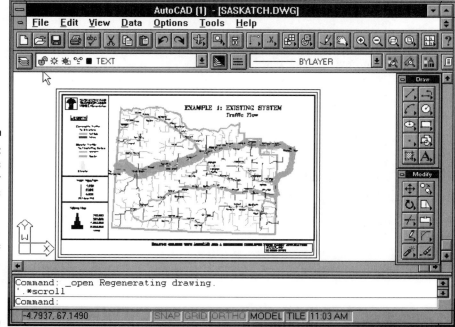

Figure 3-7:
This AutoCAD for Windows drawing area contains a sample drawing of traffic flow in Saskatchewan, Canada.

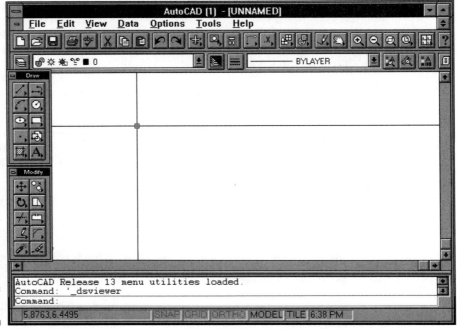

Figure 3-8:
The
AutoCAD for
Windows
command
line in its
default size,
positioned
at the
bottom of
the screen.

The command line dates back to a long-ago time in the mists of computer history, when computer screens that used graphics were still relatively new. The idea behind the command line is that you use one main, text-only screen for communicating with the program; a second, graphics-only screen shows you the results of the commands you enter. The fairly recent adoption of graphical screens, *graphical user interfaces* (or *GUIs*), and direct manipulation of on-screen elements by using a mouse has relegated the AutoCAD command line to its current status as something of a lost relic from the "good ol' days" of computerdom.

The command line is especially challenging if your main experience in using PCs is with Windows rather than DOS. (DOS users actually have a rare advantage here.) The difference between the AutoCAD command line and the hated DOS command line that most Windows users try to avoid is that the former need not be your main vehicle for interacting with AutoCAD. You can instead use the menu bar and icons to find and enter most of your commands and then use the command line primarily as an accelerator to quickly enter those commands you use most.

By using the command line, you can quickly instruct AutoCAD to perform functions via your keyboard that otherwise require opening several menus and navigating your way through one or more dialog boxes. And unfortunately, you *must* use the command line to carry out a number of functions that you cannot perform in any other way. (Drat!) If you treat it as a productivity tool and an adjunct to the menus whenever possible, however, the command line actually helps you more than it frustrates you. (Well, most of you anyway.)

AutoCAD actually makes learning how to use the command line fairly easy. After you choose a command from the menus, for example, AutoCAD echoes that command on the command line, preceding the command with an underscore character: _DDRMODES, for example, is how the AutoCAD command line displays the command to open the Drawing Aids dialog box. Just watch the command line as you use the menus and dialog boxes and remember those commands that you use most — or write 'em down if you're a card–carrying member of the MTV generation (short attention span and all that, you know . . .). Then enter the command directly from the command line whenever you need to employ that function swiftly.

You can even make the command line expand to fill the entire screen. (You can also panic those *really* inexperienced AutoCAD users by doing this on their screens when they're not looking! Yes!) You drag the command line out of its position at the bottom of the screen by grabbing an edge and then dragging it upward. The entire command line becomes a separate, small window. Then click the upward-pointing arrow in the upper right corner of the command line window, and — presto! — the command line expands to take over the entire screen, as shown in Figure 3-9.

(Unlike in the DOS version of AutoCAD, you can scroll up and down in this screen through all the commands you've entered during your entire current session in AutoCAD for Windows — not just the last several that are all the DOS-crowd can access this way.) Click the double-headed arrow in the upper right corner of the screen to return the command line to its previous size and position.

```
□                              AutoCAD - Command Line                                      ▽▲
CDATE          19920927.18332225                      (read only)                          ▲
CECOLOR        "BYLAYER"
CELTSCALE      1.0000
CELTYPE        "BYLAYER"
CHAMFERA       0.0000
CHAMFERB       0.0000
Press RETURN to continue:
CHAMFERC       0.0000
CHAMFERD       0
CHAMMODE       0
CIRCLERAD      0.0000
CLAYER         "0"
CMDACTIVE      1                                      (read only)
CMDDIA         1
CMDECHO        1
CMDNAMES       "SETVAR"                               (read only)
CMLJUST        0
CMLSCALE       1.0000Under construction.
CMLSTYLE       " "                                    (read only)
COORDS         1
CVPORT         2
DATE           2448893.77334583                       (read only)
DBMOD          0                                      (read only)
DELOBJ         1
DIASTAT        1                                      (read only)
DIMALT         Off
DCTMAIN        " "
DCTCUST        " "
DIMALTD        2                                              ▷
Press RETURN to continue:
Command: *Cancel*
Command: _copyclip
Select objects:
Command: circle
3P/2P/TTR/<Center point>:                                                                  ▼
```

Figure 3-9:
The AutoCAD for Windows command line in its expanded size and position.

Menus versus the command line

Some experienced AutoCAD users — especially those who are long-time DOS users — think that menus, icons, and so on are for wimps. New users, on the other hand, may want to get rid of that seemingly annoying command line altogether. But each feature actually has a useful purpose all its own.

For learning AutoCAD, menus and other parts of the graphical user interface are great. You can just mouse around on-screen until you locate the exact command, icon, or dialog box you need.

To get fully up to speed in AutoCAD, however, you really do want to learn to use the keyboard to enter your most common commands. (Unless, of course, your typing speed makes a dead tortoise look swift in comparison.) So a good tactic is to memorize any commands you use frequently that *aren't* represented by an icon in the toolbars displayed on-screen and then use the command line to enter them without fussing your way through the menus.

Looking for Mr. Status Bar

The *status bar,* at the very bottom of the screen, tells you several important bits of information about the drawing you're working on, some of which may not make sense at first glance. These elements include the current *coordinates* of the mouse cursor; whether *snap*, *grid*, and *ortho modes* are on or off; whether you're in *model space* or *paper space*; and whether *tile mode* is on. Figure 3-10 pinpoints these areas of the status bar. If you're new to the program, these areas bear some explanation. The following list does just that:

- ✔ **Coordinates of the cursor:** The current *cursor coordinates* are extremely important in CAD (computer-aided design, as you may recall), because they actually relate the drawing to the real-world object or scene the drawing represents. In a CAD drawing of a soft drink can, for example, the top of the can should be about 5 inches, or 12.5 centimeters, from the bottom of the can. After you set up AutoCAD correctly for your drawing, the cursor coordinates on the status bar reflect the real-life dimensions of the object or scene you're working on.

- ✔ **Snap, grid, and ortho modes:** You can bring order to the AutoCAD drawing area by telling it to *snap* the cursor to certain "hot spots," en-abling you to more easily draw objects a fixed distance apart; by making it display a *grid* of dots to align objects with; and by setting *ortho* mode, which makes drawing straight horizontal and vertical lines easy. The snap, grid, and ortho buttons appear on the status bar in dark text if the mode is on, in gray text if the mode is off.

- ✔ **Model/paper space and tile modes:** Briefly, *model space* is where you create and modify objects; *paper space* is a different mode that enables you to arrange elements in your drawing for printout. *Tile mode* is a system variable that controls model space and paper space; you turn tile mode off to turn paper space on. (This seemingly backward setup is necessary for compatibility with previous releases of AutoCAD that didn't know anything about paper space.) See Chapter 14 for fuller descriptions — in excruciating detail — of these settings.

- ✔ **Time.** Knowing the time is nice, so AutoCAD shows you the current time right there in the status bar.

Figure 3-10:
The status bar in AutoCAD for Windows.

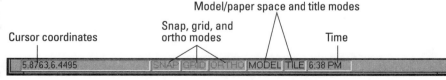

Cursor coordinates

Snap, grid, and ortho modes

Model/paper space and title modes

Time

A Bright Light and a Dim Bulb

Although AutoCAD is highly configurable, you're likely to want to use all the parts of the program's screen. Two optional features, however, take up a great deal of screen space, but differ radically in the value they offer you. One if these screen hogs is not strictly necessary but is highly useful; the other is clumsy and hard to use, but it's a real necessity for running some older programs.

Taking the aerial view

The *aerial view* is a feature idea borrowed from third-party utilities and included as a built-in feature of AutoCAD for Windows. (AutoCAD for DOS does not include an aerial view feature, but it is inexpensive to buy as an add-on if you still insist on sticking to that version.)

The aerial view is flexible and powerful — but unfortunately, like the toolbar, it takes up valuable space in the drawing area. And it floats on top of *everything;* if you open a dialog box, the aerial view, which is also sort of like a dialog box, pops up right on top of it — plop! But the aerial view is truly indispensable while you're learning how to use the Pan and Zoom features and otherwise navigate your way into and out of complicated drawings. Figure 3-11 shows the Aerial View window.

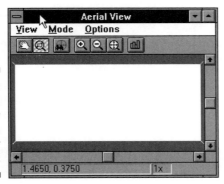

Figure 3-11:
The Aerial
View
window in
AutoCAD for
Windows.

Because it takes up so much screen space, you'll probably want to turn the aerial view on and off frequently. The button with the airplane-shaped icon, in the middle of the standard toolbar (just to the right of the arrow-shaped Undo and Redo buttons), turns aerial view on and off; just click it to make the Aerial View dialog box appear and disappear.

Snapping to the side-screen menu

Figure 3-12 shows the *side-screen menu,* or *side menu* for short. AutoCAD introduced the side-screen menu several years ago sort of as an evolutionary step between the pure command-line approach found in earlier versions of AutoCAD and the "real" Macintosh-style menus that Windows, AutoCAD, and every other program now use. The side-screen menu has largely served its purpose and is on the way out. It will undoubtedly hang on for a long time, however, because many people are used to it and because so many third-party programs place their options in this menu.

The side-screen menu is used extensively by *AutoLISP* programs — those written in a special AutoCAD programming language — and by *digitizers,* which are drawing tablets you use to control AutoCAD as well as for drawing. Digitizers tend to incorporate drivers that use side-screen menus to control the program. A healthy debate continues between those who love and hate digitizers; but for most users, they're on the way out, too. (Digitizers are great for tracing old paper drawings and for freehand sketching, but as a way to control AutoCAD itself they're not worth the trouble to buy, hook up, learn, and use.)

Side-screen menu

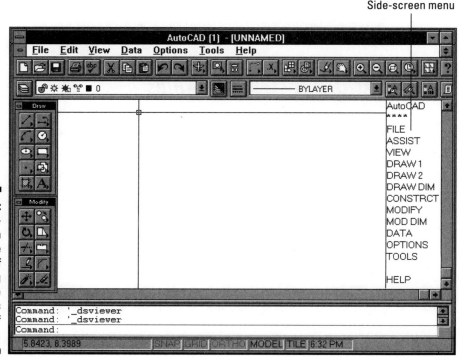

Figure 3-12:
The side-screen menu, at the right side of the drawing area, in the Windows version of AutoCAD.

The side-screen menu displays a main menu, as shown in Figure 3-12, and secondary menus that appear after you make a choice from the main menu. Choices from the secondary menus may cause other secondary (or tertiary?) menus to appear, and so on. One problem with all these secondary menus (and so on) is that the last menu you use stays on-screen until you choose the `AutoCAD` item at the top of the side-screen menu. Choosing this item makes the side-screen menu revert to its main menu.

The side-screen menu in the DOS version of AutoCAD can be used as a menu accelerator, because that version doesn't have menu shortcuts such as Alt+F+S to save, as does AutoCAD for Windows. But using the side-screen menu this way is pointless in the Windows version. If you do need the side-screen menu, however, it's always available. Just choose <u>O</u>ptions⇨<u>P</u>references from the menu bar, and then choose Screen Men<u>u</u> to turn on the side-screen menu.

What Really Makes AutoCAD Tick?

In reading about and using AutoCAD, you encounter two topics very frequently: *system variables,* which are very old, and *dialog boxes,* which in their current, highly usable forms are relatively new. System variables and dialog boxes are closely related; understanding them and how they work together can dramatically speed your ascent to proficiency in AutoCAD.

Setting system variables

System variables are settings that AutoCAD checks before it decides how to do something. If you set the system variable SAVETIME to ten, for example, AutoCAD automatically saves your file every ten minutes; if you set SAVETIME to 60, the time between saves is one hour. Hundreds of system variables control the operations of AutoCAD.

Of these hundreds of system variables in AutoCAD, more than 40 system variables control dimensioning alone. (*Dimensioning* is AutoCAD's automatic generation of labels that show the distance between two points. Different professions, and different professionals, have very different standards for how dimensions on their drawings should look. Using dimensions is described in detail in Chapter 11.)

AutoCAD, like most programs, has certain settings that you can change. AutoCAD is different from many other programs, however, in that you can access and change its settings directly. (Many programs hide their variables behind dialog boxes, icons, and so on so that you don't change them directly.) Just type **SETVAR** on the command line, followed by the variable name and then the new value you want for the variable. Then press Enter. Figure 3-13 shows the first 20 or so system variables in AutoCAD. (You can access this list by typing the command **SETVAR,** followed by **?** for the variable name, and then pressing Enter to specify that you want to list all variables.)

The capability to change a system variable directly is very powerful and worth learning the names and appropriate range of settings for the system variables that you use regularly. But expecting you to remember literally hundreds of variables, how they work, and how they interact with one another is just too much—even for all you "power users" out there. This is where dialog boxes come in.

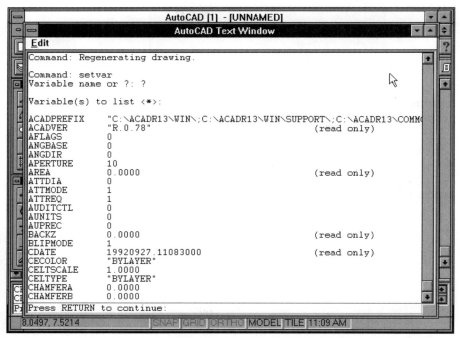

Figure 3-13:
Some of the system variables in AutoCAD.

Dancing with dialog boxes

AutoCAD's dialog boxes are an easy way to control collections of related system variables, much like a dashboard controls a car's functions. By using dialog boxes, you can handle all the related settings that may otherwise be confusing if you changed them directly through system variables.

The best single example of the power inherent in using dialog boxes to set system variables can be demonstrated through the set of dialog boxes that enable you to manage dimensions. Because you can specify so many different elements about each dimension, AutoCAD enables you to create *dimension styles,* which are named groups of dimension settings you can choose via a single menu command. The Dimension Styles dialog box, as shown in Figure 3-14, controls dimension styles.

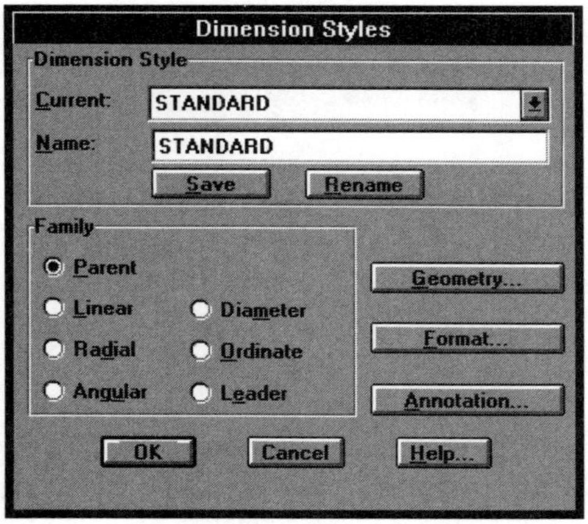

Figure 3-14:
The Dimension Styles dialog box.

To access this dialog box, choose Data⇨Dimension Style, or type **DDIM** on the command line and press Enter. Each of the options in the right-hand corner of the Dimension Styles dialog box — Geometry, Format, and Annotation — opens another dialog box, each of which in turn controls several more system variables.

The Help option for each dialog box describes what that dialog box does and the system variables that the dialog box controls. If you find yourself changing one setting regularly, you can use Help to find the name of the system variable that holds that setting and then change the value in the system variable quickly and directly from the command line. For complicated tasks such as creating new dimension styles, however, you're best off sticking to the dialog boxes.

Fun with F1

Both the DOS and Windows versions of AutoCAD feature powerful Help systems. Each includes a searchable database of topics, information on how to use Help, and an overview of what's new in Release 13. The Windows version also includes a Quick Tour of AutoCAD and a tutorial called Learning AutoCAD. Both versions are context-sensitive: That is, if you access Help in the middle of executing a command, Help for that specific command appears first. (You can then navigate from there to anyplace else in the Help system.)

Figure 3-15 shows the AutoCAD Help menu.

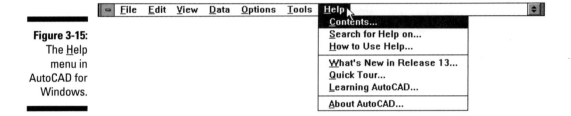

Figure 3-15:
The Help
menu in
AutoCAD for
Windows.

The Windows version of AutoCAD offers several Help features lacking in the DOS version: hot key access to Help, graphics in the Help screens, the on-line overview of AutoCAD, and the interactive tutorial. The Help system in AutoCAD for Windows is very much worth whatever time you need to take learning how to use it.

You can even annotate Help and put bookmarks in it. (And, no, I don't mean the kind made of cheap cardstock that you place between the pages of books such as this one to keep your place; these are *electronic* versions of those more tangible varieties.) Bookmarks are probably worthwhile only if you make a big deal of them and then distribute the resulting bulked-up file to all the other AutoCAD users in your organization. Then, of course, you must be prepared to redo them the next time you upgrade AutoCAD. Check out the Bookmark entry in the AutoCAD Help system if you really want (and think you need) instructions on how to use bookmarks; because you're unlikely to use them in the normal course of human events, they're not covered any further in this book.

Extra-sensitive Help

No, *extra-sensitive Help* isn't some kind of new, improved psychotherapy. It's just another term for *context-sensitive Help,* which is probably the most useful kind of Help you'll find in AutoCAD for Windows. You access context-sensitive Help in AutoCAD in two ways: by pressing F1 or by choosing the Help button in a dialog box.

If you're in the middle of entering a command, you can access Help by pressing the F1 key. Help then appears for that command. This kind of context-sensitive Help doesn't work if you're choosing items from the menus, however, unless you're to the point where the command line displays something.

If you simply hold the mouse cursor over the Circle icon in the Draw floating toolbar and then press F1, for example, the overall Help screen titled Contents appears. But if you click the Circle icon, a command appears on the command line. If you choose Help at this point, a specific Help screen for the Circle command appears. Figure 3-16 shows AutoCAD Help for the Circle command

You can access Help for dialog boxes by pressing the Help button in a dialog box. This Help feature is otherwise identical to Help for other parts of AutoCAD.

Anytime you use Help in the Windows version of AutoCAD, you can return directly to the main AutoCAD screen by pressing the Alt+Tab key combination to cycle through your currently running tasks.

A typical Help screen contains several *live areas,* which enable you to move around in the Help system, as well as *dead areas,* which just kinda lie there and contain information. (If the latter start to decompose a bit, don't worry; no smells exist in cyberspace!) The live areas of the Help screen include the following elements:

✔ **Menu bar:** Each Help window has its own *menu bar* that you can use to control Help in general. The most important function here is the Print Topic option on the File menu.

✔ **Toolbar:** Help even has its own *toolbar* for use in navigating through the Help system by using the following buttons:

• The *Contents* button provides a guide to menu entries and commands you can enter by using the keyboard.

• The *Search* button opens a window that enables you to type in an entry or select the entry from a scrolling list. You can then choose the Go To button in the Search window to move to a secondary topic.

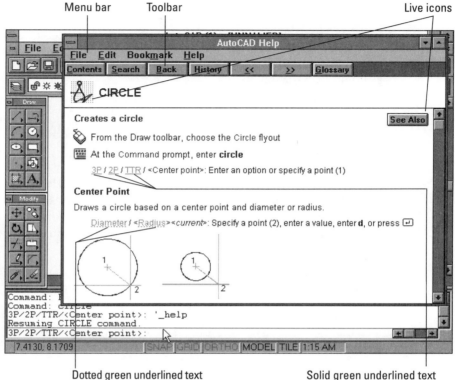

Figure 3-16:
The AutoCAD
Help screen
for the Circle
command in
AutoCAD for
Windows.

- The *Back* button returns you to previously viewed Help screens visited during the current session. Back is something you are likely to use often, because it keeps you from feeling lost in the Help system.

- The *History* button accesses a list of topics viewed in the current session.

- The << button takes you to the topic just before the current topic in alphabetical order — which is also the topic immediately above the current one in the Search scrolling list.

- The >> button takes you to the topic just after the current topic in alphabetical order — which is also the topic immediately below the current one in the Search scrolling list.

- The *Glossary* button displays the Windows Help Glossary.

✔ **Live icons:** Some of the icons in the Help screens are considered *live*—that is, they *do* something. (Unlike some supposedly "live" people I could name). Holding the mouse pointer over one of these icons turns the pointer into a hand with a raised index finger (a rude gesture in some cultures!), indicating that something happens after you click the mouse button at that point:

- Clicking the graphic in the upper left corner of the Help screen moves you up a level in the Contents hierarchy.

- Clicking the See Also icon opens a pop-up window containing a list of topics related to the currently selected item.

✔ **Solid green underlined text:** Text underlined in solid green is linked to other topics related to that described in the current Help screen. Clicking solid green underlined text opens a new window that gives you additional information.

✔ **Dotted green underlined text:** Text underlined in a dotted green line opens a pop-up box containing a definition of the underlined term.

If you have enough free space on-screen that you can afford to waste some of it, you may want to keep the Help screen open on top of whatever else is on-screen. To do so, just press F1 to access AutoCAD Help and choose Help⇨Always on Top from the Help menu bar. You'll never get anything done with that Help screen floating around on top of whatever you're trying to work on, but you'll always know exactly *what* it is you're trying to do! Seriously, though, except for looking neat, Always on Top is a pretty useless option; few AutoCAD users have enough extra screen space to set aside for perpetual on-screen Help.

Contentment through contents

You can access the same Help screens a couple other ways. Pressing F1 whenever you're not in the middle of any specific command or choosing Help⇨Contents from the main menu bar opens a Help screen that enables you to access Help for menu items, for commands, or for system variables, as shown in Figure 3-17. This feature is pretty useful, and just clicking around in it is a good way to learn some basics of AutoCAD.

The search is on

Choosing Help⇨Search for Help On from the main menu bar, or choosing Search from within any AutoCAD Help screen, opens a Search dialog box containing a long, scrolling list of topics. Unfortunately, this dialog box contains literally hundreds of topics, and finding the one you need can be very difficult unless you already know the command name, menu name, or system variable name you want.

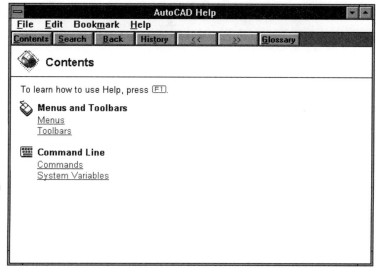

Figure 3-17:
The AutoCAD
Help Contents
screen.

If you harbor only the vaguest idea of the topic you seek — say, different ways to output your drawing file — you can expect to spend a great deal of time clicking around in the Search dialog box. As you learn more details about how AutoCAD works, however, the Search option becomes more valuable to you.

The mechanics of using Search also can be a little difficult to master. To locate the topic you want in the scrolling list of Search items, you must *scroll,* or *drag,* the button in the scroll bar up and down, up and down. . . . Merely typing the first few letters of a potential search item doesn't jump you down to it on the list, as it does in some programs. Then, if you simply click an item in the list, nothing happens; you must *double-click* it to get anywhere. What's more, after you *do* finally double-click an item, you don't even get immediate Help for it; instead, a list of topics *related* to the double-clicked item appears in a separate scroll box lower in the same dialog box. (Aarrgh!)

Unfortunately, only one item often appears in this second box, and moving the mouse down to double-click yet again seems like extra work for so little reward. This is really just a minor quibble, however, and something you'll probably get used to much quicker than I did. After you double-click the item in this separate area, the Help you need quickly appears in a regular AutoCAD Help screen. (At last!) Figure 3-18 shows a Help Search dialog box with a search already in progress.

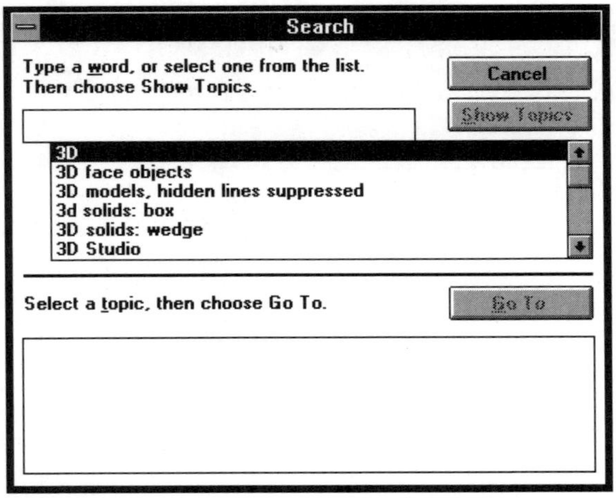

Figure 3-18:
The AutoCAD
Help system's
Search
dialog box.

What's new in Release 13

If you're an experienced AutoCAD user, What's New in Release 13 is an especially valuable Help menu option. Just open the Help menu and choose What's New in Release 13 to access a dialog box containing an overview of all the new features and commands in this release. Therein you can find detailed instructions on using this What's New in AutoCAD Release 13 dialog box to your best advantage. Or click the New Features option to see just what new functions actually are to be found in Release 13. Or click Command Summary to learn how to access one of these new functions.

Figure 3-19 shows the What's New in AutoCAD Release 13 dialog box, which currently displays the New Commands dialog box that appears after you choose the Command List option. Recommended.

Taking the Quick Tour

The Quick Tour feature of AutoCAD Help also is pretty useful for becoming familiar with the program. (Unfortunately, it displays a different "look and feel" than does the What's New in Release 13 tutorial.) You can access the Quick Tour by choosing Help⇨Quick Tour from the main menu. You can probably skip the first choice in the Quick Tour, which tells you how to use the tutorial. At the top level, you click a choice to go to it, but each chapter is sequential; you tour through each chapter by using the left- and right-arrow buttons.

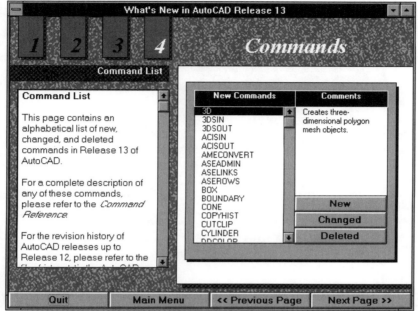

Figure 3-19:
The New
Commands
dialog box is
accessed
from the
What's New
in AutoCAD
Release 13
dialog box.

Each Quick Tour topic screen includes a Show button that displays or demonstrates the topic in question. The quick tour doesn't cover all possible AutoCAD topics (what does?), but it's a good learning tool for those functions it does describe. Figure 3-20 shows a Quick Tour screen that explains paper space.

Learning AutoCAD

The AutoCAD Help system tutorial is intended to be a bigger deal than either of the two features described in the preceding sections. To access it, choose Help⇨Learning AutoCAD from the main menu bar. Then set aside some time to go through all of it (it's pretty self-explanatory). Unless you already know AutoCAD pretty well, this tutorial is a worthwhile investment of your time.

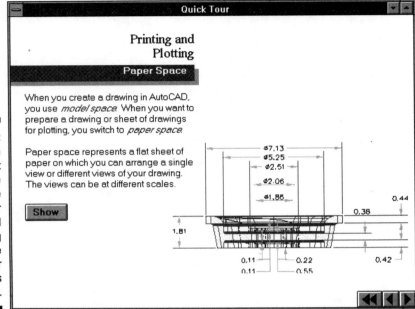

Figure 3-20:
You can
learn about
paper space
from the
Quick Tour
Printing and
Plotting
screen in the
AutoCAD for
Windows
Help system.

And if that's not enough help . . .

The Help system in AutoCAD for Windows Release 13 also contains the entire Release 13 Command Reference on-line. And the CD version of Release 13 contains the program's entire set of manuals on-line, as well as providing the printed versions. Don't *read* the manuals on-line for long, however; use the on-line version for searching and jumping around. If you really need to read big sections, grab the printed versions. By reading from paper instead of from a glowing, flickering screen, your eyes are much less likely to feel like hard-boiled eggs halfway through a section. (Better yet, grab this book.)

Chapter 4

Take Control of AutoCAD

In This Chapter

▶ How AutoCAD works

▶ How AutoCAD looks

▶ How AutoCAD draws

*Y*ou can customize a ton of features in AutoCAD, but you absolutely *must* configure a few AutoCAD settings correctly before you can even start doing productive work. Even working through examples is hard unless you have a few of the program's customization options set up correctly. So use this chapter to fix up AutoCAD and make it look sharp and act cool — just the way you want it to.

AutoCAD was one of the first PC graphics programs available, so its developers had to make some best guesses in deciding how things should work in the program. They tried hard, but in several cases, they guessed wrong. Starting with Release 12, AutoCAD at least opened the door for you to configure some aspects of the program — enough so that it now works to some extent like a standard Mac or Windows program. *Some*, but, alas, not all. So . . . follow the instructions in the remainder of this chapter to make AutoCAD work at least sort of as it should. Kinda. Maybe. (Fingers crossed.)

It's not my (de)fault

Your copy of AutoCAD is currently set up as it is for many reasons. Autodesk can change the default settings created at installation for different versions of AutoCAD and for different releases. The AutoCAD dealer, CAD manager, or other person who set up your system may have changed some things around. The third-party program you're using also may change certain default settings. Finally, if you or anyone else has used your version of AutoCAD at all, it's more than likely that a few settings have changed.

This book doesn't assume that a feature of your AutoCAD program is at some fixed,

(continued)

(continued)

default setting until it suggests that you change it. This book tells you what these settings mean and how to reconfigure them. If some of the settings are already set correctly on your system — because they are the default setting or because someone already reconfigured your program to match the correct settings — that's one less thing for you to worry about.

After you understand these settings and what they control — no mean feat, because AutoCAD is one of the most configurable programs around — you can always change them yet again if you need to.

Left to its own devices, AutoCAD can seem to be working against you. But with some effort, you can turn things around.

How to Make AutoCAD Work with You

If you're experienced in working with a graphical user environment such as Windows, Macintosh, or even a typical DOS drawing program, using the mouse has probably become second nature to you. You simply click a command, an object, or almost anything else on-screen to *select* (or highlight) it; then you click something else to select that item instead. To select two items, click the first, press and hold the Shift key, and then click the second. (Ditto for the third, fourth, and so on.)

But not in AutoCAD! Oh, no! AutoCAD works exactly the opposite of every major graphics environment or program known to man, woman, child, or computer nerd. But never fear! This chapter helps you fix whatever you can and work around what you can't. Then you can get AutoCAD on your side and get to work.

Why is AutoCAD so weird?

As is true of so many other questionable practices in computing, AutoCAD's odd style of user interaction is an attempt to maintain *backward compatibility* — the same commands and working style — with earlier versions of the program — or, in other words: "Gee, we did a *really* bad job of interface design in the previous 17 versions; better not change anything now, or our users may be upset."

As a pioneering CAD program with devoted users, AutoCAD carries a great deal of baggage. AutoCAD's command-driven style of interaction is buried deep in the program's source code; no one now has the guts to try to forge in and change it.

The problem is that almost anyone who uses other Windows programs — even many expe-

(continued)

(continued)

rienced AutoCAD users — would prefer that AutoCAD be brought up to speed with the rest of the computing world. The configuration options that you learn to change in this section go partway toward making the program more user-accessible. In the meantime, we can only hope that future versions of the program become more and more like other programs for Windows and so many other graphical environments.

Making AutoCAD work like other programs

Using a graphical interface such as Windows can be likened to driving a car: After you learn to do it, you don't think about the details any longer. But to make AutoCAD work right, you must explicitly specify to the program certain details that may, to you, seem obvious. (Ah, but not to AutoCAD! At least until you set them . . .) You must, therefore, correctly configure the following settings, called *selection settings*, to make AutoCAD work more intuitively:

- ✔ **Noun/Verb Selection:** AutoCAD's built-in mode of interaction calls for you to enter a command and then choose the objects to which the command applies. In Windows, you normally select objects first and *then* specify the command. AutoCAD calls the Windows method *Noun/Verb Selection.* You should turn on this option. The following two sections describe how to activate Noun/Verb Selection and other selection settings.

  Some advanced AutoCAD commands do *not* work on objects you already selected, even if Noun/Verb Selection is turned on. These commands ignore your current selection after you enter the command and ask you to make a new selection.

- ✔ **Use Shift to Add:** In other programs, clicking different items changes the current selection; you must press and hold the Shift key to add additional items to the selection. AutoCAD, on the other hand, adds items to the current selection after you click each subsequent item; if you hold Shift to click a second item, that item is actually *deselected* and removed from the current *selection set.* (Hmmm. Maybe the programmer working on this feature got the Shift scared out of him? Naaaaahhhh.) This crazy feature, of course, drives non-AutoCAD veterans nuts! To make the Shift key work as it does in Windows, turn on the Use Shift to Add option.

- ✔ **Press and Drag:** To create a selection window in AutoCAD, you click one place in the drawing area, *let go of the mouse button,* and then click again somewhere else. In doing so, you establish the two corners of the selection window. To enable the click-drag-release style of windowing that the rest of the world is used to — in which you click the mouse button, hold it down as you move the mouse, and in this way draw a rectangle around the objects you want—you must turn on the Press and Drag option.

✔ **Implied Windowing:** If you turn on the Implied Windowing option, AutoCAD enables you to use selection windows in two different ways: If you drag from left to right, everything inside the window is selected; if you drag from right to left, everything inside *and crossing* —that is, partly in and partly out of—the window is selected. This feature takes practice to use effectively but is well worth the trouble to learn. On the other hand, if you don't turn this feature on, well, believe me — you *don't* want to know what it takes to establish a selection window if you leave this option turned off. So just go ahead and turn it on.

✔ **Object Grouping:** Although the Object Grouping selection setting is not a "fix-it" item, as are the previous four settings, it's a neat new feature that you should be sure to enable. In Release 13, AutoCAD adds the capability to create named groups of objects and select them by typing in the name. You can lump together all the executive's desks in a building, for example, and name them *Executive Desks*. (Then, if you're paid late for the drawing, you can specify that all objects in the Executive Desks group be made out of particle board. Heh, heh, heh…)

Macintosh user's gloat note

If you're a longtime Mac user, you're no doubt feeling smug right now. And you're right; everything described here as *how Windows works* and *the right way to do things* was first popularized by the Macintosh and such programs as MacWrite and MacPaint, starting waaaay back in 1984.

This book, however, addresses DOS and Windows users here and elsewhere, because that's where the action in CAD is these days. Maybe the PowerPC will change things and the next release of AutoCAD will come out for the Macintosh first — or at least second. Until then, Mac users reading this book must settle for feeling slightly superior whenever user interface considerations are mentioned.

Setting selection settings from the Object Selection Settings dialog box

To set selection settings from AutoCAD's Object Selection Settings dialog box, follow these easy steps:

   1. **Choose Options ⇨ Selection from the menu bar. (Or type** DDSELECT **on the command line and press Enter.)**

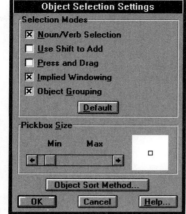

Figure 4-1:
The Object
Selection
Settings
dialog box.

The Object Selection Settings dialog box appears (see Figure 4-1).

Release 13 uses the word *object* to refer to a single, selectable element in the drawing; previous releases use the word *entity* to mean the same thing. Despite its science-fictional implications, *entity* was one term in previous versions that I liked. Oh well.

2. **Click the Noun/Verb Selection check box to turn on this setting (if currently off).**

   The setting is on if an *X* appears in the check box, as shown in Figure 4-2. (In this figure, for example, Use Shift to Add and Press and Drag, which were turned off in the preceding figure, have been turned on.)

3. **Click the Use Shift to Add check box.**

4. **Click the Press and Drag check box.**

5. **Click the Implied Windowing check box.**

6. **Click the Object Grouping check box.**

7. **Click the OK button to accept the changes and close the dialog box.**

Good news: The Selection Modes area of the Object Selection Settings dialog box also contains a Default button. Choosing Default makes these settings revert back to the original AutoCAD default settings. (By the way, the default settings are Noun/Verb Selection, Implied Windowing, and Object Grouping on and Use Shift to Add and Press and Drag off, as shown in Figure 4-1.) *Bad news:* The Undo command doesn't work for the Default button, so write down your current settings before choosing Default if you think that you may need them again. *Even more bad news:* Not every dialog box includes a Default button, so don't get used to it.

Figure 4-2:
X marks the
spot; these
selection
settings are
all turned on
now.

Setting selection settings from the command line

You're likely to change these selection settings only infrequently, so using the menus to set them is probably your best bet. When you want to change your settings a year from now, you're far more likely to remember how to do so from the menus if you did it that way in the first place. But if you're a *real* keyboard fan, just follow these steps to set selection settings from the command line:

1. **At the command line, type** PICKFIRST 1 **and then press Enter to turn on Noun/Verb Selection.**

2. **Type** PICKADD 0 **and press Enter to turn on Use Shift to Add.**

   (And don't ask me why, but 0 means *on* for the Use Shift to Add option, but it means *off* for all the other options. That means, of course, that if you want to turn *off* any of these options by using the command line, type the appropriate command and a 0 instead of a 1 — except for PICKADD, in which case . . . well, you get the idea.)

3. **Type** PICKDRAG 1 **and press Enter to turn on Press and Drag.**

4. **Type** PICKAUTO 1 **and press Enter to turn on Implied Windowing.**

5. **Type** PICKSTYLE 1 **and press Enter to turn on Object Grouping and associative hatching.**

   (You learn more about hatching in Chapter 12.)

To turn off any of these selection settings from the command line, type the appropriate command for the setting and **0** (or **1** for that nonconforming PICKADD fellow) and press Enter.

Object sort methods . . . sorta, kinda . . .

AutoCAD stores the different objects in your drawing in a database-style format, which is just AutoCAD's way of keeping things organized. Each separate object is called, appropriately enough, an *object* — a highly overused but accurate enough word.

AutoCAD maintains a set of sorted keys, kinda like ID tags, for the objects in your drawing. In crowded

drawings, however, the number of such keys can become an issue. If selecting the objects you want in a crowded drawing is difficult, use the Object Sort Method button in the Object Selection Settings dialog box to increase your options for sorting the objects, which makes selecting objects much easier — though not without some increase in the size of your drawing and a slow-down in its loading speed.

Getting saved

Yeah, you know about all those little things in life you wish you'd done way back when you had the chance: filling out your taxes before midnight on April 15; getting your brakes fixed before that nasty little accident; backing up your hard disk before it crashes forever. Well, setting the *save interval* is another one of these little things.

AutoCAD saves your drawing whenever a designated number of minutes has passed since your last save. If you save your drawing yourself before the automatic save kicks in, the save timer starts over again from that point. If you don't use the keyboard or mouse, however, AutoCAD actually stops checking to determine whether the specified amount of minutes has passed and, conse-quently, doesn't save your drawing anymore. So make sure that you remember to save your drawing yourself if you're planning to step away from your ma-chine for a while. Otherwise, you risk lost data should the power go out while AutoCAD's automatic save takes its own little R&R break.

Here's the quick version for setting this option: To change the save interval by using the menus in AutoCAD for Windows, choose Options ➪ Preferences. Then choose Every, press Tab to highlight the Minutes field, and then set the number of minutes you want between saves.

To change the save interval by using the command line in either AutoCAD for DOS or Windows, type **SAVETIME** at the command line and press Enter. (*Note:* In AutoCAD for DOS *only,* you can activate the SAVETIME command by choos-ing the Options ➪ Auto Save Time from the main menu.) However you enter the SAVETIME command, the completed sequence appears on the command line as follows:

```
Command: SAVETIME
New value for SAVETIME <120>: 10
```

Note: AutoCAD offers a default value for many options at the command prompt. If you simply press Enter at the prompt instead of typing something, AutoCAD uses the default. The default value appears on the command line in angle brackets (< >). The <120> in the preceeding line, for example, means that 120 is the default value here.

After you enter the SAVETIME command, AutoCAD prompts you for the save interval, and then it automatically saves the drawing anytime you wait longer than that interval between saves. Ten minutes is usually a good choice, but any interval you choose works. AutoCAD saves the drawing in the currently se-lected directory under the name AUTO.SV$.

Keyboard and mouse activity is what drives the mechanism that performs the saves automatically, which is why the automatic saves cease taking place if you walk away from your computer for a while. This is kind of like having a remote control that works only on weekdays; using it solves part of your problem, but not all of it. So always — *always!* — remember to save your drawing before you ever walk away from your computer for *any* reason!

Getting a grip

Grips are little handles that show up on objects after you select the object. Grips enable you to grab an object and manipulate it. Grips are cool. Having grips turned on is a Good Thing.

Like so many other features in AutoCAD (sigh), grips don't always work exactly as you'd expect them to. Chapter 8 discusses grip editing in detail. For now, however, you just need to know how to turn them on. You can do this by following these steps:

1. **Choose Options ⇨ Grips from the menu bar. Or type** DDGRIPS **on the command line and press Enter.**

    The Grips dialog box appears, as shown in Figure 4-3.

2. **Click the Enable Grips check box to turn on this feature.**

3. **Click the Enable Grips Within Blocks check box to turn off this feature.**

    You can turn this option back on later if you need to edit within a block. (See Chapter 15 for more about playing with blocks.) An empty check box means that the feature is turned off, as shown in Figure 4-3.

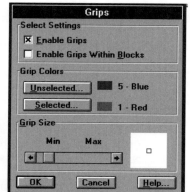

Figure 4-3:
The Grips
dialog box.

 If you want, you can also change the Grip Colors in the Grips dialog box. Grip colors help identify whether a grip is on and ready for use (blue) or on and activated as a handle (red). Unselected grips are also called *cool grips* and should be kept in a background color such as the default blue. Selected grips are called *hot grips* and should be flagged with an attention-getting color such as the default red. Choose the relevant button to open the Select Color dialog box, which enables you to make these changes (and is pretty self-explanatory in how it works). The Grip Size, too, can be changed by moving the slider box near the bottom of the Grips dialog box from Min to Max; the example window to the left of the size bar shows you the size increases or decreases of the grips as you change this option.

 You can also use the command line to enable and turn off grips — especially if you're an experienced AutoCAD for DOS user who is sometimes inflicted with "GUI fatigue" and you sometimes need to go back to the old-style AutoCAD routines as a remedy. The following steps describe the keyboard commands you use to turn grips on and grips-in-blocks off:

1. **At the command line, type** GRIPS 1, **and then press Enter.**

   This command turns on grips. To turn them off, you use a 0 instead of a 1.

2. **Type** GRIPBLOCK 0, **and then press Enter.**

   This command turns off grips within blocks; to turn them back on, you use a 1 with the command instead of a 0.

Making AutoCAD Look Good

With a little work, AutoCAD can be coaxed into responding exactly the way you want it to. (Don't you wish you had this kind of control over some of the people you know?) You can also make AutoCAD *look* right as well as act right.

At some point, you are sure to want to set up the appearance of specific drawings or a group of drawings. If you feel confident enough to tackle this task right now, jump ahead to Chapter 5. If you don't yet feel that confident just yet, however, stay with me right here for a while; this section discusses how you can make AutoCAD itself look the same every time you start it.

AutoCAD's appearance is an area in which the differences between the DOS and Windows versions of the program are very strong. The DOS version doesn't present a very attractive appearance, and you can't do much about changing it either. The Windows version, on the other hand, not only looks better, but its appearance is also far more configurable than its DOS counterpart. The Windows version, in fact, can be configured to look much like the DOS version, like a strictly Windows program, or somewhere in-between. This section deals with the appearance of the DOS and Windows versions in separate parts.

Rearranging the face of AutoCAD for DOS

In AutoCAD for DOS, your only options for changing the appearance of the screen are pretty big ones: You can turn on or off the status line, the command line, and the side-screen menu area.

You are very unlikely to want to turn off the status line, because it shows you exactly where the cursor is in your drawing and what layer you're in — very important information indeed. (Besides, who wants to lose status?) You may want to turn off the command line, but for only one reason: if you really need all your screen space and are willing to press the F1 key to toggle back and forth to the text screen whenever you want to enter a command or see AutoCAD's response.

Turning on and off the side-screen menu, however, is a real issue. Because it occupies valuable screen space in a strip down the right side of the screen, many users prefer this menu to be absent most of the time and turn it on only occasionally to run AutoLISP programs. Unfortunately, to remove (or to restore) the side-screen menu in AutoCAD for DOS, you must undertake a complicated configuration process. The handy little steps offered at the end of this section, however, should make that process as painless as possible.

Cosmetic surgery via third-party applications

Third-party applications can make a big difference in the appearance of AutoCAD; they can add menus and dialog boxes and set customization defaults in specific ways, which may be matters of substance or merely of style. If you use a third-party application, some of the information in this book may not apply directly to your working environment. If so, look for visible differences and adjust around them.

As mentioned in Chapter 2, the side-screen menu is an old, broken-down hanger-on from the bad ol' days before pull-down menus — and the more difficult programming style needed to make them work — became popular. The side-screen menu is easy for developers to use, but it doesn't really work very well, which puts more of the burden of retaining and working with it on the user. So for most AutoCAD functions, pull-down menus, dialog boxes, and icons have largely replaced the side-screen menu.

Many utility and add-on programs, however, still use the side-screen menu. And if you use a digitizer tablet to control AutoCAD, you may need the side-screen menu as an intermediary between digitizer choices and AutoCAD commands. For either situation, you need to have the side-screen menu available at least some of the time. But because it takes up valuable screen space, you want to hide it away whenever you can. Refer to the easy — or not-so-easy — instructions that follow (we're getting closer now, I promise!) to get that screen-hogging side-screen menu out of your way.

You can set all three configuration options — turning on and off the status line, command prompt, and screen menu area — during AutoCAD's initial configuration process. To change these options later, however, you must actually eliminate the ACAD.CFG file — to trick AutoCAD into thinking that it hasn't been configured yet — and then reconfigure the program. The following steps (just one more paragraph first — I swear!) show you how to do this as quickly as possible.

If you did not configure AutoCAD yourself in the first place, you may need help in reconfiguring it correctly, because every system can require you to make different configuration choices. If you are generally familiar with DOS and AutoCAD, you can go ahead and give the following steps (almost there!) a shot and then simply restore your previous ACAD.CFG configuration file if AutoCAD doesn't work correctly. If you are mostly *unfamiliar* with DOS or AutoCAD, however, I strongly advise you to get help from whoever initially configured your system before you attempt to follow these steps:

1. **At the regular DOS prompt (*not* the AutoCAD command line), rename your ACAD.CFG file to ACADOLD.CFG.**

   Your ACAD.CFG file may be located in the directory C:\ACADR13\DOS. *Do not* under any circumstance delete this file; you may need the original file in case something goes wrong with the reconfiguration. The following commands are the ones I used to rename this file on my system:

   ```
   C:>CD \ACADR13\DOS
   C:\ACADR13\DOS>REN ACAD.CFG ACADOLD.CFG
   ```

2. **Start AutoCAD by typing** ACAD **at the DOS prompt and pressing Enter.**

   AutoCAD does not start normally. Instead, AutoCAD displays its configuration screen and then prompts you for the video display and screen configuration, as shown in Figure 4-4.

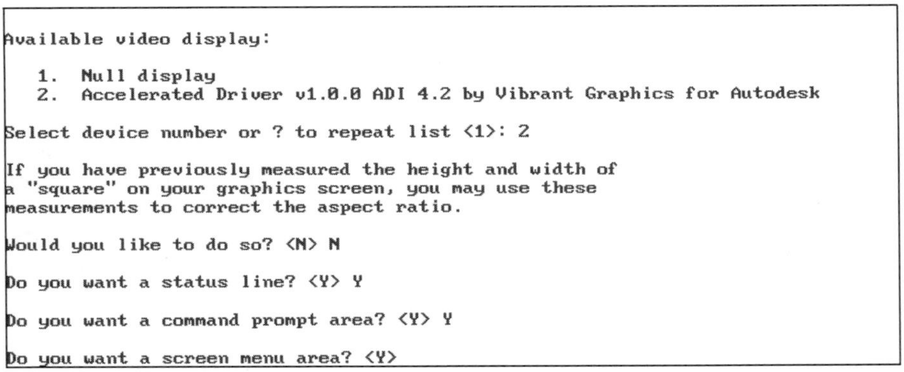

Figure 4-4:
AutoCAD for
DOS asks
about your
screen
preferences
when
reconfiguring
the program.

```
Available video display:

   1.  Null display
   2.  Accelerated Driver v1.0.0 ADI 4.2 by Vibrant Graphics for Autodesk

Select device number or ? to repeat list <1>: 2

If you have previously measured the height and width of
a "square" on your graphics screen, you may use these
measurements to correct the aspect ratio.

Would you like to do so? <N> N

Do you want a status line? <Y> Y

Do you want a command prompt area? <Y> Y

Do you want a screen menu area? <Y>
```

3. **Choose the same driver and configuration that you used in initially configuring AutoCAD.**

   If you don't know what these are, make the choices that seem to make sense for your system or consult the person who originally configured the program for you. For later use, write these settings down after you learn them.

4. **Where AutoCAD asks whether you want to correct the aspect ratio, press** N, **unless you are specifically aware of what your system needs.**

5. **Where AutoCAD asks whether you want a status line, press** Y **to keep the status line or press** N **to get rid of it.**

   Unless you have specific reasons to get rid of it, I *highly* recommend that you keep the status line.

6. **Where AutoCAD asks whether you want a command prompt area (the command line), press** Y **to keep the command prompt area or press** N **to get rid of it.**

    Again, unless you have specific reasons to get rid of it, I strongly recommend that you keep the command line area.

7. **Where AutoCAD asks whether you want a screen menu area (the side-screen menu), press** Y **to keep the side-screen menu area, or press** N **to get rid of it.**

    So just go ahead and press N to get rid of the side-screen menu area unless you think you have a specific need for it. (At least that's my thought on the subject.) Of course, if you find that you really do need the side-screen menu later, you must go through this entire process all over again to turn it back on. (Hey, nobody ever said AutoCAD configuration was easy!)

8. **Where AutoCAD asks you for the available digitizer, choose the digitizer or mouse you are using from the list provided.**

    AutoCAD considers a mouse to be a digitizer. Do not choose option 1, None, unless you are using neither a mouse nor a digitizer tablet.

    Answer any follow-up questions to this one in whatever way applies to your devices. (As you answer these and following questions, the screen scrolls to reveal its additional prompts.)

9. **Where AutoCAD asks you for the available plotter, choose the plotter connected to your system from which you want to print.**

10. **Where AutoCAD asks you for the default login name, press Enter to accept the one it provides.**

    Take note of what this default log-in name is (write it down if you need to) *before* you press Enter to accept it.

11. **Where AutoCAD asks whether you want to enable file-locking, press** N **unless you have a specific reason to say yes.**

    Note: File locking is a feature used in networked versions of AutoCAD and is not discussed further in this book. If you share AutoCAD drawings across a network, get the person who manages the network to tell you what to enter here.

12. **Where AutoCAD presents a menu asking you what to do next, choose** 0, **Exit to drawing editor.**

    But you don't actually exit yet; you still must answer one more question.

13. **Where AutoCAD asks whether you want to keep configuration changes, press** Y **to keep the changes.**

    You then return to the main AutoCAD screen.

If you respond with wrong answers during this configuration process, AutoCAD may not work correctly. If this occurs, you can fix the problem by restoring your previous configuration file: Simply exit back to DOS and copy the old configuration file over the new one. On my system, the commands to do this are shown in the following example:

```
C:\>CD \ACADR13\DOS
C:\ACADR13\DOS>REN ACAD.CFG ACADNONO.CFG
C:\ACADR13\DOS>REN ACADOLD.CFG ACAD.CFG
```

Now restart AutoCAD. And then, please, get whatever assistance you need before attempting to reconfigure AutoCAD again. (I won't tell anyone either. Promise!)

Touching up AutoCAD for Windows

In AutoCAD for Windows, you can change the program's appearance from within the program itself, so you don't need to reconfigure the entire program to make different elements of the screen appear and disappear. Whereas the DOS version requires major surgery to make it appear the way you want it to, all AutoCAD for Windows needs is a little dab or two of makeup here and there.

Modifying the location and appearance of the toolbars and the command line in AutoCAD for Windows is just a matter of manipulating their windows. Making the side-screen menu appear and disappear, however, is somewhat more complicated, but this section shows you how to do it.

Although the side-screen menu is no longer very practical for controlling AutoCAD itself — menus, dialog boxes, and icons work far better — it's still used by some utility programs written in AutoLISP (the original AutoCAD programming language) and by some digitizers (those silly tablets used both for drawing and for controlling AutoCAD, remember?). So you may want to turn on the side-screen menu whenever you run utilities or use a digitizer and then turn it off again after you no longer need it for these functions and want to save screen space.

1. **Choose Options ⇨ Preferences from the menu bar. Or type** PREFER-
   ENCES **on the command line and press Enter.**

   The Preferences dialog box appears. (Figure 4-5 displays the Preferences dialog box with the side-screen menu in the background.)

2. **With the System panel displayed, click the Screen Men<u>u</u> check box to turn the side-screen menu on or off.**

   If an *X* appears in the check box, the side-screen menu is turned on; if no *X* appears, the side-screen menu is gone from your screen.

3. **Click <u>O</u>K to exit the Preferences dialog box.**

   The side-screen menu now either appears or disappears, depending upon the check box selection you made.

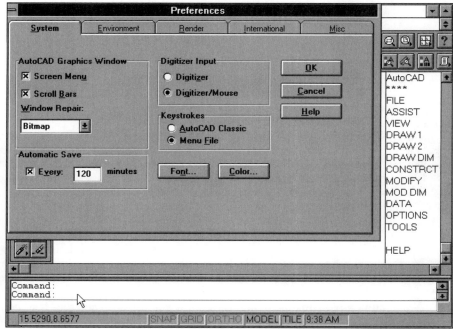

Figure 4-5:
The
AutoCAD for
Windows
Preferences
dialog box
with the
side-screen
menu in the
background.

Making AutoCAD Quicker on the Draw

You can spend the rest of your career fine-tuning how AutoCAD draws — if you really want to, that is. You don't want to, of course, or you'd be reading *AutoCAD Disassembled: Vol. XXIII* instead of this book. But you do need to know how to set a couple drawing-related settings to do much of anything. This section tackles those particular settings, providing you with just enough info to get you started, and the book harps on them again later as necessary.

Turning on running object snaps

In most drawings, different objects touch each other, usually at specific points such as the endpoint of a line, the center of a circle, or the intersection of two existing objects. Drawing becomes much easier if these points act as *hot spots* for the mouse pointer. That is, the move pointer is pulled toward these areas, which enables you to more easily draw objects so that they touch each other. *Object snaps* give you the flexibility to control which points on each object draw the cursor to them.

Don't feel bad if you become confused over the difference between the *snap grid* and *object snaps*. Because they both have *snap* in their names, the distinction can sometimes seem a little tricky. (Kinda like if you're cooking and you ask your significant other for the thyme; if she says "5:30" instead of handing you a jar of spice, this is not really her fault.) The snap grid makes objects snap to points a predefined distance apart in the drawing area, while object snaps force objects to snap to certain locations on other objects. But don't worry: The more you use AutoCAD, the less often these terms confuse you.

What can be even more confusing is that you can also use other, specific snaps over and above the snap grid and object snaps whenever you're actually drawing. But these aren't involved in your setup procedures, and Chapter 6 describes these in detail anyway, along with other specific drawing techniques, so I'll try not to trip you up any more here by adding these to the mix now. (So why did I bring them up in the first place, you wonder? Ummmm, maybe . . . perversity? Naaaahhhh!)

Okay, back to the subject. And if you're a new user, listen up, because object snaps are *really* important. If you don't use object snaps, you can draw lines that *look* as if they connect, but in truth, they don't *really* connect. And as you build up your drawing, these nasty little unconnected lines can cause you more and more problems — and they show you up as an amateur if someone else edits your drawing later. What's more, that's just in *two-dimensional* (2D) drawings. In *three-dimensional* (3D) drawings, unconnected objects that merely look as if they're touching from one point of view may actually be inches, meters, or even *miles* apart if viewed from a different angle.

This discrepancy becomes evident because, without the benefit of object snaps, lines can too easily be set up at *totally* different distances from one another — and they show it! — if you add in that oh-so-important third dimension. So use your object snaps to avoid this unfortunate problem; they enable you to draw connecting lines quickly and accurately — making such lines much harder for you to mess up, even if you try.

Important object snaps available in AutoCAD include those to the endpoint of a line, the midpoint of a line, the intersection of two objects, and the center of a circle. Using object snaps all the time takes a little self-discipline until you get good at using them, so try out the steps in the following section a few times and then use them in your own work whenever possible until they become second nature.

Using the Running Object Snap dialog box

The most comprehensive way to manage object snaps is by using the Running Object Snap dialog box. Open this dialog box often and use it to control exactly which object snaps are on.

1. **Choose Options ⇨ Running Object Snap from the menu bar. Or type DDOSNAP on the command line and press Enter.**

   Another way to open this dialog box is to press and hold the right mouse button for a second or so.

   The Running Object Snap dialog box opens, as shown in Figure 4-6.

   To open the Running Object Snap dialog box by using keyboard shortcuts in Windows, press Alt+O+O.

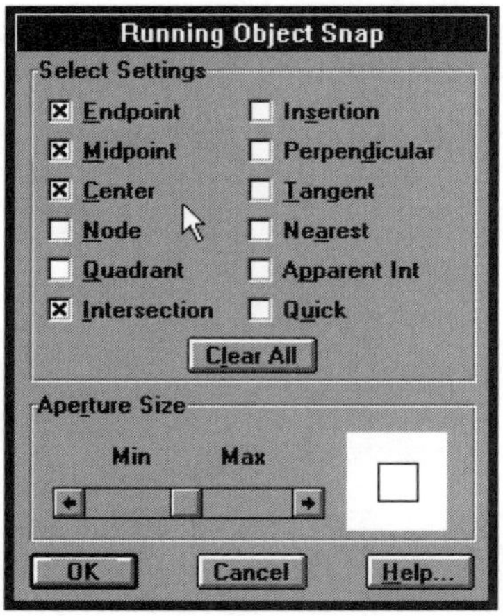

Figure 4-6:
The Running
Object Snap
dialog box.

Running Object Snap
Select Settings
☒ Endpoint ☐ Insertion
☒ Midpoint ☐ Perpendicular
☒ Center ☐ Tangent
☐ Node ☐ Nearest
☐ Quadrant ☐ Apparent Int
☒ Intersection ☐ Quick
Clear All
Aperture Size
Min   Max
OK   Cancel   Help...

2. **Click the different settings check boxes to set the ones you want and clear the ones you don't want.**

   A good initial working set is to have the Endpoint, Midpoint, Center, and Intersection options turned on, as shown in the figure.

You can use the Clear All button to clear all the current object snap settings and then just click the ones that you want to set. Even if this takes more mouse clicks in some cases, starting from a clean slate may be quicker than thinking about which snaps are already set after you first open the dialog box and which of those need to be turned off.

Setting object snaps by using the command line

You can set and clear object snaps from the command line, too. This procedure is fast after you get good at it, but it's hard to learn. So until you do, follow these steps:

1. **Type** OSNAP **on the command line and then press Enter.**

2. **Type at the command prompt the snap modes you want and press Enter.**

   This is the tricky part, because you must type in at least the first few letters of the name of each object snap mode you want to use. The following example shows what to type to set the endpoint, midpoint, center, and intersection snaps:

   ```
   Command: osnap
   Object snap modes: end, mid, cen, inter
   ```

Loading up linetypes

AutoCAD forces you to load linetypes into your DWG file before you can access them. This is a Bad Thing that you must work around. Load up a working set of linetypes *before* you need them so that you can do your work with fewer interruptions.

Each linetype you load takes up a few kilobytes of RAM (random access memory), whether you actually use the linetype or not. So don't load up a huge set of linetypes unless you really need them. On the other hand, having a few too many linetypes is better than having a few too few.

Using the Select Linetype dialog box

Most users find the Select Linetype dialog box their best vehicle for managing linetypes. (If you use a number of different linetypes from different sources, however, you may also want to learn to use the LINETYPE command, as described in the following section.)

To load a working set of linetypes, follow these steps:

1. **Choose Data ⇨ Linetype from the menu bar. Or type** DDLTYPE **on the command line and press Enter.**

   The Select Linetype dialog box appears.

   You can also open the Select Linetype dialog box from the object properties bar; just click the Linetype icon, which displays three different horizontal lines and is located right in the middle of the bar.

2. **To load linetypes, choose the Load button at the bottom of the dialog box.**

   The Load or Reload Linetypes dialog box appears, as shown in Figure 4-7.

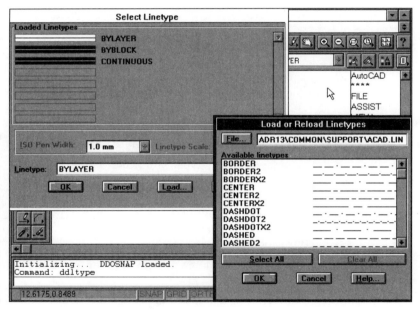

Figure 4-7: The Load or Reload Linetypes dialog box is accessed from the Select Linetype dialog box.

3. **Choose the linetypes file you want and then click OK.**

   In many cases, you need the default linetypes file ACAD.LIN in the SUP-PORT subdirectory. If so, the file is already chosen for you and appears in the text box at the top of the dialog box, so you can skip this step. To find a different linetypes file, however, you must click the File button. You can then use the dialog box that appears to locate the specific linetypes file you want (with the file extension LIN). The only linetypes file available, however, is ACAD. LIN unless you've installed others on your system.

4. **Choose from the Available Linetypes list of the Load or Reload Linetypes dialog box any linetypes in the file you selected that you want to load.**

   Scroll up and down through the list to locate the linetypes you want. Click a linetype to select it from the list; click it again to remove it. To select more than one linetype at a time, press and hold the Shift key as you click each linetype to add it to your selection set. Continue until you highlight all the linetypes you want to load.

   If you need to load a large number of linetypes, click Select All to highlight all the linetypes. Then hold the Shift key and click the ones you *don't* want; this removes them from the selection set.

5. **Click OK to load the selected linetypes and return to the Select Linetype dialog box.**

6. **Click OK in the Select Linetype dialog box to complete the process.**

Using the keyboard to load linetypes

Using the keyboard to manage linetypes is faster than using the dialog box, but only if you remember the required commands. Follow these steps to load linetypes by using the keyboard:

1. **Type LINETYPE on the command line and press Enter.**

2. **Type LOAD on the command line and press Enter to load linetypes.**

3. **Type the name(s) of the linetypes you want to load.**

   Choices available in the default file, ACAD.LIN, include BORDER, CENTER, DASHDOT, DASHED, DIVIDE, DOT, HIDDEN, and PHANTOM. Variations of these linetypes, such as BORDER2 and BORDER2X, also are included, as are a number of ISO-compliant linetypes. (Figure 4-7 shows how some of these linetypes look.)

4. **Type FILE on the command line and press Enter to choose the linetype file you want.**

   The Select Linetype File dialog box appears. Choose the linetype file you want to use from this dialog box..

5. **Load more linetypes by repeating steps 2 through 4, or press Enter to exit.**

Getting the layered look

Layers are the most important tool you have in AutoCAD for organizing your drawings. Imagine for just a moment how your body would look if it didn't have a skeleton. (*That* should wake you up!) Well, that's exactly what your AutoCAD drawing is like without layers: a pulsating, jumbled mass that can't do very much. Putting different elements of your drawing on different layers, therefore, such as text on one layer and dimensions on another, is an important factor in creating perfect AutoCAD drawings.

You needn't make all your layer decisions up front, however, because AutoCAD enables you to add a layer, or rename an existing layer, at any point in the drawing cycle. (Deleting a layer, however, is harder work.) You should always create at least a couple of additional layers as you start drawing so that you aren't forced to just stick everything in layer 0 and thus end up with a spineless blob of a drawing, like that hapless body without its skeleton. (Blecchh!)

The Layer Control dialog box is not one of AutoCAD's best features. A number of the odd little differences between AutoCAD and other programs come to the fore in this one place. But if you are a new user of AutoCAD, trust me; the current Layer dialog box is *much* better than that of previous versions of the program. And after you get used to this version's dialog box, it's really not too bad to use.

As you create new data, it goes on the layer that is designated "current." (Initially, layer 0 is the current layer.) You can make the data on a layer invisible by turning off that layer; you can prevent data on a layer from being updated by freezing it. You can modify or erase data on any visible layer that's not frozen.

AutoCAD enables you to specify different colors and linetypes for different objects. Use this capability to distinguish and organize different types of objects. But the best way to use colors and, in many cases, linetypes is to assign to everything on a specific layer the same color and linetype. That way, you can flag the different layers in your drawing by the colors and linetypes in them. If you haven't done so already, use the information in the preceding section, "Loading up linetypes," to load a working set of linetypes. Then you're ready to define your initial working set of layers.

Layer usage — that is, what exactly goes on each layer — and *layer names* are a big deal in AutoCAD, because drawings from different people don't work well together without a consistent layer usage and naming scheme. If your work-place uses a set of standard layer names, learn what it is and then use it. Otherwise, you'll need to figure out your own approach and stick with that. Dimensions in your drawings, for example, usually should be placed on their own separate layer, and that layer should always be assigned a consistent name, such as DIMENSIONS. This way, you can easily add parts of one drawing to another. If you need to share drawings with others, you need only to rename your layers to match their names and then get back to work.

Unfortunately, making mistakes in creating layers is far too easy to do, so you'll need to just keep on trying until you finally get it right. By following the steps in this section, you can actually create and name a layer and then modify it to use a specific color and linetype. If you're in a hurry to create many layers, you can go ahead do all the creating and naming first and then make all your color and linetype assignments afterward.

Creating and modifying layers with the Layer Control dialog box

Using the Layer Control dialog box is your best bet to create, edit, and manage layers. It's a little hard to use, however, so make sure that you follow these steps carefully:

1. **Choose Data ⇨ Layers from the menu bar. Or type DDLMODES on the command line and press Enter.**

   The Layer Control dialog box appears, as shown in Figure 4-8.

   You can also open the Layer Control dialog box from the object properties bar by clicking the Layers icon, which displays three stacked planes (geometric, not air) and is located at the far left end of the bar.

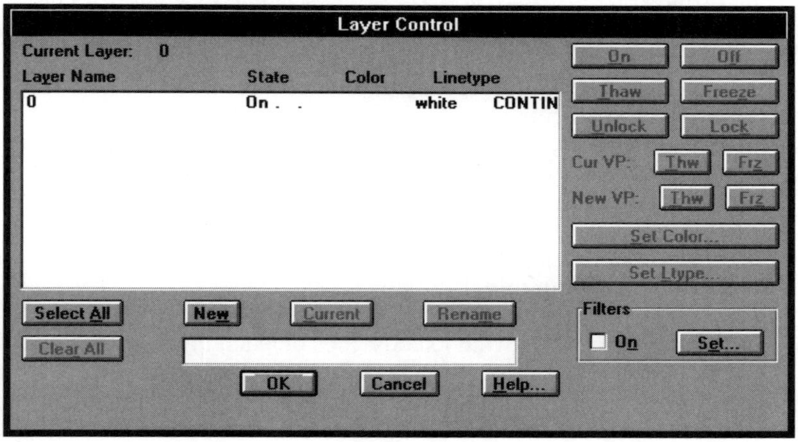

Figure 4-8:
The Layer
Control
dialog box.

Layer Control				
Current Layer: 0				On / Off
Layer Name	State	Color	Linetype	Thaw / Freeze
0	On . .	white	CONTIN	Unlock / Lock
				Cur VP: Thw / Frz
				New VP: Thw / Frz
				Set Color...
				Set Ltype...
Select All New Current Rename				Filters □ On Set...
Clear All				
OK Cancel Help...				

2. **Type the new layer name in the text box near the bottom of the dialog box.**

   A good starting set of layer names, in addition to 0, of course, may be GEOMETRY, TEXT, and DIMENSIONS.

3. **Choose the New button located just below the Layer Name list at the center of the dialog box.**

   The new layer name appears in the Layer Name list. If, for example, you type **GEOMETRY**, that appears in the list as the name of your new layer.

   The headings at the top of the Layer Name list further describe your layer. The default State for this new layer is On, the Color is white, and the linetype is CONTINUOUS. Now, however, you can modify these settings in the layer.

   Do not click the New button until after you type the layer name. And do not click the OK button at this point either; if you do, you exit the dialog box.

4. **Click the layer name you want to modify to highlight it in the Layer Name list.**

5. **Choose the Off button to keep the layer off after you return to your drawing.**

   If a layer is off, your drawing does not display or print it.

   If you click the Off button, the word Off replaces the word On under the State heading in the Layer Name list.

6. **Click the Freeze button to freeze the selected layer after you return to your drawing.**

   If you freeze a layer, your drawing does not display it. Unlike with the Off setting, if you update the drawing, you do not regenerate the frozen layer. Because each layer takes time to regenerate, freezing layers saves update time. And if you create a print or plot of the drawing, you do not print the layer.

   If you click the Freeze button, the letter F appears under the State heading in the Layer Name lists.

7. **Click the Lock button to lock the layer after you return to your drawing.**

   Locking a layer prevents you from modifying the objects on it. You *can* create new objects on a locked layer, however, and you can display, regenerate, and print the layer.

   If you click the Lock button, the letter L appears under the State heading in the Layer Name list.

8. **Click the Set Color button to change the color you want to use on the layer.**

   The Select Color dialog box appears. Choose the color you want to use by clicking it in this dialog box. The nine Standard Colors listed at the top of the dialog box are the most transferrable from one system to another. If you are using a white background in the drawing area, objects drawn in the color named white appear black on-screen.

If you change the color of a layer, the name of the new color appears under the Color heading in the Layer Name list.

9. **Click the Set Ltype button of the Layer Control dialog box to change the linetype to use on the layer.**

The Select Linetype dialog box appears (refer to Figure 4-7). Choose the linetype you want to use from the Loaded Linetypes list at the top of the dialog box. If the linetype you need doesn't appear on this list, you must load it. Refer to the preceding section, "Loading up linetypes," for info on how to load a linetype.

If you change the linetype, the name of the new linetype appears under the Linetype heading in the Layer Name list.

10. **Click the Current button to designate the layer as the Current Layer — that is, one in use after you return to your drawing.**

The name of the Current Layer appears near the top of the Layer Control dialog box. Any new objects you create on your drawing are put onto the current layer, but you can edit objects on any layer that's on and not frozen or locked.

11. **To create another layer, return to step 2 and repeat this process.**

12. **To exit the Layer Control dialog box after you finish creating layers, click OK.**

Figure 4-9 shows the Layer Control dialog box with three new layers in it. The GEOMETRY layer is the first one to be edited, so it is On and Current; other layers are frozen and locked.

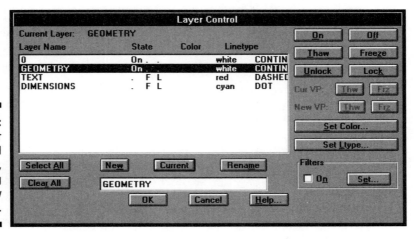

Figure 4-9:
The Layer Control dialog box, displaying three new layers.

The Layer Control dialog box normally sorts the layer names in alphabetical order. If you create new layers, however, AutoCAD initially adds them to the existing list in the order in which you create them. After you exit the dialog box, AutoCAD then sorts all the layers alphabetically by layer name; so your layers are likely to appear in a different order the next time you open the dialog box. (This is important to remember, because this surprise resorting may make you think that some of your layers have disappeared when they've actually only been scrolled off the part of the Layer Name list that is visible on-screen. And I don't want you to *resort* to doing anything drastic if this occurs. Ouch—sorry.)

To work more quickly, create all your layers first by using the Ne<u>w</u> command. Then change the settings by highlighting one or more layers and clicking the appropriate button: <u>O</u>n or O<u>ff</u>, <u>T</u>haw or Free<u>z</u>e, or <u>U</u>nlock or Loc<u>k</u>. The Layer Name list immediately updates all the highlighted layers with their new settings.

Creating and modifying layers from the command line

Creating and modifying a layer from the command line is fast but complicated. Not only do you have a number of options but they also work differently than do those of the Layer Control dialog box. Instead of selecting a layer and then specifying whether it's On or Off, for example, you first choose On or Off and *then* type in the name(s) of the layer(s) you want to turn on or off.

If you like this style of interaction, you may prefer to use the command line rather than the dialog box to set up your layers. You may also want to commit these commands to memory if you use the DOS version of AutoCAD, because AutoCAD for DOS has no object properties bar to enable you to modify layer properties quickly.

Follow these steps to create and modify a layer from the command line:

1. **Type** LAYER **on the command line and press Enter.**

2. **Type** NEW **and press Enter.**

3. **Type the name of the layer(s) you want to create, such as** GEOMETRY,TEXT,DIMENSIONS, **and press Enter**.

Don't put spaces between the layer names or between any other items you enter in a list at the command line; AutoCAD interprets spaces as returns. Use commas, with no spaces, to separate names in a list on the command line.

The initial settings for your newly created layer(s) are On, thawed, and unlocked; the color is white; and the linetype is continuous.

The following example is what appears on-screen after you create three new layers named GEOMERTY, TEXT, and DIMENSIONS:

```
Command: layer
?/Make/Set/New/ON/OFF/Color/Ltype/Freeze/Thaw/LOck/Unlock:
      new
New layer name(s): geometry,text,dimensions
```

If you get stuck while working within the LAYER command, you can type **'ddlmodes** (or choose <u>D</u>ata ➪ <u>L</u>ayers) to open the Layer Control dialog box. (The apostrophe in front of **ddlmodes** tells AutoCAD that you are not interrupting the LAYER command, just doing something else for a moment.) This can help you finish what you started. From the Layer Control dialog box you can, for example, load linetypes that you can then assign to layers within the LAYER command.

4. **To create additional layers, type NEW and press Enter, and then type the name of the layer and press Enter again.**

   After you create all the layers you want, you can then modify their settings as necessary.

5. **To turn off one or more layers, type OFF and press Enter, and then type the name(s) of the layer(s) you want to turn off and press Enter again, as shown in the following example:**

```
?/Make/Set/New/ON/OFF/Color/Ltype/Freeze/Thaw/LOck/Unlock:
      off
Layer name(s) to turn Off: text,dimensions
```

   If a layer is off, your drawing does not display or print it. If you update the drawing, you also regenerate the layer.

6. **To freeze one or more layers, type FREEZE and press Enter and then type the name(s) of the layer(s) you want to freeze and press Enter again, as shown in the following example:**

```
?/Make/Set/New/ON/OFF/Color/Ltype/Freeze/Thaw/LOck/Unlock:
      f
Layer name(s) to Freeze: text,dimensions
```

   Notice in this and several following examples that only the first letter or two that you type actually appears at the command prompt. You may type just these letters instead of the entire command. In most cases, you need type only the letters that appear in uppercase type in commands in the command prompt.

   If you freeze a layer, your drawing does not display it. Unlike with the Off setting, if you update frozen the drawing, you do not regenerate the layer (which saves update time).

7. **To lock one or more layers, type** Lock **(or** Lo**) and press Enter, and then type the name(s) of the layer(s) you want to lock and press Enter again, as shown in the following example:**

```
?/Make/Set/New/ON/OFF/Color/Ltype/Freeze/Thaw/LOck/Unlock:
       lo
Layer name(s) to Lock: text,dimensions
```

You can't modify objects on a locked layer until you unlock the layer. You *can* create new objects, however, and you can display, regenerate, and print the layer.

8. **Type** COLOR **and then press Enter to change the color of one or more layers.**

The command line prompts you for the color to use. Enter a color name. The most transferrable colors are the standard ones: red, yellow, green, cyan, blue, magenta, white, 8 (gray), and 9 (reddish-brown). Although most PC's can display 256 colors — and some can display thousands or millions of colors — these eight are the only ones that will show up on every PC that can run AutoCAD.

The command line then prompts you for the layer name(s) to apply the color to. Type the name(s) of the layer(s) you want to apply the color to and press Enter.

Repeat this step for each layer you want to change color.

The following example shows how the command line appears as I change the Text layer to the color red and the Dimensions layer to the color cyan:

```
?/Make/Set/New/ON/OFF/Color/Ltype/Freeze/Thaw/LOck/Unlock: c
Color: red
Layer name(s) for color 1 (red) <0>: text,0,geometry
?/Make/Set/New/ON/OFF/Color/Ltype/Freeze/Thaw/LOck/Unlock: c
Color: cyan
Layer name(s) for color 4 (cyan) <text>: dimensions
```

9. **Type** LTYPE **and press Enter to change the linetype of one or more layers.**

The command line prompts you for the linetype to use. Type a linetype name and press Enter.

If you need to review the available linetypes, type **?** and a list of available linetypes appears in a text window. After you find the name of the linetype you want, type **LTYPE** and press Enter again to return to the prompt for the linetype name and then enter the linetype name at the prompt and press Enter. Finally, double-click the text window to close it (in Windows) or press the F1 key to return to the drawing area (in DOS).

The command line then prompts you for the layer name(s) to apply the linetype to. Type the name(s) of the layer(s) to which you want to apply the linetype and press Enter again.

Repeat this step for each layer in which you want to change linetypes.

The following example shows how the command line appears as I change the Text and Dimensions layers to use the dashed linetype:

```
?/Make/Set/New/ON/OFF/Color/Ltype/Freeze/Thaw/LOck/Unlock: l
Linetype (or ?) <CONTINUOUS>: dashed
Layer name(s) for linetype DASHED <0>: text
?/Make/Set/New/ON/OFF/Color/Ltype/Freeze/Thaw/LOck/Unlock: l
Linetype (or ?) <CONTINUOUS>: dashed
Layer name(s) for linetype DASHED <0>: dimensions
```

10. **Type** SET **and press Enter to choose the current layer.**

The command line prompts you for the layer to make current. Type a layer name and press Enter again, as shown in the following example:

```
?/Make/Set/New/ON/OFF/Color/Ltype/Freeze/Thaw/LOck/Unlock:
      l
New current layer <0>: geometry
```

And you're done! (Yes!)

The 5th Wave   By Rich Tennant

Chapter 5

Setup Comedy

● ●

In This Chapter

▶ How to set units and angles

▶ How to set limits

▶ How to set up a grid and snap interval

▶ How to scale dimensions and linetypes

▶ How to save your drawing as a prototype

▶ Seven steps to setup

● ●

*W*ell, you've heard of standup comedy, so why not *setup* comedy? (Okay, so it should be *sit*up comedy; so sue me.) Unfortunately, AutoCAD setup can too often become a comedy of errors — if not performed correctly.

AutoCAD does a lot for you. But the pleasure it provides is not without an occasional jolt of pain. People who most often feel that pain haven't set up their drawings correctly. Although not fatal, this affliction can cause you to hate any and all of the following: yourself, your boss, your client, and, above all, AutoCAD. The remedy is uncomplicated: Learn the steps to set up your drawing correctly. Doing right by your setup saves you trouble down the road.

Why you need to set up AutoCAD correctly is partly because AutoCAD *is* so flexible and partly because, well, you're doing *CAD*. In this context, the following three key reasons help explain why AutoCAD drawing setup is important:

✔ **Smart Paper:** The big advantage of CAD over paper drawings is that a CAD drawing is much easier to modify. In CAD, for example, erasing is easy. CAD's biggest advantage is that the screen can act as *smart paper*. Smart paper enables you to erase and modify any drawings that need fixing. And after you set up AutoCAD correctly, you can draw in the same units you'd find in real life — feet and inches, meters, or whatever you use. AutoCAD can then calculate distances and dimensions for you and add them to the drawing. You can make the mouse pointer snap directly to "hot spots" on-screen, and a visible, resizeable grid gives you a better sense for the scale of your drawing. This smart paper function, however, works well only if you tell AutoCAD how you set up your specific drawing. So AutoCAD can't really do its job until you tell it how to work.

✔ **Dumb Paper:** The biggest disadvantage of CAD is that it takes you a step away from the real paper your drawing ends up on. Creating a great drawing on-screen that fits only awkwardly onto the paper you need to print it on is all too easy. After you finish creating your drawing on the smart paper AutoCAD provides on-screen, you must print it out on the *dumb paper* used for thousands of years. Then you must deal with the fact that people use certain standard paper sizes and drawing scales. Most people also like everything to fit neatly on one sheet of paper.

AutoCAD can impose limits on your on-screen drawing work that help your drawing better translate to paper (the dumb kind, that is). But the program can't do this until you provide it with some information about *how* to translate data from screen to paper. If you set up AutoCAD correctly, good printing results automatically; if not, printing time can become one colossal hassle.

✔ **It Ain't Easy:** AutoCAD does not do its setup for you. It provides the tools, but it doesn't make doing the setup yourself easy. This particular deficiency is one of the biggest in AutoCAD. You must figure out on your own how to make the program work right. If you just plunge in without carefully setting it up, your drawing and printing efforts are sure to wind up a real mess. You may, in fact, end up with a virtually unprintable drawing (and probably mutter a few unprintable words in the process, too).

Fortunately, although the steps to performing your setup correctly are overly complex, you can master them with a little attention and practice. If you are somewhat familiar with AutoCAD, skip to the end of this chapter and use the section "Seven Not-So-Deadly Steps to Setup" — as well as Appendix C — to help you in your setup work. If you're new, read through this chapter once and then use the setup section and Appendix C for reference.

An AutoLISP routine called MVSETUP asks you to enter units, a scale factor, and a paper size and then sets units and limits for you. MVSETUP, however, is clumsy to operate, and doesn't set the linetype sizing variable LTSCALE or the dimensions sizing variable DIMSCALE — nor give you any clue how to do so. This chapter doesn't use MVSETUP.

While you're working in AutoCAD, always keep in mind what your final output will look like on real paper. Even your first drawings should look just like hand-drawn ones — only better.

Taking Your Measurements

The type of units used for measuring distances and angles may not be something you change much, but when you do need to change them, it's an important change. You may also need to change the precision with which AutoCAD displays units and the direction in which AutoCAD measures angles. The program provides a handy dialog box for changing units, and you can make changes from the command line as well.

Choosing your units

The *units* used within a drawing are the same units of measurement the real world uses. You draw an eight-foot-high line, for example, to indicate the height of a wall and an eight-inch-high line to indicate the cutout for a doggie door (for a Dachshund, naturally). The on-screen line may actually be only two inches long, but AutoCAD indicates that it is eight feet long if that's how you set up your drawing. This is an easy and natural way to work once you understand that you can plot a drawing out at another scale setting.

For units, you choose a *type* of unit — Scientific, Decimal, Engineering, Architectural, and Fractional — and a *precision* of measurement. Engineering and Architectural units are in feet and inches, while Engineering units are decimal and Architectural units are fractional. For metric measurements, use one of the other types of units: Scientific, Decimal, or Fractional. You can change the type or precision of units later without causing much trouble in your drawing.

Changing linear units in the Units Control dialog box

You can choose and change the type of units you use in your drawing by changing settings in the Unit Control dialog box. To access this dialog box to choose units (and control how angles are measured), follow these steps:

1. **Choose Data⇨Units from the menu bar. Or type** DDUNITS **at the command line and press Enter.**

   The Units Control dialog box appears, as shown in Figure 5-1.

2. **Choose from the Units area the unit option you want for your drawing.**

   You can choose a unit by clicking the round circle in front of the unit-type name (these are called *radio buttons* or *option buttons* in computerese, if you didn't already know that.) As you select different options, the appear-

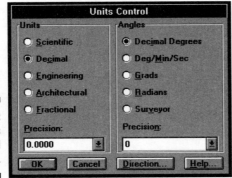

Figure 5-1:
The Units
Control
dialog box.

ance of the text in the Precision drop-down list box changes to reflect exactly how AutoCAD displays that choice on-screen:

Scientific:	0.0000E+01
Decimal:	0.0000
Engineering:	0'-0.0000"
Architectural:	0'-0 $^{1}/_{16}$"
Fractional:	0 $^{1}/_{16}$

The default choice is Decimal, because it's unitless (in case you don't like all those little inch and foot marks all over your drawing). But choose the type of unit representation that is appropriate for your own work. Engineering and Architectural units are displayed in feet and inches; the other units have no dimensions and work well for either feet and inches or metric units, as you prefer.

3. From the Precision list box, choose the degree of precision you want.

For Architectural and Fractional units, the choices are whole units, such as 0, $^{1}/_{2}$, $^{1}/_{4}$, and so on. (Figure 5-2 shows the precision choices for Architectural units.) For the other three units, the choices are the number of decimal places you can use.

Too much precision actually slows down a drawing, because AutoCAD tries to calculate where the cursor is to an increasing number of decimal places. A grosser — that is, less precise — precision setting helps AutoCAD move faster. So be gross for now; you can always act a little less gross later.

4. Choose OK to exit the dialog box and lock in your unit choices.

Changing linear units by using the UNITS command

Using the Units Control dialog box really is the easiest way to set units; neat features such as the Precision drop-down list box, which changes to reflect the currently selected units, make this dialog box the best way to go. But if you change units much, or just love to use the keyboard, you may want to learn how to update your units choice from the command line. Use the following steps to change units at the command line:

1. At the command line, type UNITS **and then press Enter to start the Units command.**

An AutoCAD text window opens and shows you examples of all the different formats. (I *told* you to use the dialog box, but did you listen? Nooo!) This text window, with some choices already made, is shown in Figure 5-3.

2. Choose from the Report formats list the Units you want to use in your drawing by typing the number of your choice at the on-screen prompt and pressing Enter.

The choices, with examples, are as follows:

1. Scientific:	0.0000E+01
2. Decimal:	0.0000
3. Engineering:	0'-0.0000"
4. Architectural:	0'-0 $^1/_{16}$"
5. Fractional:	0 $^1/_{16}$

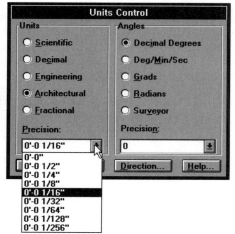

Figure 5-2:
Precision
choices for
Architectural
units in the
Units
Control
dialog box.

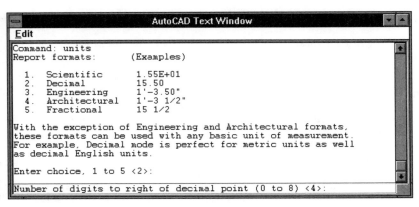

Figure 5-3:
The text
window that
appears
after you
enter the
UNITS
command
on the
command
line.

AutoCAD thinks in inches! If you're using Engineering or Architectural units (feet and inches), AutoCAD understands any coordinate you enter as a number of inches. Learn to swiftly find the ' (apostrophe) character on your keyboard so that you can quickly specify feet if that's what you mean.

3. **Choose the degree of precision you want by entering a value at the prompt at the bottom of the text screen.**

For Engineering and Architectural units, AutoCAD asks you for the denominator of the smallest fraction to display. The choices are 1, 2, 4, 8, 16, 32, 64, 128, and 256, representing 1 unit, $1/2$ unit, $1/4$ unit, and so on. For the other three unit types, the choices are the number of decimal places you can use. The larger the fraction — 1 is largest, $1/2$ is the next largest, and so on — the faster AutoCAD draws, so don't specify a greater degree of precision than you really need.

After you specify the precision of the units you're using, AutoCAD starts asking you questions about angles. If you want to change the manner of display, precision, or direction of angular measurements, use the directions in the following section on using a dialog box to set up angles. If you don't want to change anything about angles at this point, press Ctrl+C to cancel the command. Then click the control box in the upper left corner to close the text window (in Windows) or press the F1 key (in DOS) to return to the drawing area. AutoCAD preserves the choices you already made.

Calculatin' all the angles

In AutoCAD, you also specify *angular units* — the way in which angles are measured, such as a circle having 360 degrees — and the direction in which you draw them. If you use decimal degrees, setting a precision of one degree (no fractions of a degree), and treat a horizontal line pointing to the right as an angle of zero degrees (as in architecture), you need make no changes here. Otherwise, fire away.

In AutoCAD, you choose the units in which AutoCAD measures angles. You choose a *type* of angular unit — Decimal Degrees (the most common), Deg/Min/Sec (useful mainly if you're planning a sea voyage), Grads, Radians, and Surveyor — and a *precision* of measurement. You can also choose the *direction* in which angles are measured. If you set these options now but change your mind after you start your drawing, you can change angular units, precision, and direction later without causing much trouble for your drawing.

The easiest way to set and change angular units and direction is by using the Units Control dialog box. To use the dialog box to control how angles are measured, follow these steps:

1. **Choose Data⇨Units from the menu bar. Or type DDUNITS at the command line and press Enter.**

   The Units Control dialog box appears. (Refer to Figure 5-1.)

2. **Choose from the Angles area of the dialog box the angular units you want to use in your drawing.**

   Just click the round circle — the radio, or option, button — in front of the unit you want to choose. As you select different options, the appearance of the text in the Precision drop-down list box changes to reflect how AutoCAD displays that choice as follows:

Decimal Degrees:	0
Deg/Min/Sec:	0d
Grads:	0g
Radians:	0r
Surveyor:	N 0d E

   The default choice is Decimal Degrees, because it's unitless (again, no little measurement marks all over your drawing). You should, however, choose the angular unit you really need.

3. **From the Precisio<u>n</u> drop-down list box, choose the degree of precision you want for your drawing.**

   For Deg/<u>M</u>in/Sec and Sur<u>v</u>eyor units, the choices are whole degrees; degrees and minutes; degrees, minutes, and seconds; and degrees, minutes, and seconds plus additional decimal places of precision for the seconds. (See Figure 5-4.) For the other three units, the choices are the number of decimal places you can use.

   Too much precision actually slows down a drawing, because AutoCAD tries to calculate angles to an increasing number of decimal places, so don't specify a degree of precision you don't really need.

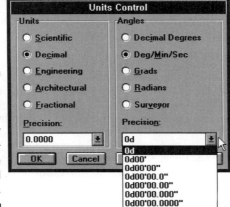

Figure 5-4:
Precision
choices for
Deg/<u>M</u>in/
Sec angular
units in the
Units Control
dialog box.

4. **To change the base direction from which AutoCAD measures angles, or to change the orientation of angular measurement (clockwise or counter-clockwise), click the <u>D</u>irection button below the Precisio<u>n</u> drop-down list.**

   The Direction Control dialog box appears, as shown in Figure 5-5.

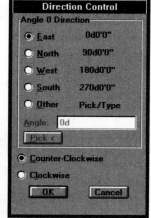

Figure 5-5:
The Direction
Control
dialog box.

5. **Choose the Angle 0 Direction you want: East, North, West, South, or Other.**

   The Angle 0 Direction is the direction that AutoCAD uses as 0 for angular measurements. East is to the right on-screen, North is up, West is left, and South is down. Architects, for example, tend to use East as the Angle 0 Direction; that way, flat things are at 0 degrees and straight up is 90 degrees, which fits architectual usage. Others tend to use North as the Angle 0 Direction, which fits compass measurement, a generally well-understood usage. You can choose a preset direction, choose Other to select a direction on-screen, such as 45 degrees (Northeast), or type in a specifc direction.

6. **Choose the direction in which AutoCAD measures angles: Counter-Clockwise or Clockwise.**

   Architects tend to use a counter-clockwise measurement so that angles are measured "from the ground up"; others tend to use clockwise.

7. **Choose OK to exit the dialog box and activate your choices.**

Set Some Limits!

With AutoCAD, you can put as much stuff on-screen as you could ever want. You can draw, annotate, set dimensions, and move things around 'til the cows come home. But after you've so painfully created this drawing, you may find that you can't print, use, or edit the drawing. This problem crops up mainly if the shape and size of the on-screen drawing are such that the drawing just doesn't fit very well on the paper you intend to print on.

You use these AutoCAD drawing limits (set via the LIMITS command) to specify how big an area you want to draw on. The area you specify must be big enough to hold the object you're drawing but should also fit easily onto a printout, using a standard drawing scale, of course.

A few thoughts on paper

You may already know what you need to know about the paper sizes used in your profession and in your office's printers and plotters; but if not, here are a few important facts.

The standard paper sizes are lettered *A, B, C, D,* and *E.* Their sizes are as follows:

- *A* = 8 ½" x 11" (standard letter size in the U.S.)

- *B* = 11" x 17"

- *C* = 17" x 22"

- *D* = 22" x 34"

- *E* = 34" x 44"

Knowing the following relationships should make using the tables later in this chapter — as well as switching among paper sizes — easier for you:

- *C* paper is double the length and width of *A* paper.

- *D* paper is double the length and width of *B* paper.

- *E* paper is double the length and width of *C* paper.

Because printing to a large printer, such as an *E*-sized pen plotter, is expensive and time-consuming, you may often find yourself sending *check prints* to a standard office printer as a test. (The words *print* and *plot* are now used more or less interchangeably; if a difference exists, it's that *printing* uses a laser printer while *plotting* uses a pen plotter.)

To maintain correct proportions and layout, you can make check prints for *C* or *E* paper on standard *A* paper (for example, 8 ½" x 11" copier paper) and check prints for *D* paper on standard *B* legal paper. Reading some of the lettering may be hard if printing this small, but such a printout preserves the correct proportions of your drawing.

Determining your limits

Tying together all the elements necessary for an acceptable drawing — the size of the actual objects you're drawing, the size of the paper you print on, and other important quantities such as the grid display and snap grid you use — is in no way an easy task. (See the section "Making Your Screen Smart," later in this chapter, for details on grid and snap.)

You can spend quite a bit of time calculating and experimenting with all the elements of your drawing. But instead, you can just use the handy helpmates I've included in this book as your guide: Tables 5-1 and 5-2, which are partial lists, or the complete lists in Appendix C. Under *Limits* in Table 5-1 or 5-2, find the area that easily fits the size of the object(s) you want to draw. Then coordinate that with the Paper Size you plan to use and the Drawing Scale to which you want to draw the printout. Taking all these elements into account should result in a single set of figures that you can use to set up your drawing. How to use the numbers in these tables is explained in more detail in the rest of this chapter and in Appendix C.

Table 5-1 Picking Limits — Architectural Units, Horizontal Orientation

Paper Size	Drawing Scale	Limits	Grid	Snap	Linetype & Dimension Scale
8½"x11"	¼"= 1'	44'x34'	4'	1'	48
8½"x11"	½"= 1'	22'x17'	2'	1'	24
8½"x11"	1" = 1'	11'x8½'	1'	6"	12
11"x17"	¼"= 1'	68'x44'	4'	1'	48
11"x17"	½"= 1'	34'x22'	2'	1'	24
11"x17"	1" = 1'	17'x11'	1'	6"	12

Table 5-2 Picking Limits — Mechanical and Other Units, Horizontal Orientation

Paper Size	Drawing Scale	Limits	Grid	Snap	Linetype & Dimension Scale
8½"x11"	1cm = 1m	25mx20m	1m	50cm	100
8½"x11"	5cm = 1m	5mx4m	20cm	10cm	20
8½"x11"	10cm = 1m	2.5mx2m	10cm	5cm	10
11"x17"	1cm = 1m	40mx25m	1m	50cm	100
11"x17"	5cm = 1m	8mx5m	20cm	10cm	20
11"x17"	10cm = 1m	4mx2.5m	10cm	5cm	10

Catching your limits

The following steps offer detailed instructions for setting limits. Notice that you can start the limits command from a menu choice but that all the action takes place on the command line; in spite of the importance of the topic, AutoCAD has no dialog box for setting limits, although the Plot Preview dialog box may prove useful for checking limits and paper size. So just follow these steps to set your drawing limits:

1. **Choose Data⊅Drawing Limits from the menu bar to start the Limits command. Or type LIMITS on the command line and press Enter.**

   The LIMITS command appears on the command line, and the command line displays the following at the bottom of the screen:

   ```
   Command: 'limits
   Reset Model space limits:
   ON/OFF/<Lower left corner> <0'-0",0'-0">:
   ```

   The value at the end of the last line of the prompt is the default value for the lower left corner of the drawing limits; it appears using the units and precision that you selected in the Units Control dialog box — for example, 0'- 0" if you selected Architectural units with precision to the nearest inch.

2. **Type the lower left corner of the limits you want to use and press Enter.**

   The usual value to enter at this point is **0,0.** (That is, type a zero, a comma, and then another zero, with no spaces.) Or you can just press Enter to accept the default value. You can adjust the limits later if you want.

   AutoCAD now prompts you for the upper right corner of the limits:

   ```
   Upper right corner <1'-0",0'-9">:
   ```

3. **Type the upper right corner of the limits you want to use and press Enter.**

   Use the Limits column in Table 5-1, Table 5-2, or Appendix C to pick an upper right limit that works for your drawing size, scale factor, and paper size.

   If you enter feet and not inches, you must also enter the foot designator, such as **6'**; otherwise, AutoCAD assumes that you mean inches.

Making Your Screen Smart

So just what does it mean for a computer screen to be smart? No, not knowing how to tie its shoelaces or spell "cat." Basically, it means that the screen helps you do what you want. Although a computer can't interpret verbal commands, it can provide controls to enable the user to specify important settings right there on-screen. In drafting, the screen should provide visible *tick marks* for orientation and draw the cursor to specific spots where objects are more likely to be located. AutoCAD performs all these feats through its *grid* and *snap interval* settings.

The *grid* is simply a set of visible, evenly spaced dots that give some orientation as to how your drawing places its objects in relation to one another on-screen.

The *snap interval* is a bit trickier to set. The snap interval forces the mouse cursor to snap to invisible hot spots a certain distance apart on-screen, enabling you to easily align objects a predetermined distance apart.

The relationship between the grid and the snap interval should be close. In other words, the grid and the snap interval should either be the same distance apart, or the snap interval should be an even fraction of the grid distance ($\frac{1}{2}$, $\frac{1}{4}$, or $\frac{1}{12}$, for example). In this way, the grid serves as a visual reminder of the snap interval.

You nearly always want a grid in your drawing, because it's so useful in orienting objects to each other. You may not always want to use a snap interval, however, because some drawings, such as a contour map, don't contain objects that align on specific points.

You can set your grid to work in one of two ways: to help with your drawing or to help with your printout. You set a grid that helps with your drawing a logical number of measurement units apart. Grid points, for example, may be 30 feet (10 yards) apart on a drawing of a football field. A grid that helps with your printout is different; you space this kind of grid so that a grid square represents a one-inch square on your final printout.

In either case, the snap interval should be set at anywhere from the same value as the grid to any even division of it: One-half, one-fourth, and one-twelfth work well for architecture; one-half and one-tenth work well for mechanical drawings and for other disciplines. Good starting points for grid and snap intervals for specific drawings are provided in Tables 5-1 and 5-2 earlier in this chapter, and in Appendix C.

Setting grid and snap intervals in the Drawing Aids dialog box

If you're just learning about grid spacing and snap intervals, learn to use the Drawing Aids dialog box first. By using the dialog box, you can quickly note and adjust the relationship between the grid and snap intervals. You're likely to want to change these settings often, however; if you do, you may also want to learn some of the techniques of using the command line to set these, as described in the following section.

To set the grid and the snap intervals by using the Drawing Aids dialog box, follow these steps:

1. **Choose Options⇨Drawing Aids from the menu bar. Or type DDRMODES on the command line and press Enter.**

   The Drawing Aids dialog box appears (see Figure 5-6).

   The dialog box has four parts, but you only need to concern yourself with the Snap and Grid sections. Some of the other settings are nerd stuff that you can probably live a long time without ever needing to think twice about — and aren't covered in this book anyway.

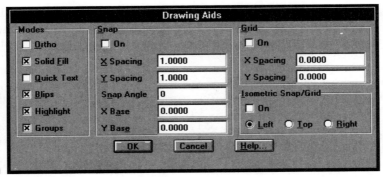

Figure 5-6:
The Drawing
Aids dialog
box.

2. **Click the On check box in the Grid section to turn on Grid.**

   This creates a grid with spacing between grid points, set to the snap distance, as described in step 4.

3. **Enter the X Spacing for the grid in the accompanying text box.**

   Use Table 5-1 or 5-2 or Appendix C to select a grid spacing that maps to one plotted inch, based on your drawing size, scale factor, and paper size. Or just enter a value that makes sense to you in relation to the size of the objects you're drawing and your screen area; you probably want to have at least a 10 x 10 grid to start.

   X measures horizontal distance; Y measures vertical distance. Legend has it that the mathematician Rene Descartes devised this scheme after watching a fly walk on a patterned ceiling. (This would be a better story if he thought it up at a horse race, but I don't think you can put Descartes before the horse. . . .)

   Don't change the Y Spacing. The Y spacing automatically changes to equal the X spacing; this creates a square grid, which is just what you want for now. (Maybe later you'll want a different X value in your grid, but this is fine 'til then.)

4. Click the On check box in the §nap section to turn on Snap.

This creates default snaps one unit apart.

5. Enter the X Spacing for the snap interval in the accompanying text box.

Use Table 5-1 or 5-2 or Appendix C to select a snap spacing that works best for your drawing, or just enter a value that makes sense to you; any value that's an even fraction of the grid spacing works.

Don't change the Y Spacing. The Y spacing automatically changes to equal the X spacing; this creates drawing snaps an equal distance apart in the X and Y directions, which is just what you want for now.

As long as you have the Drawing Aids dialog box open, you may as well turn off §lips (in the Modes section). The §lips setting determines whether AutoCAD leaves little blips on-screen to mark points you select as you draw. One common reason for doing a redraw is to get rid of blips, however, and starting a redraw takes a moment — time you don't need to waste. So turn off §lips right now by clicking the check box to remove the X (if one is there), unless, of course, you *really* like them.

Setting grid and snap intervals from the command line

If you change these settings much — for example, if you switch frequently between detail work on a small part of your drawing and large-scale work on the whole thing at once — learning how to change grid and snap settings from the command line is definitely worth the effort. Follow these steps to do use the command line to change these settings:

1. Type GRID at the command line and press Enter.

The following prompt appears:

```
Grid spacing(X) or ON/OFF/Snap/Aspect/ <0'-0">:
```

2. Type the value for the grid spacing at the prompt and press Enter.

Use the suggested values from Table 5-1, Table 5-2, or the more complete list in Appendix C.

Remember to indicate feet (by entering an apostrophe after the number) whenever you use the command line if you use Architectural or Engineering units that are measured in feet and inches and you don't want a grid spacing in inches.

3. **Type** SNAP **at the command line and press Enter.**

The following prompt appears:

```
Snap spacing or ON/OFF/Aspect/Rotate/Style <0'-1">:
```

Don't worry about the options on the command line labeled *Aspect*, *Rotate*, and *Style*; you can look them up in your AutoCAD manual in the unlikely event you ever need them.

4. **Type the value for value for the snap spacing at the prompt and then press Enter.**

Use the suggested values from Table 5-1, Table 5-2, or the more complete list in Appendix C.

Use an even division of the grid spacing for your snap setting. Values of $1/2$, $1/4$, and $1/12$ of the grid spacing work well, for example, if you're using feet and inches; values of $1/2$ and $1/10$ of the grid spacing work well if you're using metric units or miles.

You can quickly turn on or off the grid and snap spacings by entering the commands **GRID ON, GRID OFF**, **SNAP ON**, and **SNAP OFF** at the command line. Press F7 to toggle the grid setting on and off; press F9 to toggle the snap spacing on and off. You can also click the snap button in the AutoCAD for Windows status bar to toggle snap on and off; the same goes for the grid button and the grid setting.

Scaling, Scaling, over the Bounding Main . . .

Even though *you* know from the tables earlier in this chapter what scale your drawing is in, AutoCAD doesn't know it until you tell it. This situation is fine as long as you're just drawing shapes, but you may want to use different *linetypes* (patterns that make some lines look different from others) and you may want to add *dimensions* (measurements that show the size of the things you're drawing.)

To help AutoCAD handle these changes correctly, you need to tell it your *scale factor* — how much it should magnify or shrink the appearance of linetypes in your drawing. If AutoCAD doesn't know what scale factor to use, dimensions can come out very tiny or VERY LARGE, and lines can look waaaay too big or too small.

The scale factor that works best for linetypes is found in a system variable called LTSCALE (as in LineType SCALE). The scaling factor that works best for dimensions is found in a system variable called DIMSCALE. Chapters 2 and 3 offer more information on system variables.

You can start the LTSCALE command from a menu choice, but you can finish it only from the command line. You can also set the linetype scale in the Select Linetype dialog box. You can set DIMSCALE from the command line or through a complicated dimensioning dialog box. This section describes how to set them both from the command line, for simplicity's sake. You can change either of these at any time.

To set the linetype scale from the command line, follow these steps:

1. **Type** DIMSCALE **on the command line and press Enter.**

   AutoCAD responds with a prompt asking you for the dimension scale. The value already listed at the end of the prompt is the current dimension scale setting (the default), as shown in the following example:

   ```
   New value for DIMSCALE <1.0000>:
   ```

   DIMSCALE is only the most important of the dozens of variables that affect how dimensions look. Because DIMSCALE affects many of the other variables, it may be the only one you need (if you're lucky). To delve further into this complex topic, see Chapter 11.

2. **Type the value you want for the dimension scale on the command line and press Enter.**

   This value is the scaling factor for dimensions that's appropriate for your drawing, as listed in Tables 5-1 and 5-2 and Appendix C.

3. **Type** LTSCALE **on the command line and press Enter.**

   AutoCAD responds with a prompt asking you for the scale factor. The value at the end of the prompt is the current linetype scale setting, as in the following example:

   ```
   New scale factor <1.0000>:
   ```

4. **Type the value you want for the linetype scale on the command line and press Enter.**

   This value is the scaling factor for linetypes that's appropriate for your drawing, as listed in Tables 5-1 and 5-2 and Appendix C.

You should print a couple of check prints of your drawing at an early stage — *before* you draw many objects — to make sure that everything works out the way you expect. Include dimensions, text, a couple different linetypes, and graphics to test all the key elements of your drawing.

Creating the Primordial Prototype

I bet you didn't notice this, but *every* drawing you create in AutoCAD is based on a *prototype* — a file that AutoCAD checks to decide what initial setup to use. The program provides you with a default prototype that is all most people ever use. This prototype, however, overlooks one of the more subtle but powerful features of AutoCAD.

To save yourself a great deal of time, create a new prototype every time you set up a drawing so that you can reuse it later. Eventually, you'll want to have a set of prototypes for each paper size and scale factor combination that you use. You may also want to include a basic set of layers and a suitably scaled *title block* — an area that describes drawing facts such as the drafter's name and company name — in each prototype drawing.

After you finish the initial setup work on a new drawing, save that drawing under a special name somewhere where you won't normally find it. In AutoCAD, the default prototype is located in the \ACAD\SUPPORT directory. You can place your custom prototypes in the same directory, along with the default prototype, or in a different subdirectory that you set aside just for this purpose.

After you save your drawing as a prototype, make sure that you save it again under its regular name in the directory you want. That way, any additional changes you make end up in the drawing proper, not in the prototype.

You can initiate the save process from either the menus or the command line. In either case, you use the Save As dialog box to save your work. Follow these steps to save your drawing as a prototype:

1. **Choose File⇨Save As from the menu bar. Or type** SAVEAS **at the command line and press Enter.**

   The Save Drawing As dialog box appears, as shown in Figure 5-7.

2. **Navigate to the directory where you save prototypes by selecting that directory from the Directories list.**

   If you created your drawing from scratch, you are probably already in the directory that holds the AutoCAD default prototype ACAD.DWG. On my system, ACAD.DWG is located in \ACADR13\COMMON\SUPPORT.

3. **Save the file as a prototype under an appropriate name by typing the new filename in the File Name text box and clicking OK.**

   It may seem cryptic at first glance, but a name such as ESIZ48SC, which includes the paper size (ESIZ, or E size) and scaling factor (48SC), actually may help you find the prototype you need later. Remember to use the DWG extension as part of the filename.

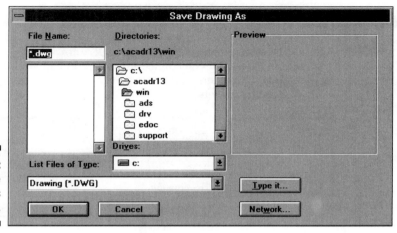

You can use any drawing as a prototype, but you're unlikely to remember all the settings in every drawing you create. That's why creating a few specific drawings as prototypes and not using them as anything else, as described in this section, is a good practice.

4. Choose File⇨Save As again.

The Save Drawing As dialog box reappears.

5. Navigate to the directory where you want to save your drawing, as described in step 2.

This should be a directory you've designated for your current project. It should *not* be the same directory in which you store your prototypes.

6. Save the file under an appropriate name, as described in step 3, and click OK.

To the extent possible given the eight-character filename limit of DOS and Windows, use a filename that indicates the purpose of the drawing. BANKPLM4.DWG, for example, may be a good name for the fourth drawing in a set that shows the plumbing for a bank building.

Seven Not-So-Deadly Steps to Setup

Of the hundreds of commands available to you in AutoCAD, you really need concern yourself with only seven commands for setting up your drawing correctly. Use Table 5-3 to find both menu-driven and command line versions of these seven basic steps to setup.

Table 5-3	Seven Serviceable Setup Steps	
Step	*Menus/Dialog Boxes**	*Command Line*
Units & Angles	Data⇨Units; or DDUNITS command	UNITS command
Limits	Data⇨Drawing Limits	LIMITS command
Grid	Options⇨Drawing Aids; or DDRMODES command	GRID command
Snap	Options⇨Drawing Aids; or DDRMODES command	SNAP command
Linetype scale	Data⇨Linetype; or DDLTYPE command	LTSCALE command
Dimension scale	Data⇨Dimension Style, Geometry button; or DDIM command	DIMSCALE command
Save prototype drawing	File⇨Save As; or SAVEAS command	SAVEAS command

* The commands that start with "DD" access dialog boxes; other commands work on the command line.

After you know the basic steps of setup, you can get off to a much better start on your AutoCAD drawings. Just keep in mind the following tips:

✔ Saving your drawing as a prototype requires no special procedures; just save it someplace away from your regular drawings.

✔ For the linetype scale and dimension scale, use the value you find in Table 5-1 or 5-2 earlier in the chapter, or the more complete list in Appendix C.

Part II
Let There Be Lines

It was Wayne's therapist, in fact, who suggested he purchase an AutoCAD program.

In this part...

Setting up the program correctly makes AutoCAD work better, but all the setup in the world doesn't get your drawing done. Points, lines, circles, and other elements of *geometry* make up the heart of your drawing. And AutoCAD offers many different ways to draw. After you draw your lines, you sometimes must go back and make a few changes in them. And in the process, you probably need to zoom in and out and pan all around to see how the entire drawing is coming together. Editing and viewing also are important parts of the drawing process; this part covers it all.

Chapter 6
Ready, Set, Draw!

*Y*ou're never off the hook entirely when it comes to AutoCAD setup, so this chapter starts out with a quick look at the minimal amount of setup you need to create a simple drawing in AutoCAD. Then it's off to the races with some of the more meaty aspects of CAD: drawing on-screen, drawing from the command line, using different kinds of snaps, and a look at a couple different ways to control how the lines you draw on-screen appear and how you organize them.

Snappy Setup

The easiest way to set up your drawing correctly is to use an existing drawing that's as similar as possible to the one you're going to create. This tip helps explain why so many drawings look alike and why offices often adhere to strict standards concerning the drawings created on a project. You can actually waste far more time perfecting — or trying to save — an AutoCAD drawing than you would a hand-drawn one. So using a copycat approach — that is, starting with an existing drawing to use as a template for your new one — often is a good idea.

But many times you may just need to start from scratch to fit the specific needs of your drawing — or to avoid inheriting junk that *your* ever-so-special drawing simply doesn't need. This section, therefore, helps you quickly set up your drawing correctly by reviewing with you all those little basics you need to remember about AutoCAD setup. (For the complete story on AutoCAD and drawing setup, however, see Chapters 4 and 5.)

Note: Most of the setup instructions in this section involve typing at the command line instead of selecting items from menus and dialog boxes. This is for two excellent reasons: Showing commands takes up less page space than showing dialog boxes (and this is a Dummies book, not the Encyclopaedia · AutoCADia), and besides, learning how to perform common tasks efficiently from the keyboard is *good* for you (yeah, right!). And as setup tasks are among the most common you can expect to perform in AutoCAD, knowing how to tackle them from the command line can really speed your work along much faster than it'll go if you waste your time messing with all those silly little dialog boxes. After you actually *create* such drawing elements as layers, however, managing and modifying them by using dialog boxes becomes much easier than dealing with the command line, so never fear — you get to see many more dialog boxes later in the chapter.

Setting selection settings . . . selecting set- . . . er, whatever

Unless you're an experienced AutoCAD user who doesn't want to change to the more modern way of operating, as is standard in Windows applications, you should set your selection settings as described in the following steps. If you're sticking with old-style selection settings, the following note is for you.

Note: The balance of this book assumes that these are the settings you use, so you may need to be really flexible in interpreting the detailed instructions in some of these procedures if you still use the old AutoCAD-style settings. You need to set your selection settings only once, so in spite of my admonition of only a section ago, these steps use a dialog box instead of the command line. (Sigh, how soon I forget . . .)

To set your selection settings, follow these steps:

1. **Choose Options⇨Selection from the menu bar.**

   The Object Selection Settings dialog box appears.

2. **Click all the following check boxes to turn on each selection setting:**

   - Noun/Verb Selection
   - Use Shift to Add
   - Press and Drag
   - Implied Windowing
   - Object Grouping

3. **Click OK to exit the dialog box and put your settings into effect in your drawings.**

Getting a grip on your drawing

AutoCAD grips are different from grips found in other drawing packages, but they're also powerful and flexible. You can easily turn them on and off from the command line by following these steps:

1. **To turn on grips, simply type** GRIPS 1 **on the command line and press Enter.**

2. **To turn off grips again, type** GRIPS 0 **on the command line and then press Enter.**

Shooting with loaded linetypes

After you set your selection settings and get a grip on your drawing, loading a few linetypes is the next logical step. Using the command line is the quickest way to load linetypes. (See, no more of that sissy dialog box stuff now!) The easiest way to manage linetypes overall, however, is to use the Select Linetype dialog box . . . er . . . (Oops — I lied. Oh, well . . .) Well, at least you can access the Select Linetype dialog box by typing **DDLTYPE** at the command line. And we're talking about loading the critters now, so the command line it is! (Any objections? I didn't think so.)

Follow these steps to load linetypes by using the command line:

1. **Type** LINETYPE **at the command line and press Enter.**

2. **At the** ?/Create/Load/Set **prompt, type** LOAD **and then press Enter.**

3. **At the** Linetype(s) to load **prompt, type the names of the linetypes you want to load and press Enter.**

After you finish step 3, the command line looks as follows:

```
Command: LINETYPE
?/Create/Load/Set: LOAD
Linetype(s) to load: BORDER,DASHED,DOT
```

AutoCAD now opens the (sigh) Select Linetype File dialog box.

4. In the dialog box, click the ACAD.LIN file (or whatever other file contains the linetypes you want) to select it.

(On my system, ACAD.LIN is in the directory \ACADR13\COMMON\SUPPORT.)

5. Choose OK to exist the dialog box.

Lay (er)ing it on thick

As is true of the other settings discussed so far, creating an initial working set of layers is most easily done from the command line. But, once again, *managing* layers is more easily accomplished by using the Layer Control dialog box (grrrr!), which, thankfully, you can access directly by typing **DDLMODES** at the command line (ahhhhh!).

To create layers by using the command line, follow these steps:

1. Type LAYER at the command line and then press Enter.

2. Type NEW at the prompt that appears, and then press Enter again.

3. At the New layer name(s) prompt, type the names of the new layers you want to create and press Enter.

The following example shows how the command line looks after you create three new layers named GEOMETRY, TEXT, and DIMENSIONS:

```
Command: LAYER
?/Make/Set/New/ON/OFF/Color/Ltype/Freeze/Thaw/LOck/Unlock: NEW
New layer name(s): GEOMETRY,TEXT,DIMENSIONS
```

Limiting factors (limits, grids, snap intervals, and scales — oh, my!)

Setting the appropriate limits for your drawing, as well as the grid, snap interval, and scaling factors to match, is one of the most important steps you can take in creating an accurate, easy-to-print drawing. Setting just the right limits and related parameters, however, is not easy without some help. So use Appendix C to determine the appropriate limits for the size of the objects you are trying to draw as well as the size of the paper on which you want to print the drawing. (Or check out Tables 5-1 and 5-2 in the preceding chapter if you'd rather flip backward than forward to the appendixes.)

To set your drawing's limits and related parameters, follow these steps:

1. **To set limits for your drawing, type** LIMITS **on the command line and press Enter.**

   AutoCAD displays a line that reads Reset model space limits and then a prompt line with options.

2. **Press Enter to accept the default lower left corner limits of 0-0; if this value does not appear at the prompt, type it and press Enter.**

3. **At the next prompt, type the limits you want for the upper right corner of your drawing and press Enter.**

   The following example is appropriate for drawing a football field that is 100 yards long and 50 yards wide, with 10-yard-deep end zones:

   ```
   Command: LIMITS
   Reset Model space limits:
   ON/OFF/<Lower Left corner> <0.0000,0.0000>: 0,0
   Upper right corner <12.0000,9.0000>: 200,125
   ```

I calculated the LIMITS value in the preceding example by finding the most nearly appropriate entry in Appendix C and multiplying by five to obtain limits that leave plenty of space for the football field. (A multiplication factor of four would have worked, too, but would not have left much space beyond the end zones.) If you need to multiply an entry to get appropriate limits, make sure that you multiply the values for the grid, snap intervals, linetype scale, and dimension scale by that same factor.

Now you need to set the appropriate visible grid and snap intervals for the limits.

4. **To set the grid for your drawing, type** GRID **at the command line and press Enter.**

5. **At the prompt, type the value for the grid spacing you want and press Enter.**

6. **To set the snap interval, type** SNAP **and then press Enter.**

7. **At the prompt, type the value for the snap setting you want and press Enter.**

You can set the grid and snap interval either on a flexible, seat-of-your-pants basis or so that each grid square represents one plotted inch on the printout. Flying by the seat of your pants is more flexible, but occasionally your buns get burned. So either use values that make sense or use the tables in Appendix C to find values that set the size of a grid square to one plotted inch.

The following example uses seat-of-the-pants values for a football field. Setting a visible grid with dots ten yards apart and a snap grid with snap points one yard apart seems to make sense for initial work.

```
Command: GRID
Grid spacing(X) or ON/OFF/Snap/Aspect <2.0000>: 10
Command: SNAP
Snap spacing or ON/OFF/Aspect/Rotate/Style <1.0000>: 1
```

Now you want to set the scale for your linetypes and dimensions. Scaling linetypes and dimensions is all too easy to forget up front, but such an onerous omission can really jump up and bite you in a tender spot at output time. And you really don't want your client to be standing around as a bad printout rolls off the pen plotter and you must frantically leaf through *AutoCAD For Dummies* to determine what you did wrong, now do you? So just go ahead and set these scale settings right now, while you're thinking of it. Okay?

8. **To set the linetype scale factor for your drawing, type** LTSCALE **on the command line and press Enter.**

9. **At the prompt, type the new scale factor you want and then press Enter.**

AutoCAD displays the words Regenerating drawing and then the command prompt reappears.

10. **To set the dimensions scale factor, type** DIMSCALE **and press Enter.**

11. **At the prompt, type the new value you want for the dimensions scale factor and press Enter.**

Unlike with grid and snap settings, you can't set the linetype and dimension scaling by guessing and then expect to end up with a useful result. Use the tables in Appendix C to find values that make sense for your drawing.

The following example uses values that make sense for a football field:

```
Command: LTSCALE
New scale factor: <1.0000>: 500
Regenerating drawing.
Command: DIMSCALE
New value for DIMSCALE: <1.0000>: 500
```

How do you determine the exact linetype scale and dimension scale? By calculating the *dimension scale factor* for the drawing. The dimension scale factor is simply the number by which you multiply one side of the drawing's scale to calculate the other. In a drawing in which the scale is 1cm = 1m, for example, the dimension scale factor is 100 (1cm × 100=1m). For this drawing, the table entry in Appendix C shows 100; if you multiply the entry by 5 to get the correct limits, the drawing's scale factor becomes 1cm = 5m, and the dimension scale factor, also multiplied by 5, becomes 500. (If this is confusing, don't worry; that's why the table is in Appendix C — so that you can just look up appropriate values instead of needing to refigure this each time for yourself.)

Zooming in on the results

Now that all your other settings are, well, *set*, you can use the ZOOM command to zoom in on the drawing so that your screen displays the entire grid. (Zooming just gives you a closer-up or farther-away view of your drawing.)

Having your screen display your entire grid as you start your drawing can be pretty useful, and you probably will want to zoom out to that view at various times during your work so that you can examine your entire drawing at once. Two simple commands give you a view of your drawing that displays not only the entire grid, but also a little room around the edges. The first command zooms out so that the grid fills your drawing area; the second command zooms out an additional 10 percent to give you a little working room around the edges of the drawing. Both commands require that you type ZOOM on the command line, but that shouldn't confuse you at all if you simply follow these steps:

1. **Type** ZOOM **on the command line and then press Enter.**

2. **To show your entire grid on-screen, type** ALL **at the prompt and press Enter.**

   AutoCAD displays the words `Regenerating drawing` and then a new command prompt appears.

3. **Type** ZOOM **on the command line a second time and then press Enter.**

4. **At the prompt, type** .9X **to give yourself a little working space, and press Enter again.**

The following example shows the command line with these commands entered:

```
Command: ZOOM
All/Center/Dynamic/Extents/Left/Previous/Vmax/Window/
      <Scale(X/XP)>: ALL
Regenerating drawing.
Command: ZOOM
All/Center/Dynamic/Extents/Left/Previous/Vmax/Window/
      <Scale(X/XP)>: .9X
```

In this example and elsewhere in AutoCAD, just press the spacebar at the command prompt to repeat the preceding command.

How to Draw

The rudest shock for the novice user of AutoCAD is the level of complexity involved in using AutoCAD as opposed to using a most other drawing programs. (Well, actually the rudest shock is probably the price — *ten times* what a standard drawing program costs; the *second* rudest shock is the additional complexity.) AutoCAD's difficult setup procedures and its numerous methods of controlling what's happening on-screen can be quite daunting without help. At no point is the program's complexity more apparent than when you're simply trying to draw something — anything! — on-screen.

In AutoCAD, you can draw either by using the mouse or by entering commands from the command line. Each drawing option offers its own special advantages. But to really make AutoCAD sing, you want to use a combination of the two methods. The command line is good for entering data about the initial part of the drawing and its main elements; the mouse is good for adding more elements that depend on the initial ones, for editing, and for adding text, dimensions, and annotations.

Drawing on command

Whenever AutoCAD users talk about using the command line to "enter geometry," they mean something quite different from merely using the command line to enter commands. You can enter commands from the command line anytime if you want; in fact, how you enter commands in AutoCAD is just a matter of deciding which of the following methods is fastest for you to use and easiest for you to remember:

  ✔ Choose the command from a menu.

  ✔ Use Windows keyboard shortcuts to choose the command from a menu (AutoCAD for Windows only).

  ✔ Click an icon to launch the command (AutoCAD for Windows only).

  ✔ Enter the command from the command line by using the keyboard.

 Entering geometry from the command line, on the other hand, means using the command line to specify the actual coordinates of points on your drawing. This method enables you to draw complicated shapes, with great accuracy, without ever picking up the mouse. (Unless you become really, really confused in placing your points on-screen, in which case your drawing is likely to wind up looking like particularly ugly graffiti.)

Experienced AutoCAD users can undoubtedly work faster than you can (rank novice that you are at this point), especially creating a new drawing, because they are quite accustomed to using the command line to quickly enter coordinates for their drawing. Entering drawing coordinates from the command line effectively, in the lofty manner of these AutoCAD experts, requires that you learn the following different ways to enter keyboard coordinates:

  ✔ Absolute entry of X,Y coordinates.

  ✔ Relative entry of X,Y coordinates.

  ✔ Relative entry of polar coordinates.

X,Y coordinates are two-dimensional coordinates defined by the Cartesian coordinate system. A specific point, called the *origin*, is defined as being 0,0. Other points are defined by moving first in an *X,* or right/left, direction, and then in a *Y,* or up/down, direction.

You define the X,Y coordinates on-screen when you specify a drawing's limits; limits make the on-screen coordinates meaningful to the drawing you create by matching traditional paper sizes. The grid you define shows some of the points in the X,Y map, and the snap grid you define — if you turn on the snap grid — tells you which points in the X,Y map you can select with the mouse.

The following sections further define the two types of X,Y coordinates as well as the third type of coordinates — polar coordinates.

Absolute coordinates

Absolute coordinates are an unvarying description of a point's location. If the lower left corner of your drawing is 0,0, for example, the absolute coordinates 2,1 take you 2 units to the right of the lower left corner and 1 unit above it. No matter where on-screen you're working at a given time, the absolute coordinates 2,1 describe that same location. If you try to draw a line from 2,1 to 2,1, it doesn't go anywhere; it starts and ends at the same point.

The following example displays the commands you would enter on the command line to draw a three-unit-wide square starting at 2,4, using absolute coordinates:

```
Command: LINE
From point: 2,4
To point: 5,4
To point: 5,7
To point: 2,7
To point: 2,4
To point: C
```

Instead of entering point coordinates such as 2,4 from the keyboard, you can enter them by clicking at the appropriate point on-screen with the mouse.

Note: You can always complete a line command for a triangle, square, or other shape by typing **C,** for *close,* at the last prompt on the command line for that command. The **C** closes the shape.

In case you've forgotten my advice from waaay back in Chapter 4, remember *not* to use spaces on the command line, because AutoCAD interprets them as returns. A definite no-no!

Figure 6-1 shows the screen with a square drawn on it by using absolute coordinate commands.

Relative coordinates

Relative coordinates describe where a point is in relation to the previous point you specified. A set of relative coordinates is designated by preceding the coordinates with the @ symbol. If the first point you specify is 0,0, for example, you can move to 2,1 from the command line two ways: by entering the absolute coordinates 2,1 or by entering the relative coordinates @2,1. Now if at this point (pun most certainly intended) you enter the absolute coordinates 2,1 again, you won't go anywhere; but if you enter the relative coordinates @2,1, you move right two units and up one.

The following example displays the commands you would enter on the command line to draw a four-unit-wide, two-unit-high rectangle starting at 6,6, using relative coordinates:

```
Command: LINE
From point: 6,6
To point: @4,0
To point: @0,2
```

```
To point: @-4,0
To point: @0,-2
To point: C
```

You can always complete a line command for a triangle, square, or other shape by typing **C,** for *close,* at the last prompt on the command line for that command. The **C** closes the shape.

Figure 6-2 shows the screen with a rectangle drawn on it by using relative coordinate commands.

Polar coordinates

Polar coordinates are always relative, because they describe the angle and distance of one point from the previous point. The angles you enter for polar coordinates depend on the angle direction you specify; the default in AutoCAD assumes that an angle straight up is 90 degrees, an angle to the right is 0 degrees, an angle to the left is 180 degrees, and an angle straight down is 270 degrees. This default setting represents the angle directions most commonly used in architecture.

From 2,7 to 2,4   From 5,7 to 2,7

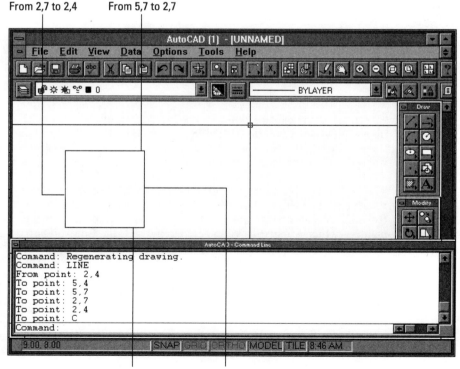

Figure 6-1:
A square
drawn from
the command
line by using
absolute
coordinates.

From 2,4 to 5,4   From 5,4 to 5,7

From @ -4,0 to @0,-2 (6,6)   From @0,2 to @ -4,0

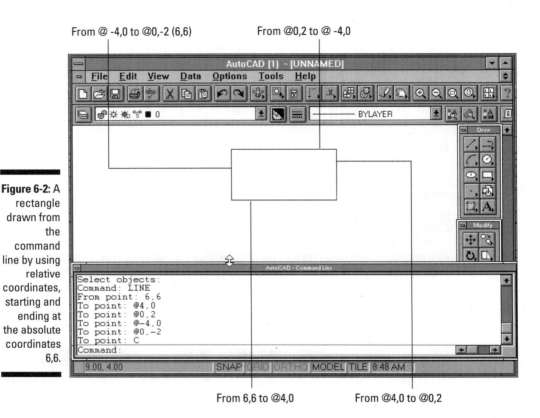

Figure 6-2: A rectangle drawn from the command line by using relative coordinates, starting and ending at the absolute coordinates 6,6.

```
Select objects:
Command: LINE
From point: 6,6
To point: @4,0
To point: @0,2
To point: @-4,0
To point: @0,-2
To point: C
Command:
```

From 6,6 to @4,0   From @4,0 to @0,2

To change the angle direction to something different, such as designating straight up as 0 degrees, type the **DDUNITS** command on the command line (and press Enter) to open the Units Control dialog box. Then click the <u>D</u>irection button in the dialog box. Chapter 5 contains more detail on changing angles this way.

The odd thing about polar coordinates is that, although they specify a point relative to the last point you entered, the *angle* you enter is absolute. No matter the direction of the last line segment you draw, the polar coordinates stay the same — which are just as you specified in the Units Control dialog box.

You specify a polar coordinate on the command line by using the @ symbol to indicate relative coordinates and the less-than symbol (<) to indicate an angle. The following example displays the commands necessary to draw an equilateral triangle, three units on a side, starting from the coordinates 5,5 and using polar coordinates:

```
Command: LINE
From point: 5,5
To point: @3<0
To point: @3<120
To point: @3<240
```

Figure 6-3 shows the screen with a triangle drawn on it by using polar coordinate commands. The callout for the final side of the triangle demonstrates why polar coordinates are so important. Some points that are easy to specify by using polar coordinates are difficult or impossible to specify using only absolute coordinates. By using polar coordinates, you can enter the exact point of the drawing and preserve the integrity of the drawing.

From @3<120 to @3<240

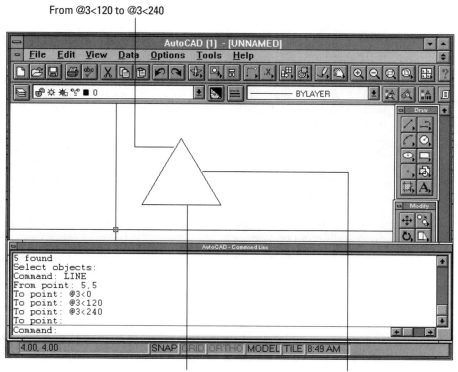

Figure 6-3:
A triangle drawn from the command line by using polar coordinates.

From 5,5 to @3<0   From @3<0 to @3<120

Getting the Look Right

Wanting different objects in your drawing to look different is a pretty natural desire. A different look — different colors, lineweights, or linetypes — can communicate important information about the characteristics of the object being drawn, about what other objects it may be like, or even about how far from the viewer of the drawing the object is located. (That is, how far the *real* object that the drawing *represents* is from the viewer; on-screen or on a print-out, the objects in the drawing are, of course, all flat — and only as far from your nose as the screen or paper.)

The ways that AutoCAD enables you to make objects look different from one another are through changes to the *color* of an object, to the *linetype* of an object, and to the *lineweight* of an object.

Linetype describes the thickness and the pattern of filled-in and empty spaces in a line. A thick solid line is distinguishable from a thin solid line, for example, and a solid line is easily distinguishable from a dotted line.

Drawing in different thicknesses is hard to do using only a pencil (unless, of course, you own one of those new *space age* pencils, with several different leads, colors, and, of course, a built-in can opener). And line thicknesses are usually rendered differently on different output devices and at different output scales. Because of these realities, CAD uses continuous, dashed, and dotted lines of every description to depict different types of objects.

In AutoCAD, *lineweight* — the thickness of a line — also communicates impor-tant information. Linetypes, however, are used more often. You may want to use a few very different lineweights, such as thin, medium, and thick, to differ-entiate between lines. If you do, make sure that the different thicknesses really do look different on your printout; if they don't, don't bother using different lineweights in your drawing at all.

Color is also used to differentiate objects, but more for on-screen differentiation than for any differentiation on the printout. That's mainly because most CAD drawings are either printed in black and white in the first place or are eventu-ally photocopied into a black-and-white version that others in the creation process must understand. So in most cases, plan to use color mainly to commu-nicate nice-to-have information rather than must-have information.

AutoCAD uses linetype and color distinctions in a pretty sensible way. Linetypes most often indicate different types of objects; color, as often as not, indicates the layer that an object is on. Sometimes the linetype, the color, and the layer mean exactly the same thing; you may draw all the trees in your drawing in dashed lines, in green, on the FOLIAGE layer. But you can also use layers to subdivide a category; you may subdivide the foliage into TREES, BUSHES, and GRASS layers, for example, all of which are green and all drawn with the same linetype.

You can also specify linetypes and colors for each individual object you create, which at first seems like a good idea because it gives you a lot of control. But this practice can quickly become cumbersome if you must create separate linetype and color drawings for each type of object, as well as remember *why* you made all the decisions for each object. Sometimes, however, you simply find it necessary to be that specific, and if that's the case, AutoCAD quite handily supports this capability; just make sure that you use it as sparingly as you can. (Or you may need a whole 'nother computer just to keep track of what all the colors and linetypes for all your different objects mean.)

Many professions and projects develop detailed standards for how to use linetypes and layers. Linetypes are very important in helping the users of your drawing understand just what you're doing; layers are very important for sharing drawings with others currently working on a project or who may later want to reuse your work. Determine what standards, if any, exist for your profession and follow them relentlessly; doing so makes it possible for you to reuse your current work in later work that you do, do do de do. (Do I feel a song coming on?)

Using that layered look

In the following example, you create two layers by using different linetypes and colors and then draw objects on these layers. The objects in this example are the outline of a swimming pool and the water in the pool (but you could plug your own names into these basic steps at any point to create your own drawings). You use the Layer Control dialog box in this example; the setup steps at the beginning of this chapter describe how to create layers entirely from the command line if you want to do that instead.

Follow these steps as a guide to creating layers for different linetypes and colors:

1. **Choose Data⇨Layers from the menu bar. Or type DDLMODES at the command line and press Enter.**

   The Layer Control dialog box appears, as shown in Figure 6-4.

2. **Type the name of the first layer, CONCRETE in this example, in the text window near the bottom of the dialog box.**

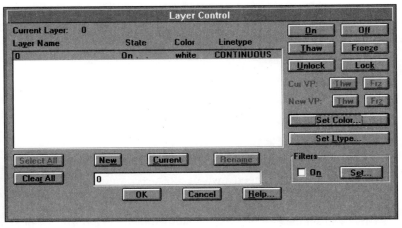

Figure 6-4:
The Layer
Control
dialog box
with only the
default layer
0 defined.

3. **Click the New button to create the layer.**

   The layer CONCRETE appears right below the default layer 0 in the list of layers in the dialog box. (*Note:* Don't click OK just yet, or the dialog box disappears and you must repeat step 1 to open it again.)

4. **Click the word CONCRETE (or whatever your layer's name is) in the Layer Name list to highlight the new layer.**

   For ease of use, you can click anywhere next to the layer name to highlight it.

5. **Click the Set Color button, located in the group of buttons to the right of the Layer Name list box, to set the color assigned to the layer.**

   The Select Color dialog box appears, as shown in Figure 6-5.

Figure 6-5:
The Select
Color dialog
box, with the
color gray
selected in
the
Standard
Colors list.

The colors available on your system may be different from those on mine, so the exact apperance of your Select Color dialog box also may be different than that shown in the figure. But that's okay; just pick any of the Standard Colors that you'd like on your system.

6. Click gray, the eighth color from the left in the Standard Colors list, to select it as the color for this layer, and then click OK.

The Layer Control dialog box reappears. In the Layer Name list, the Color for the CONCRETE layer changes to 8, which is the color number for gray. (This number also appeared in the Color text box at the bottom of the Select Color dialog box after you selected the color.)

7. Click the Set Ltype button in the Layer Control dialog box to set the linetype assigned to the layer.

The Select Linetype dialog box appears, as shown in Figure 6-6.

If you already loaded the linetypes you need for your drawing, the Select Linetype dialog box displays them in the Loaded Linetypes list. If not, click the Load button and select the linetype file and linetype you need. For this example, the linetype file is ACAD.LIN, in the subdirectory \ACAD\R13\COMMON\SUPPORT (on my machine, at least), and the linetype selected is BORDER. You can also load the linetype DIVIDE2 at this time, because you can use that linetype to indicate water in the swimming pool.

8. Click BORDER in the Loaded Linetype list to highlight and select it as the linetype for the CONCRETE layer, and then click OK.

The highlighted linetype appears as a black line on a white background; nonhighlighted linetypes appear as black lines on white backgrounds — the opposite of which you may expect from other programs. (And, yes, the program *should* also highlight the linetype name to indicate what's selected, but that would make things too easy, wouldn't it?) The name of the selected linetype also appears in the Linetype text box. You can't select two linetypes at once; if you select a second one, you deselect the first.

Note: AutoCAD selects and deselects items in lists differently than most other programs. To select a layer in a list, you click its name; other layers that are already selected are not automatically deselected. To deselect a layer, you must press and hold the Shift key as you click the layer's name. AutoCAD also highlights selected items differently than many other programs do. If you're not sure whether an item is highlighted, click a different item to highlight it and confirm what AutoCAD highlighting looks like. Then press and hold the Shift key and click the same item again to remove the highlight.

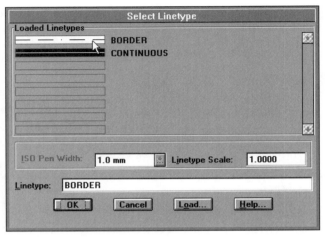

Figure 6-6:
The Select
Linetype
dialog box,
with the
linetype
BORDER
selected.

After you click OK, the Select Linetype dialog box disappears, returning you to the Layer Control dialog box. In the Layer Name list, the Linetype for the CONCRETE layer changes to BORDER, the linetype you just selected.

9. **Repeat steps 2 through 8 to create another layer called WATER with the color cyan (light blue) and the linetype DIVIDE2.**

The Layer Control dialog box reappears with your two new layers set up, as shown in Figure 6-7.

10. **Click OK to accept the new layer settings.**

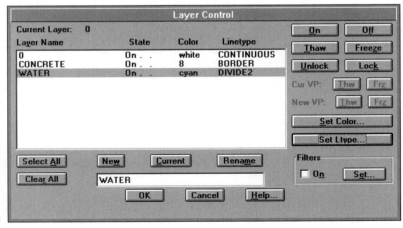

Figure 6-10:
The Layer
Control
dialog box
with new
layers
CONCRETE
and WATER.

Objective creation

If you need to specify different linetypes and colors for specific objects, you can use the Object Creation Modes dialog box to do so. You can also specify these linetype and color attributes from the command line. In many cases, you want to change the linetype and color, draw a few objects, and then return to the color and linetype assigned to the layer you're working on.

Along with linetype and color, you can also specify the text style, linetype scale, elevation, and thickness of an object before you create it. You can learn more about these additional attributes later in the book.

BYLAYER is the default attribute for both colors and linetypes. It enables you to use the color or linetype defined for a layer on objects in that layer. If an object has BYLAYER assigned as its color, for example, and is on a layer assigned the color green, that object also is green. If you later change the layer's color to, say, red, all objects on the layer that are assigned BYLAYER as their color attribute instantly become red as well

In the following example, you do your drawing on layer 0, the default layer for new objects in the standard AutoCAD drawing. You change the color and linetype by using the Object Creation Modes dialog box; and then you use the command line to change the color and linetype back to those of BYLAYER. The steps in this example can serve as a template for you to follow in creating your own objects.

To change the color and linetype of an object, follow these steps:

1. **Choose Data⇨Object Creation from the menu bar. Or type** DDEMODES **at the command line and press Enter.**

   In Windows, you can also click the Object Creation button, the first button to the right of the Linetype Control area in the object properties bar.

   The Object Creation Modes dialog box appears, as shown in Figure 6-8.

2. **Click the Color button to select the new color you want to use for your object.**

   The Select Color dialog box appears. For this example, choose magenta, the sixth color to the right in the Standard Colors list, by clicking that selection in the list, and then click OK. The Object Creation Modes dialog box reappears.

3. **Click the Linetype button to select the new linetype you want to use for your object.**

The Select Linetype dialog box appears. For this example, choose CONTINU-OUS (an unbroken line) from the Loaded Linetypes list by clicking it in the list, and then click OK. The Object Creation Modes dialog box reappears, displaying your newly chosen color and linetype, as shown in Figure 6-9.

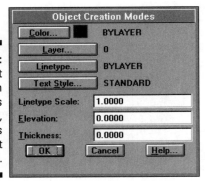

Figure 6-8:
The Object
Creation
Modes
dialog box,
displaying its
default
settings.

4. **Click OK to accept the new color and linetype settings for your objects.**

   At this point, you can draw the object or objects that use the color and linetype you specified. After you finish, you can use the command line to change the color and linetype back to the default BYLAYER attribute.

5. **At the command line, type LINETYPE and press Enter.**

6. **Type SET at the prompt and then press Enter to set a different linetype.**

7. **At the prompt, type BYLAYER as the linetype and then press Enter.**

8. **At the command line, type COLOR and press Enter.**

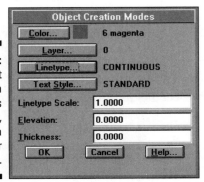

Figure 6-9:
The Object
Creation
Modes
dialog box,
displaying a
new color
and linetype.

9. **At the prompt, type** BYLAYER **again as the color, and then press Enter.**

The following lines show the commands and prompts entered to set both the linetype and the color back to BYLAYER:

```
Command: LINETYPE
?/Create/Load/Set: SET
New object linetype (or ?) <BYLAYER>: BYLAYER
?/Create/Load/Set: <Enter>
Command: COLOR
New object color <BYLAYER>: BYLAYER
```

Notice that the commands used on the command line to open the Layer Control dialog box — DDLMODES — and the Object Creation Modes dialog box — DDEMODES — are similar. The menu commands to open these dialog boxes, Layers and Object Creation, are also right next to each other on the Data menu. These similarities demonstrate the close relationship between these two ways of controlling how objects appear on-screen and in your printed drawing.

The Way You Undo the Things You Do

One of the biggest problems in drafting is the sheer ease involved in thoroughly messing up an otherwise great drawing. In a paper-and-pencil drawing, such a mistake may be irreparable. But with AutoCAD, you can fix most mistakes. (Not all, mind you, but — hey! — you can't have everything!)

The mistakes that you *can* fix in AutoCAD are mostly errors of *commission*; that is, you commit an act you shouldn't have. You may, for example, draw a square in the middle of a complex drawing and then realize — ackkkk! — you should have drawn a *circle* instead. (Silly you!) Well, no problem. Mistakes such as these are easy to fix in AutoCAD; these type of mistakes, in fact, are what the *Undo command* was designed for. (Da da da *da* ta-daaa!)

But before I discuss this modern wonder of CAD, I must take time to mention the horror of (pause for effect) the mistakes you *can't* fix easily in AutoCAD! (Cue thunder and lightning.) These mistakes are mostly errors of *omission*; in other words, you neglect to perform a setup step or set a mode setting correctly, and, as a result, your drawing becomes *very* testy to work with. If you complete a complicated drawing but neglect to set limits correctly, for example, you may find that creating a printout of your drawing that looks at all fetching becomes very, very hard. You may need to rearrange the elements in your drawing considerably or even perform complicated manipulations in paper space (described in Chapter 14), just to get a decent-looking printout.

To help you repair either kind of error, AutoCAD provides a powerful Undo/ Redo feature. Unlike the undo capabilities of many other programs, AutoCAD's Undo does — or undoes — almost anything you want, up to and including the following feats of design derring-do:

- Undo goes back a nearly unlimited number of steps.

- Undo is not affected by saves; you can save your drawing and still undo actions performed before the save.

- Undo affects almost all commands. The undo capabilities of some programs affect only specific commands; AutoCAD Undo not only undoes items you actually draw but also mode settings, layer creation, and more.

- Undo offers several different options for handling groups of commands or erasing several commands simultaneously.

This section describes the most useful features of AutoCAD's Undo capability — those you need 99.9 percent of the time. For more details and information on other, less useful features, especially should an emergency arise, check the AutoCAD on-line Help facility or the AutoCAD manuals.

AutoCAD's Undo does not work for all AutoCAD commands and does not reverse changes made to all system variables. Among the important commands AutoCAD can't undo are the following:

- CONFIG, used to configure AutoCAD.

- NEW or OPEN, used to create or access drawings.

- PSOUT, QSAVE, SAVE, and SAVEAS, used to save drawings to disk.

- PLOT, used to plot a drawing. (Because creating an Undo command that makes the printer pick up a sheet of paper and erase it would be *pretty* difficult!)

Undoing a step at a time

AutoCAD provides two kinds of undo commands for reversing a single step. The more common command is *U,* short for Undo (well, what did you expect — Unicorn?), and the less common command is *OOPS* (for obvious reasons).

OOPS reverses the last ERASE command. Just enter **OOPS** at the command line after you accidentally use ERASE to . . . uh, well, *erase* something. OOPS instantly reverses the effect of that ERASE. (This also works if you simply change your mind instead of making an out-and-out mistake.)

The Undo command, however, does much more. The simplest way to use Undo is to just keep undoing your previous actions until you work your way back to your mistake. To undo and redo a command sequence a single step at a time, follow these steps:

1. **Use one of the single-step Undo commands.**

   Your choices include the following actions:

   - Chooose Edit⇨Undo from the menu bar.
   - Press Ctrl+Z.
   - Type **U** at the command line and press Enter.
   - On the standard toolbar, click the icon that displays an arrow curved to the right (Windows only).

   The Undo capability works even across saves of your drawing. It does not, however, work after you close your drawing and then reopen it. Think twice, therefore, before you close any drawing; you may later wish you had undone something in it first. And then it's too late.

2. **Think carefully now, before doing anything else, about whether you *really* wanted to perform an Undo operation.**

   This is a *very important* warning: AutoCAD's Redo capability only redoes the *last* step that you undo; unlike the Undo command (or that annoying Energizer bunny), Redo does *not* just keep on going. In AutoCAD, as in life, you really don't want to undo much without thinking about it first. Otherwise, you can all too easily just keep undoing and undoing — and then realize too late that you've gone too far and undone valuable, even irreplaceable, work. Also far too easy to do is to undo one action, replace it with another, and only then realize that you didn't really want to undo the first action at all. Too late! If you enter another command after using Undo, Redo doesn't work. Not even a little. So after each individual Undo you perform, think — *think!* — about what you've just (un)done and make sure that you're truly glad you got rid of it, whatever it was, before you replace it.

3. **If needed, redo the step by performing a Redo operation.**

   Your choices include the following actions:

   - Choose Edit⇨Redo from the menu bar.
   - Type **REDO** at the command line and press Enter.
   - On the standard toolbar, click the icon displaying an arrow curved to the left (Windows only).

   Remember: You can redo only *once*.

Do not try to type **R** at the command line to redo a command. Redo does not work like Undo in using its initial as the command to activate it. *R*, in fact, is the abbreviation for the REDRAW command, not REDO. If you enter **R** at the command line, not only must you wait while AutoCAD redraws the screen, but you also discover that the REDO command doesn't work anymore for elements of that drawing created before the redraw.

4. **Use one of the single-step Undo commands (described in step 1) again if you want continue undoing.**

   Continue to choose Edit⇨Undo, press Ctrl+Z, enter **U** at the command line, or (Windows only) click the standard toolbar icon with the arrow curved to the right. Continue to consider, after each undo step, whether you're sure that you haven't already undone too much.

The best way to learn about AutoCAD's Undo capability is to experiment with it. Create a test drawing with different layers and other settings and create some geometry on-screen. Then use Undo to back up through your actions, watching what happens as you do so. Experimenting helps you use Undo intelligently — and not overdo it when you really need it.

Chapter 7
Tooling Around in Your Drawing

In This Chapter

▶ AutoCAD's drawing tools

▶ Lines and Polylines

▶ Freehand sketches

▶ Points and Polygons

▶ Circles and Arcs

▶ Ellipses and Splines — and more!

*A*utoCAD's main purpose, of course, is to support computer-aided design (what a concept!). And the most important activity in drafting is drawing *geometry* — shapes such as lines, circles, rectangles, and so on. Dimensions, text, and other important parts of the drawing — neat as they are — don't matter much unless the underlying geometry is right.

AutoCAD offers a small but powerful range of drawing tools. In this chapter, you learn how to get the most out of these drawing tools. You also learn — in detail — how to get what you want out of AutoCAD's user interface, whether you use the toolbars in Windows or the menus in DOS. The tips and tricks you learn in this chapter, in fact, help you navigate through all of AutoCAD.

AutoCAD's Drawing Tools

AutoCAD features relatively few types of objects to draw, but those the program does offer are quite powerful. For descriptive purposes, this chapter divides AutoCAD's drawing tools into the following three groups:

✔ Lines

✔ Points and shapes

✔ Curves

Third-party add-on packages that run with AutoCAD often add extra drawing tools to the mix; see the documentation that comes with the add-on program for information on such tools.

Note: The command line is unavoidable when using drawing commands. You can start these commands from the Draw menu in AutoCAD for DOS or the Draw toolbar in AutoCAD for Windows, but these methods simply type the command on the command line for you; you must then enter any additional options on the command line yourself. The examples in this chapter, therefore, just cut right to the chase and show you how to do things from the command line. You can start the commands any way you like though.

Table 7-1 offers an overview of all the drawing tools native in AutoCAD, describing these tools' major options and showing you how to access them from both AutoCAD for DOS (menus) and AutoCAD for Windows (toolbar). Use the table for an initial survey of what's available and as a quick refresher course if you're working along and suddenly find yourself stuck for just the command to access the tool you need. (Oh, and don't worry just yet if not all the terms on the table are familiar to you; all will become clear as you read through the chapter and use the commands. Trust me.)

Table 7-1		AutoCAD Drawing Tools and Commands		
Tool	*Command*	*Major Options*	*Draw Toolbar Entry (Windows)*	*Draw Menu Entry (DOS)*
Line	LINE	Start, end points	Line; flyouts for infinite line, ray	Line
Polyline	PLINE	Start, end points	Polyline; flyouts for 3D polyline, multiline, spline	Polyline
Ray	RAY	Start point, point through which ray passes	Ray; on Line flyout	Ray
Infinite line	XLINE	Two points through which line passes	Infinite line; on Line flyout	Construction Line
Multiline	MLINE	Justification, scale, style	Multiline; on Polyline flyout	Multiline
Sketch	SKETCH	Increment, pen, erase, connect	None	Sketch

Tool	Command	Major Options	Draw Toolbar Entry (Windows)	Draw Menu Entry (DOS)
Point	POINT	Point shape	Point; flyouts for divide, measure	Point; secondary menus for Divide, Measure
Rectangle	RECTANG	Two corners	Rectangle; on Polygon flyout	Rectangle; on Polygon secondary menu
Polygon	POLYGON	Number of sides, edge length, inscribed/circum-scribed	Polygon; flyouts for rectangle, four-sided polygon, and so on	Polyline; secondary menus for Rectangle, Polygon, 2D Solid
Circle	CIRCLE	Three points, two points, tangent	Circle; flyouts for Definition methods and Donut	Circle; secondary menus for Definition methods and Donut
Arc	ARC	Various methods of definition	Arc; flyouts for definition methods	Arc; secondary menus for Definition methods
Ellipse	ELLIPSE	Arc, center, axis	Ellipse; flyouts for definition methods	Ellipse; secondary menus for Definition methods
Spline	SPLINE	Convert polyline or create new	Spline; on Polyline flyout	Spline
Donut	DONUT	Inside, outside diameters	Donut; on Circle flyout	Donut; on Circle secondary menu

Flyouts and secondary menus

A *flyout* is not something sticky that you hang up on hot days to catch bugs and then toss out after it's full of the nasty thingies. A feature of the Draw toolbar, and other AutoCAD for Windows toolbars, a flyout is an additional row or column of icons that appears — "flies out" — after you click a particular icon. All the toolbar icons with little triangular pointers on them have flyouts. Figure 7-1, for example, shows the flyout row of icons that appears after you click the Polyline icon on the Draw toolbar.

Figure 7-1:
The Draw toolbar in AutoCAD for Windows displaying its default icons and the Polyline flyouts.

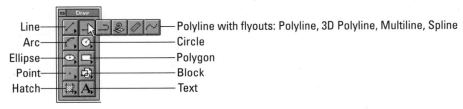

You notice in Figure 7-1 that the Polyline icon is repeated as the first flyout to the right of the icon you click to display the flyouts. You move the mouse pointer along the newly displayed icons to choose one; after you release the mouse button, the icon that the pointer is over is selected. The selected icon then replaces the previously displayed icon on the toolbar. So if you choose the Multiline flyout icon, the Multiline icon replaces the Polyline icon on the Draw toolbar.

The good news about this capability to change your toolbar icon display is that you can display your most frequently used options at any one time. The bad news is that you constantly change the appearance of your toolbars as you choose different options on the flyouts. You can fix this situation by reconfiguring the toolbar so that it displays all the options you use frequently at once, not as flyouts. To do so, see the AutoCAD documentation.

In the DOS version of AutoCAD, secondary menus are "hanging" menus that appear after you click a menu choice and disappear after you choose one of the secondary menu items or you click the mouse elsewhere. Figure 7-2 shows the Draw menu open with the Polygon secondary menu displayed. A sideways-pointing triangle next to a menu item indicates the presence of a secondary menu. (Secondary menus are often referred to as "submenus." I mention this so that, if you encounter this term, you'll know it doesn't refer to what the crew of a submarine uses to decide on dinner.)

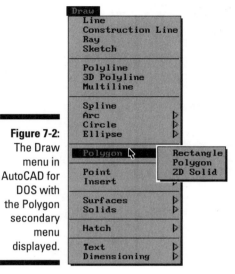

Figure 7-2:
The Draw
menu in
AutoCAD for
DOS with
the Polygon
secondary
menu
displayed.

The DOS version, in its default configuration, actually has an advantage over the default configuration of the Windows version; DOS displays more of the options you want in the actual menu instead of in a secondary menu or (as in Windows) a flyout. On the other hand, the Windows Draw toolbar is more accessible than the DOS Draw menu, so maybe things balance out here.

Commands vs. the (ooey!) GUI

So what's your best course: to enter Draw commands from the command line or to choose them from the menus or toolbars in the graphical user interface — or the *GUI*, as those of us fond of sticky treats like to call it? I recommend that you learn the command line entries for the Draw commands you use most. Choosing from the Draw menu in DOS is slow, especially if you must locate a command on a secondary menu. Choosing from flyouts in Windows also is slow, especially with the icons in the toolbar changing every time you choose a flyout. The Draw commands you enter at the command line also are almost completely consistent across the different versions and different releases of AutoCAD, so if you ever move among versions, knowing these commands reduces your learning curve considerably.

So, as I've told you I've forgotten how many times before (and will keep telling you until you commit it firmly to memory), *learn to use the command line for frequently used options and the menus or toolbars for less frequently used ones!*

Toeing the Lines

You can create a rough drawing of just about anything by using only lines, so they're worth tackling first. The following two line commands are the most important you use in AutoCAD:

- Lines
- Polylines

The following additional line commands are also available in AutoCAD:

- Rays
- Infinite lines
- Multilines
- Sketches

The sections that follow describe each of these line-related commands.

Lines (lines, everywhere a line . . .)

A *line* in AutoCAD is actually a series of one or more connected line *segments*. Each segment is a separate object. This does not seem like a big deal until you try to move or otherwise edit a multi-segment line and find that you must select each and every piece of it. To avoid such a hassle, use polylines, described later in this chapter, instead of lines if you want the connected segments to be a single object.

Your first few attempts to draw a line in AutoCAD can be very confusing, because AutoCAD keeps prompting you for additional *points*. CAD programs compose many objects in multiple connected line segments, so AutoCAD just keeps asking you for more points until you tell it to stop. You must tell it to stop by pressing Ctrl+C, Escape (in the Windows version), the spacebar, or Enter.

The LINE command doesn't offer any major options but, uses the currently selected linetype and color. The linetype selected is especially important; if the linetype is noncontinuous and the line bends often compared to the distance between dots and dashes in the line, the line can be pretty hard to follow. Setting the linetype size to an appropriate value, as described in Chapter 5, is important in making a noncontinuous line visible as it bends around.

Creating a line

The three different ways to tell AutoCAD to create a line are as follows:

- ✔ Type the LINE command on the command line and press Enter.
- ✔ Choose <u>D</u>raw⇨Line from the DOS menu bar.
- ✔ Click the Line icon (with flyout) on the Windows Draw toolbar.

Line example

The following example shows all the commands you need to enter on the command line to create a square made up of individual line segments:

```
Command: LINE
From point: 2,2
To point: 5,5
To point: 5,8
To point: 2,8
To point: CLOSE
```

Ortho mode is an important AutoCAD mode that affects lines and polylines. If ortho mode is on, you can draw lines only straight up, straight down, directly left, or directly right — and in no other direction. You can turn ortho mode on and off in the middle of a line command by preceding the ortho command with an apostrophe, as in **'ORTHO ON**. Entering the command **'ORTHO OFF** turns off ortho mode and enables you to draw lines in any direction. (The apostrophe makes the command *transparent,* meaning that you can enter it in the middle of another command.)

Polylines (wanna crackerline?)

A *polyline,* in its simplest form, is just like a line — that is, a series of connected line segments. Polylines, however, can include arcs as well as line segments. But no matter how many line segments and arcs it encompasses, a polyline as a whole is still one object. Finally, polylines offer additional options that regular lines lack: You can control the width of each segment or even specify a *halfwidth* that causes the polyline to taper along its length. (But *never* call your boss a halfwidth, even if he or she tapers along his or her length — whatever *that* means.)

After you create a polyline, you can use the PEDIT command to edit it; or you can convert the polyline to a collection of line and arc segments by using the EXPLODE command — although you lose the width or halfwidth defined for each segment if you do this, reducing the entire collection to a regular line width. (For more information about how to specify arcs within polylines, see the section "Raiders of the lost arcs," later in this chapter.)

Creating a Polyline

The three different ways to tell AutoCAD to create a polyline are as described in the following list:

- ✔ Type the PLINE command on the command line and press Enter.
- ✔ Choose Draw➪Polyline from the DOS menu bar.
- ✔ Click the Polyline icon (with flyout) on the Windows Draw toolbar.

Polyline example

The following example shows the commands you enter on the command line to create a polyline with a straight segment, an arc, and another straight segment:

```
Command: PLINE
From point: 3,2
Current line-width is 0.0000
Arc/Close/Halfwidth/Length/Undo/Width/<Endpoint of line>: 3,6
Arc/Close/Halfwidth/Length/Undo/Width/<Endpoint of line>: ARC
Angle/CEnter/CLose/Direction/Halfwidth/Line/Radius/Second pt/
        Undo/Width/<Endpoint of arc>: 4,6
Angle/CEnter/CLose/Direction/Halfwidth/Line/Radius/Second pt/
        Undo/Width/<Endpoint of arc>: LINE
Arc/Close/Halfwidth/Length/Undo/Width/<Endpoint of line>: 4,2
Arc/Close/Halfwidth/Length/Undo/Width/<Endpoint of line>:
        <Enter>
```

Figure 7-3 shows the polyline — a single object — created by these commands.

Initial line segment   Arc   Final line segment

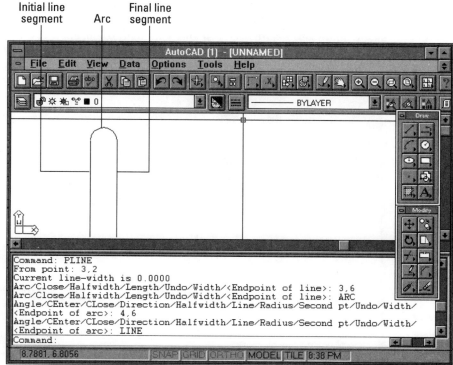

Figure 7-3:
A polyline with two line segments connected by an arc.

```
Command: PLINE
From point: 3,2
Current line-width is 0.0000
Arc/Close/Halfwidth/Length/Undo/Width/<Endpoint of line>: 3,6
Arc/Close/Halfwidth/Length/Undo/Width/<Endpoint of line>: ARC
Angle/CEnter/CLose/Direction/Halfwidth/Line/Radius/Second pt/Undo/Width/
<Endpoint of arc>: 4,6
Angle/CEnter/CLose/Direction/Halfwidth/Line/Radius/Second pt/Undo/Width/
<Endpoint of arc>: LINE
Command:
```

Rays and infinite lines (Buck Rogers, watch out!)

You can use both *rays* and *infinite lines,* also known as *xlines,* mainly as guides to construction as you create your drawing, because no real object you draw can contain a true ray or infinite line. (Nothing in real life goes on forever, although some things — a chewing out by your boss, for example — may seem to!) Even if you wanted to depict a ray or infinite line in your drawing, you'd simply use a line segment with one or two arrowheads to get the idea across.

Rays are easy to draw; you just define a starting point and then a second point through which the ray passes. AutoCAD then keeps prompting you for more of these second points, or *through-points,* so that you can draw as many rays as you want that start at the same point as the first one. You can't, however, enter an angle to specify how many angular units to offset the current ray from the previous one, which would be fun.

Infinite lines are more complex. For an infinite line, you can specify not only a *from* and a *to* point but also whether the infinite line is horizontal through a single point, vertical through a single point, and so on. Figure 7-4 shows horizontal and vertical infinite lines. Infinite lines are something that many of us are unlikely to use regularly, so I'll leave you to the tender mercies of the AutoCAD documentation or, better, to experiment in AutoCAD if you want to learn more.

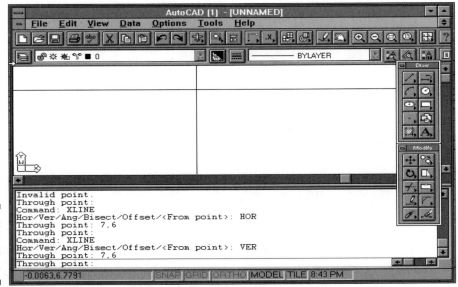

Figure 7-4: Horizontal and vertical infinite lines.

Creating a ray

The three different ways to tell AutoCAD to create a ray are as follows:

- ✔ Type the RAY command on the command line and press Enter.
- ✔ Choose Draw⇨Ray from the DOS menu bar.
- ✔ Click the Ray icon (from the Line flyout) on the Windows Draw toolbar.

Ray example

The following example shows the commands you enter at the command line to create a ray from point 3,6 through point 7,8, and on into infinity:

```
Command: RAY
From point: 3,6
Through point: 7,8
Through point: <Enter>
```

Creating an infinite line

The three different ways to tell AutoCAD to create an infinite line are described in the following list:

- ✔ Type the XLINE command on the command line and press Enter.
- ✔ Choose Draw⇨Construction Line from the DOS menu bar.
- ✔ Click the Infinite line icon (from the Line flyout) on the Windows Draw toolbar.

Infinite line example

The following example shows the commands you enter on the command line to create a horizontal and a vertical infinite line through point 7,6:

```
Command: XLINE
Hor/Ver/Ang/Bisect/Offset/<From point>: VER
Through point: 7,6
Through point: <Enter>
Command: XLINE
Hor/Ver/Ang/Bisect/Offset/<From point>: VER
Through point: 7,6
Through point: <Enter>
```

Multilines (lines aplenty)

Multilines are specialized types of lines that actually consist of several lines at once — up to 16 parallel lines seen as one object, in fact. You can use the default style multiline, which includes two elements, or you can create your own, adding additional elements as you choose. Your own multilines can vary also in the presence or absence of *joints* that appear at each vertex and in the style of *end cap* that appears at the beginning and ending of the multiline. Multilines that cross each other can create patterns to represent specific elements. Multilines are useful in architectural drawings and in drawing construction elements such as piping and geographical elements such as rivers. Drawing a river, for example, by entering a single multiline, which then appears on-screen as two lines, saves a lot of time.

If you want to use a multiline style other than the standard, two-line style, you must load it in advance. And if you want to modify the standard style before using it, you also must do so in advance. Use the MLSTYLE command on the command line to load and modify multiline styles. This command opens the Multiline Styles dialog box. This isn't anything you're very likely to do, however, so just see the AutoCAD documentation for details on how to use this dialog box to create new styles and modify existing ones if you ever need to.

You can draw multilines, in either the standard style or a new style you define, by using one of the following options:

- *Top, Zero, Bottom* specifies whether the cursor location indicates the top line of the multilines, the middle (zero) line, or the bottom line.
- *Scale* determines the distance between lines.

Creating a multiline

You can tell AutoCAD to create a multiline by using an already loaded multiline style or the standard default style in the following three ways:

- Typr the MLINE command on the command line and press Enter.
- Choose <u>D</u>raw⇨Multiline from the DOS menu bar.
- Click the Multiline icon (from the Polyline flyout) on the Windows Draw toolbar.

Multiline example

The following example shows the commands you can enter on the command line to create a multiline:

```
Command: MLINE
From point: 2,2
From point: 5,9
From point: 7,11
From point: <Enter>
```

Freehand sketches (free — free, at last!)

Creating a freehand sketch is simply drawing with the mouse. This may seem simple, but even freehand drawing involves a few options with which you need to be concerned. Sketches use a lot of memory; be careful about using too much system memory to store complex sketches.

You can use any of the following command line options in creating a freehand sketch:

- *Pen* raises and lowers the pen to enable and disenable drawing. You can't choose items from the menus if the pen is down.
- *eXit* saves the sketch and leaves the Sketch command operation.
- *Quit* leaves the Sketch command without saving the sketch.

✔ *Record* saves the sketch up to the last point sketched.

✔ *Erase* erases the sketch but stays in the Sketch command.

✔ *Connect* continues sketching from the end of the last sketched line.

✔ *. (period)* starts a drawing.

To use the SKETCH command on the command line, ignore the preceding options and follow these steps:

1. **Type** SKETCH **at the command line and press Enter.**

   At the prompt that appears, AutoCAD asks you to specify the *increment* — that is, the length of the little tiny line segments that make up your sketched line.

2. **Type at the prompt the increment length you want for your sketched lines and press Enter.**

   Experiment with different values to see what's appropriate for your drawing; use the largest value you can that still looks good. (The smaller the increment, the more tiny the lines you can draw, but the slower performance is if you need to redraw the screen or you print the sketch.)

3. **To begin drawing, click and release the mouse button before actually starting to draw.**

   After you finish drawing each line segment in the sketch, you again click and release the mouse button. (This is unlike almost any other drawing program; other programs require you to press and hold the mouse button down and drag the mouse pointer to draw.)

4. **Move the mouse pointer across the drawing area on-screen to draw the line segments of your sketch.**

   As you sketch, the line stays one color as you move the mouse a small distance; this shows that you haven't yet moved the mouse a distance longer than the length of the increment, so you haven't actually produced a line segment yet. As you move the mouse farther, the line segment changes color to indicate that it's now part of the sketched line.

5. **Continue drawing lines in this manner until you complete your drawing.**

6. **After you complete your drawing, press Enter to save your sketch.**

   If you use Quit, you lose your sketch up to that point. (If you try to use eXit, you may become confused and use Quit instead.)

After you leave the Sketch command by pressing Enter, AutoCAD tells you how many lines it saved; this information is a gentle reminder of the threat posed by all those little sketch lines in slowing down any redrawing or plotting you may want to perform.

If you plan to use sketched lines, expect to become good at it only with practice. Before sketching, experiment with the SKETCH command, and plot a drawing by using a few different increment values to find the value that produces the best-looking results without hurting speed in redraws too much. Figure 7-5 shows an example of a freehand sketch and the commands used to create it.

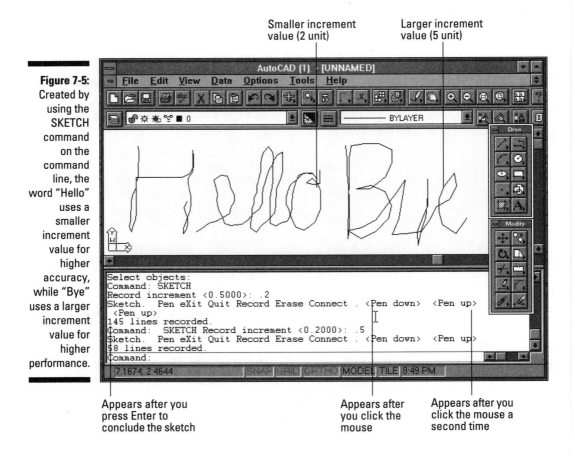

Smaller increment value (2 unit)

Larger increment value (5 unit)

Figure 7-5: Created by using the SKETCH command on the command line, the word "Hello" uses a smaller increment value for higher accuracy, while "Bye" uses a larger increment value for higher performance.

Appears after you press Enter to conclude the sketch

Appears after you click the mouse

Appears after you click the mouse a second time

Creating a sketch

You can use the following methods to tell AutoCAD to create a sketch:

- ✔ Type the SKETCH command on the command line and press Enter.
- ✔ Choose Draw➪Sketch from the DOS menu bar.

Sketch example

The following example shows you the commands to enter on the command line to create a sketch:

```
Command: SKETCH
Record increment <0.1000>: .2 <or drag a line segment on-
          screen to specify>
Sketch. Pen eXit Quit Record Erase Connect. <Pen down> <Pen
          up>
104 lines recorded.
```

In the third line of the command, <Pen down> appears after you click the mouse. <Pen up> appears in that line after you click the mouse again. The 104 lines recorded in the following line appears after you press Enter to conclude the sketch.

Scoring Points . . . and Shapes

Points and *shapes* are AutoCAD objects that enclose space and aren't curved. The following three types of objects, all of which are important, are available in this category:

- ✔ Points
- ✔ Rectangles
- ✔ Polygons

The following sections describe each type of object and now to create it.

Points (game, and match!)

Although simple in real life (and in other drawing programs), *points* in AutoCAD are complex and powerful. Before drawing a point, you must specify the *point style* and *size*; otherwise, you're stuck with the default. (And the default may not appear as you want it to on-screen or on a plot, so specify your points *before* you start drawing.)

You can use points not only to represent small objects, but also for construction purposes. You may, for example, want to create a point as something you can snap to while doing a drawing and then get rid of later.

You can specify how a point is drawn, as well as its size, by using either commands entered on the command line or the Point Style dialog box. The command line commands, PDMODE and PDSIZE, are complex and use arbitrary and hard-to-remember values. Unless you plan on using points frequently and really like the keyboard, I suggest that you use the dialog box instead.

DDPTYPE is the command that opens the Point Style dialog box (see Figure 7-6). The first line in the dialog box shows the actual point styles available. The second, third, and fourth lines add surrounding shapes to the point — a circle (second line), square (third line), or circle-in-square (fourth line).

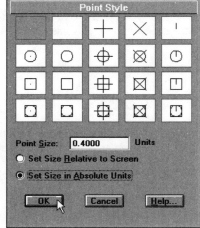

Figure 7-6:
The Point Style dialog box with the point size set in absolute units.

You can also specify the Point Size in the Point Style dialog box. You can specify the point size as a percentage of the screen size, which means the point always appears on-screen, by choosing the Set Size Relative to Screen option button, or as a number of drawing units, which means the point always appears on your printout, by choosing the Set Size in Absolute Units option button. You may want to specify point styles in screen units while working on your drawing so that they can't disappear from the screen and then respecify them in absolute units before printing so that they're sure to appear in the plot.

After you specify the point style, actually placing the point on-screen is easy; the following sections show you how to do this.

Creating a point

You can create a point by using any of the following methods:

- ✔ Type the POINT command on the command line and press Enter.
- ✔ Choose <u>D</u>raw⇨Point from the DOS menu bar (with secondary menu).
- ✔ Click the Point icon (with flyout) on the Windows Draw toolbar.

Point example

The following example shows you the commands to enter on the command line to create a point:

```
Command: POINT
Point: 2,2 <or pick a point>
```

Rectangles (oh, what a tangled wreck . . .)

Rectangles are a fairly recent addition to AutoCAD, first appearing in Release 12. Rectangles are really rather simple to create, which is nice; just pick a corner, move the mouse, and pick another corner. You don't even have any options to bother with. And you don't need to hold down the mouse cursor and drag it anywhere to create a rectangle either; just click in one corner, move the mouse to the opposite corner, and click there, too.

Unlike in other drawing programs, you don't click and drag the mouse to draw lines or create rectangles in AutoCAD; instead, after choosing the appropriate command for the object you want to draw, you click and release the mouse at the first point on screen, where you want the drawing to begin, and then you do so again at the second point, where you want it to end. (If you chose the <u>P</u>ress and Drag option in the Object Selection Settings dialog box at the time you set up AutoCAD, because you wanted AutoCAD to function like other programs in drawing objects, forget it; that setup choice affects how you *select* objects but not how you *draw* them. See Chapter 4 for details.)

Creating a rectangle

You can tell AutoCAD to create a rectangle by using the following methods:

- ✔ Type the RECTANG command on the command line (*not* RECT or RECTANGLE) and press Enter.
- ✔ Choose Draw⇨Polygon⇨Rectangle from the DOS menu bar.
- ✔ Click the Rectangle icon (from the Polygon flyout) on the Windows Draw toolbar.

Rectangle example

The following example shows you the commands to enter on the command line to create a rectangle:

```
Command: RECTANG
First corner: 4,7
Other corner: 7,4
```

If you really want to eliminate clean-up work at the end of the drawing process, make a rough drawing containing nothing but rectangles to represent the drawing's major parts. Put the rectangles on their own layer so that you can hide or get rid of it later. Set the correct limits and so on, but don't worry about actually drawing anything; just put rectangles of about the right size anywhere that geometry or text are to go. Print the result to see how it looks. You can get a good idea of the final look of your drawing in a short period of time by using this method.

Polygons (so next time, lock the cage . . .)

Moving from rectangles to *polygons* is much like moving from the sublime (that is, the very simple) to the ridiculous (that is, waaay too complex for words). Creating a triangle, a pentagon, or another polygonal shape in AutoCAD can readily be considered a minor feat of engineering in and of itself. The process involved in creating a polygon is exact, however, and relates well to what "real" drafters do. But if all your previous drawing experience is with a drawing package rather than a drafting board, drawing AutoCAD polygons can be a *real* pain.

To create a polygon, follow these steps:

1. **Type the** POLYGON **command on the command line and press Enter.**

   AutoCAD then prompts you for the number of sides you want on your polygon.

2. **Type at the prompt the number of sides you want for your polygon and then press Enter.**

   If you want to draw a triangle, for example, you type **3** at this prompt. AutoCAD then prompts you to specify either the center of the polygon (the default) or the edge of the polygon.

3. **Specify at the prompt whether you want to draw an edge of a polygon or you want to use the center point of the polygon for your drawing.**

You need to type **E** at this prompt and then press Enter to specify that you want to draw an edge. Then continue on with step 4. If you want to use the center point of the polygon, skip to the unnumbered paragraph immediately before step 6.

Now here's where you can really get in trouble, so follow along closely.

4. **At the prompt, type the coordinates for the first point of an edge for the polygon you want to create and press Enter.**

AutoCAD automatically creates a polygon with the specified number of sides — a triangle, square, pentagon, or whatever. This polygon is then resized according to the coordinate you enter in the following step.

5. **At the prompt, type the coordinates for the second endpoint of the edge of your polygon and press Enter.**

After you specify the second endpoint of the edge, you're done. This means that whatever shape you're creating is exactly *equilateral* (all sides the same length). So that second endpoint had better be in the right spot; otherwise, you can easily create a pentagon that looks as if its base is horizontal but is really tilted slightly right or left. If you want a *nonequilateral* shape, such as a right triangle, you must edit your equilateral triangle — or draw a polyline — to get it.

Creating a polygon by specifying its number of sides and what circle it surrounds or is circumscribed by is relatively easy. The circle is used to define either the distance from the polygon's center to the middle of each side — a *circumscribed polygon* — or to each vertex, or corner — an *inscribed polygon*. After entering the number of sides for your polygon, as described in step 2, you click a point on-screen or enter coordinates for the center of the polygon at the following prompt *instead of* entering an *E* to specify a polygon edge (as described in step 3, if you're on edge — as you may actually be at this point).

6. **To specify using the center point of the polygon for your drawing, type at this prompt the coordinates for the center of the polygon and then press Enter.**

Now you must tell AutoCAD whether the polygon is *inscribed in* a circle or *circumscribed around* a circle; inscribed within a circle is the default setting.

7. **At the prompt, type** C **if you want the polygon circumscribed around a circle and then press Enter. If you want the polygon inscribed in a circle, type** I **at the prompt and press Enter or just press Enter.**

Finally, you must enter the radius of the circle, either by entering a number from the keyboard or by clicking a point on-screen. If you use the keyboard to enter a number at the command line, a polygon of the right size and with a horizontal base appears. If you pick a point, the polygon's exact alignment depends on the point you pick. Again, if using this latter method, you can easily end up with a slightly misaligned shape.

8. **At the prompt, type the value you want for the radius of the circle and press Enter.**

   AutoCAD draws the polygon.

If you want to turn your equilateral polygon into a nonequilateral one, you must grab the offending corner and drag it to the right spot on-screen to make the shape you want. You find more information about this particular task in Chapter 8.

Creating a polygon

You can tell AutoCAD to create a polygon by using any of the following methods:

- ✔ Type the POLYGON command on the command line and press Enter.
- ✔ Choose Draw⇨Polyline⇨Polygon from the DOS menu bar.
- ✔ Click the Polygon icon (with flyout) on the Windows Draw toolbar.

Polygon examples

The following example shows you the commands to enter on the command line to create a polygon, as shown in Figure 7-7:

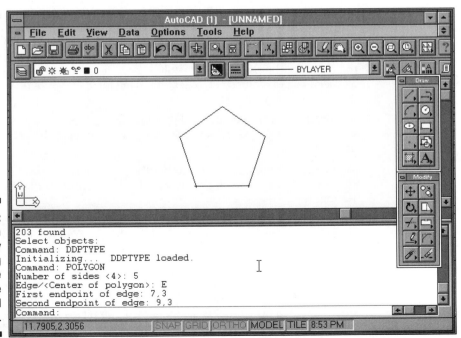

Figure 7-7: Creating a pentagon by specifying one side at the command line.

```
203 found
Select objects:
Command: DDPTYPE
Initializing...   DDPTYPE loaded.
Command: POLYGON
Number of sides <4>: 5
Edge/<Center of polygon>: E
First endpoint of edge: 7,3
Second endpoint of edge: 9,3
Command:
```

```
Command: POLYGON
Number of sides: 5
Edge/<Center of polygon>: E
First endpoint of edge: 7,3
Second endpoint of edge: 9,3
```

The following example shows you the commands to enter at the command line to create a polygon by specifying its bounding, or inscribed, circle:

```
Command: POLYGON
Number of sides: 3
Edge/<Center of polygon>: 4,8
Inscribed in circle/Circumscribed about circle (I/C) <I>: I
Radius of circle: 2
```

(Throwing) Curves

AutoCAD features a strong selection of curved objects for your drawing needs, as well as many ways to define them. Because you are provided so many ways to create curves, and because getting them to the right spot requires a fair amount of thought, you may want to consider drawing all your curved objects at once for a while, especially if you're an inexperienced AutoCAD user, until you get good at creating and placing them. The important curve-shaped objects for most AutoCAD users are as follows:

- Circles
- Arcs

Other curved objects available in AutoCAD that are not as important to most users as circles and arcs include:

- Ellipses
- Splines
- Donuts

The following sections describe each command. You will probably need to practice drawing all of these shapes, however, except perhaps circles, if you really want to get them right.

(Will he go round in) circles...

AutoCAD offers an easy way to draw circles in AutoCAD, and it also offers . . . *other* ways. The easy way is to define the center point of the circle and then to define the radius. You can also define a circle by entering one of the following options of the command (for those "other" ways):

- ✔ **3P** represents any three points on the circumference.
- ✔ **2P** represents the endpoints of a diameter of the circle.
- ✔ **TTR** represents two tangents and a radius.

Any of these commands can be useful for getting just the right circle into just the right spot on-screen, but you may find yourself doing what I do, which is creating the circle you want by using the center point/radius method and then moving it to just the right spot, as described in Chapter 8.

Creating a circle

You can tell AutoCAD to create a Circle by using any of the following methods:

- ✔ Type the CIRCLE command on the command line and press Enter.
- ✔ Choose Draw⇨Circle from the DOS menu bar (with secondary menus).
- ✔ Click the Circle icon (with flyout) on the Windows Draw toolbar.

Circle examples

The following example shows you the commands to enter on the command line to create a circle from a center point and radius:

```
Command: CIRCLE
3P/2P/TTR/<Center point>: 7,7
Diameter/<Radius>: <4.0000>: 2
```

The following example shows you the commands to enter at the command line to create a circle from two tangents and a radius:

```
Command: CIRCLE
3P/2P/TTR/<Center point>: TTR
Enter Tangent spec: TAN TO <Pick a circle or object with a
          tangent>
Enter second Tangent spec: TAN TO <Pick a circle or object
          with a tangent>
Radius <4.0000>: 2
```

Arcs (the 'erald angels sing . . .)

Arcs are, quite simply, parts of circles. By the time you finish learning about all of the many ways to define arcs, you may just end up drawing circles where you want an arc and then using correction fluid to cover over everything but the desired arc on your printout.

As it does with circles, AutoCAD offers you an easy way to define arcs. Just specify three points on-screen to define the arc, easy as one-two-three. These points tell AutoCAD where to start the arc, how much to curve it, and where to end it.

Sounds pretty easy, right? So where's the problem? Well, the trouble is that you often must specify many arcs more exactly than is possible using this method. AutoCAD helps you specify such arcs, true, but the procedure ain't easy.

You can start your arc by specifying the center of the arc or the start point. If you specify the center, AutoCAD asks you to specify the start point of the arc. AutoCAD defines arcs counter-clockwise, so pick a start point in a clockwise direction from the end point. After you specify the center and start point, AutoCAD presents several options you can choose, including the following:

- ✔ **Angle:** This option specifies the angle used by the arc. A 180-degree angle, for example, is a semicircle.

- ✔ **Length of chord:** This option specifies the length of the straight line connecting the endpoints of the arc. If you know the exact length, select Length of chord as the option you want.

- ✔ **Endpoint:** This option specifies where the arc ends. It is the default option and is often the easiest to use.

If you specify the start point as the first option, you then can choose among the following three command line options as well:

- ✔ **Center:** This option takes you back to the preceding options. Enter Angle, Length of chord, or Endpoint, as described above.

- ✔ **End:** This option specifies the endpoint of the arc. You then need to define the angle the arc covers, its direction, its radius, or its center point.

- ✔ **Second point:** This is the default option. The second point you choose is *not* the endpoint; instead, it's a point on the arc that, along with the start and endpoints, defines the arc's *curvature* — that is, how much it curves. After you enter the second point, you must enter an endpoint to complete the arc.

Creating an arc

You can tell AutoCAD to create an arc by using any of the following methods:

- ✔ Type the ARC command on the command line and press Enter.

- ✔ Choose Draw⇨Arc from the DOS menu bar (with secondary menus for different ways to define the arc).

- ✔ Click the Arc icon (with flyouts for different ways to define arc) on the Windows Draw toolbar.

Arc examples

The following example shows you the commands to enter on the command line to create an arc by specifying three points on the arc:

```
Command: ARC
Center/<Start point>: 1,1
Center,End/<Second point>: 2,2
End point: 3,3
```

The following example shows the commands to enter on the command line to create an arc starting from the center and specifying an angle, as shown in Figure 7-8:

```
Command: ARC
Center/<Start point>: C
Center: 4,4
Start point: 6,4
Angle/Length of chord/<End point>: ANGLE
Included angle: 90
```

Ellipses (S. Grant?)

Ellipses, like arcs, are complex. An ellipse is like a warped circle with a major (long) axis and a minor (short) axis to determine its length, width, and degree of curvature. After you start to draw an ellipse, AutoCAD presents the following options at the prompts on the command line:

- ✔ **Arc:** This option generates an elliptical arc rather than a full ellipse. You define an elliptical arc just as you do a full ellipse. The following methods for creating an ellipse apply to either.

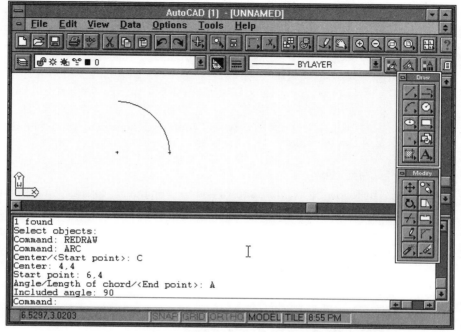

Figure 7-8:
Drawing an
arc by
specifying
its center,
its start
point, and
an angle.

✔ **Center:** This option requires that you define the center of the ellipse and then the endpoint of an axis. You can then either enter the distance of the other axis or specify that a rotation around the major axis defines the ellipse. If you choose the latter, you can enter (or drag the ellipse to) a specific rotation for the second axis that, in turn, completely defines the ellipse.

✔ **Isocircle:** This option creates an *isometric circle* — something you're unlikely to use; check the AutoCAD documentation if you need details.

✔ **Axis endpoint 1:** This option requires that you define one axis by entering its end points and the other by entering a distance or rotation.

These options are confusing to learn by reading; try doing it to get a feel for ellipses. If you need to draw an ellipse, you are likely to specify it by using one of these methods.

Creating an ellipse

You can tell AutoCAD to create an ellipse by using any of the following methods:

- ✔ Type the ELLIPSE command on the command line and press Enter.
- ✔ Choose Draw⇨Ellipse from the DOS menu bar (with secondary menu for definition methods).
- ✔ Click the Ellipse icon (with flyout for definition methods) on the Windows Draw toolbar.

Ellipse example

The following example shows you the commands to enter on the command line to create an ellipse:

```
Command: ELLIPSE
Arc/Center/<Axis endpoint 1>: 4,4
Axis endpoint 2: 8,4
<Other axis distance>/Rotation: .25
```

Other curved objects

A *spline* is a curve that passes near or through a number of points in a smooth way. You're unlikely to need splines when getting started with AutoCAD. See the AutoCAD documentation when you're finally ready to vent your spline.

Designating it as a *donut* (hold the coffee, please...) is a simple way to define a single object that consists of two concentric circles with the space between them filled. But watch out; drawing a donut is likely to draw some cops, too! (Sorry...) Creating a donut can be a time-saver in some cases, but it's certainly not the most important command to learn. In fact, you're unlikely to use the DONUT command much; if you do need it, you can usually figure it out through trial and error (donuts work a lot like circles), or see the AutoCAD documentation for details.

Okay, so now you know how to create all kinds of shapes by using various AutoCAD tools and commands. Ah, but what if you don't want to use these shapes *exactly* as created? What if you want to *change* them in some way — to move them to different locations on-screen, for example, or even alter their very appearance? Why, in those cases, you must learn how to edit! And that's the subject of the following chapter! (Coincidence? I think not . . .)

Chapter 8
Edit It

*E*diting may be the hardest to learn and hardest to use function in AutoCAD. Editing in any version of AutoCAD is really different from the editing you do in other programs — and it's even inconsistent among some of its own commands. Those users with a historical perspective of AutoCAD updates over the last several years, however, recognize that editing in AutoCAD has come a long way since the program's early days; for most of your work, you can now actually use editing techniques that are similar to, if somewhat more complicated than, those of many other programs. As for those who may not be as familiar with AutoCAD (the rest of you), well, you may find yourself checking this book, your AutoCAD books and manuals, and other sources every now and then for guidance.

The preceding two chapters describe the techniques and commands you use for creating new objects; this chapter discusses editing those existing objects. In your everyday "real" work, you move back and forth freely between the two operations, so you are likely to find yourself using the techniques from these three chapters freely as well.

After you successfully scale the learning curve for AutoCAD editing, you can do almost anything you want with your drawings — much more so than is possible in other, less powerful programs. So stick with it until it all starts to make sense.

The Selective Service

The usual reason for selecting an object is so that you can somehow modify it or change it. The change may even involve getting rid of it entirely. You may also select an item so that you can learn something about it or its properties. For all these reasons, understanding how the selection process works is an important first step in mastering AutoCAD editing.

This section discusses all the different ways that AutoCAD selects things. Taking the time to learn about and experiment with these different methods is really worth the effort, because much of AutoCAD's power is unavailable to you if you don't know how to select objects correctly. So try to follow closely through this section, and practice — as many times as necessary — any tasks that may at first seem confusing to you. Your work should become better and faster as a result.

Getting the settings right

To access the most selection options possible in AutoCAD, you must turn on some settings that, by default, remain turned off until you activate them yourself. That's because AutoCAD has evolved over many years from a primitive program containing only a dull, retrograde, small number of ways to select objects to a highly advanced program offering an exciting, forward-looking, large number of ways to select objects. Unfortunately, the default selection settings are mostly the ones you don't want or need most of the time. To access those you do want, you must make a few adjustments to get them just right.

The Object Selection Settings dialog box contains all these settings, just ready for you to fix. Your best bet is to turn on all the options in the dialog box. Just type **DDSELECT** at the command line and press Enter, or choose Options⇨ Selection from the menus to access the dialog box. Click all the check boxes to turn on all the dialog box's options (except those already turned on, of course). Figure 8-1 shows how the dialog box looks after you finish. The object selection settings affect the creation of a *selection set* (a group of selected objects). You find more details about this dialog box, its settings, and the system variables that back it up in Chapter 4.

Picking objects one at a time

One way to select objects is to pick them one at a time. The Use Shift to Add option of the Object Selection Settings dialog box, which controls the setting of the PICKADD system variable, controls this option.

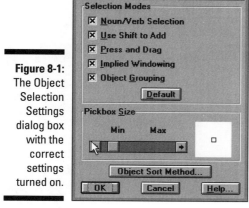

Figure 8-1:
The Object
Selection
Settings
dialog box
with the
correct
settings
turned on.

If the Use Shift to Add option is off, you build up a selection set just by picking objects one at a time. In most programs, you can select only one item at a time using this method; if you select one object and then another, the first object is deselected and the second one selected. Only the object you select last remains selected. But in AutoCAD, with Use Shift to Add turned off, *all* the objects you select, one at a time, remain selected and are added to the set, no matter how many you highlight. Whatever command you choose next affects every selected object.

With the Use Shift to Add option turned on, however, things get almost back to normal. If you pick one object and then another, only the second object stays selected. You must pick an object, *press and hold the Shift key,* and *then* pick another object to build up the selection set as you select more objects, adding additional selections to the set each time you do this. Be careful, however; with a few of the less frequently used AutoCAD commands, that old, Shiftless style still applies, even with this option turned on. For those commands, pressing Shift is a waste of effort.

The most confusing difference between selected objects in AutoCAD and those in other programs involves *grips* (which are described in detail in the section "Grip editing," later in this chapter). In most other programs, only selected objects display grips, or *handles*, at certain points surrounding the objects. In AutoCAD, however, a selected object retains its grips even *after* you deselect it. To the new user, the object probably looks as if it's still selected. In AutoCAD, the only clue you can trust to indicate whether you've actually selected an object — and that it is still selected — is the special dotted linetype the object acquires. The currently selected object in Figure 8-2, for example, displays the dotted linetype to indicate that is it still selected. *Never* assume that an object is currently selected just because it displays grips.

Figure 8-2:
Selected and unselected objects: The circle is unselected and the rectangle was previously selected but is now deselected, while the line is currently selected, as shown by its dotted linetype.

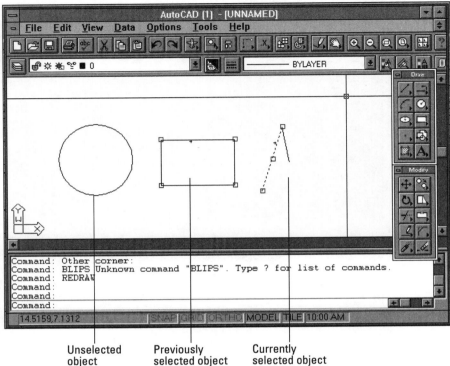

Unselected object

Previously selected object

Currently selected object

How much is that object in the window?

The Implied Windowing option in the Object Selection Settings dialog box (backed up by the PICKAUTO system variable) enables a powerful AutoCAD feature called, appropriately enough, *implied windowing.* Leaving out the history lesson, what this feature does is to enable you to use two different types of *selection windows* easily — albeit one involves a small learning curve to master. A selection window, by the way, is simply a window that you draw — by picking first one corner then picking the opposite corner — to select objects within the window. With the Implied Windowing option on, you can either use a *bounding window,* the kind of selection window other programs use, or a special type of selection window called a *crossing window.* You can determine which type of selection window you use just by varying how you move the mouse.

In most graphics programs, you can select a group of objects by dragging the mouse to open a window around them. Everything that's totally inside the window is then selected; everything that is only partly in the window or that's entirely outside the window isn't selected. To use this kind of selection window in AutoCAD, just start with the mouse pointer on the *left* side of the screen, click and hold the mouse button to begin drawing the window, and drag the mouse to the *right* side of the screen, making sure that you fully enclose in the window that's created every object you want to select. Then release the mouse button. Every object that is now fully enclosed by the window is selected; other objects are not.

With using implied windowing, you can also use a crossing window for object selection. Just like the window described in the preceding paragraph, a crossing window also selects objects as you drag a window around them. But with a crossing window, you can also select objects that are *only partially* in the window. A crossing window thus enables you to select large objects that may not be entirely visible on-screen, just by capturing a piece of them within your selection window. To use a crossing window in AutoCAD, just start the mouse pointer on the *right* side of the screen, click and hold the mouse button to begin drawing the window, and then drag your mouse to the *left* side of the screen to create the window, making sure you enclose at least part of any object you want to select within the window. Then release the mouse button. Every object that is fully enclosed by the window or that is *partly enclosed* by the window is now selected.

To create a *bounding window* in which to select objects that are *fully within* the window, drag the mouse *from the left* side of the screen *to the right* side. To create a *crossing window* in which to select objects that are *fully or partially within* the window, drag the mouse *from the right* side of the screen *to the left* side. These two types of selection windows, therefore, are distinguished only by the direction in which you drag the mouse on-screen.

Figures 8-3 and 8-4 show a *bounding window* and a *crossing window*, respectively, in action.

If the P̲ress and Drag option in the Object Selection Settings dialog box (also controlled by the PICKDRAG system variable) is turned on (an X appears in its check box), you create any selection window by pressing the mouse button down at the starting corner of the window, dragging the mouse to its destination, and releasing the mouse button at the ending corner of the window, as described in the preceding paragraphs.

If the P̲ress and Drag setting is turned off (its check box is empty), you create instead any selection window by clicking and releasing the mouse button in the starting corner of the window, moving the mouse to its destination without pressing the button, and then clicking and releasing the mouse button again at the ending corner of the window.

Creating a selection window, as you've no doubt figured out by now, is much like drawing an object; the difference is that, to draw an object, you must first enter a drawing command on the command line, choose a command from the draw menu, or click a drawing icon on a toolbar. Creating a selection window requires no such preliminary — just click and mouse away!

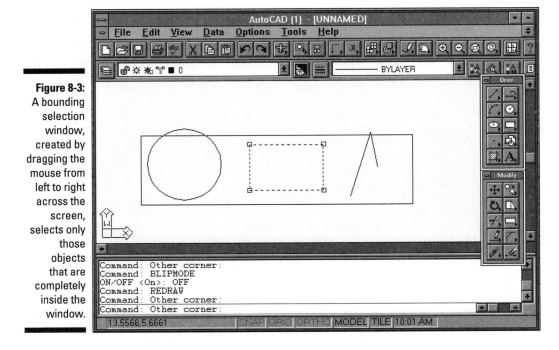

Figure 8-3:
A bounding selection window, created by dragging the mouse from left to right across the screen, selects only those objects that are completely inside the window.

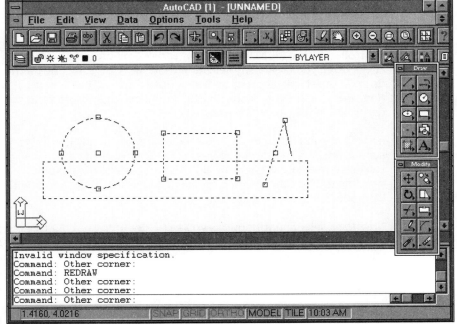

Figure 8-4:
A crossing selection window, created by dragging the mouse from right to left across the screen, selects objects that are completely or only partially inside the window.

Using the SELECT command

Some selection methods aren't available until after you enter a command — a process called *command-first editing.* (You find more information about *command-first editing* in the section "Command performances," later in this chapter.) You can circumvent this command-first editing, however, and use a wider variety of selection methods by entering the SELECT command at the command line.

Entering the SELECT command enables you to use a very wide range of methods to select objects. After you finish selecting objects and terminate the command, however, the grips and selection highlights disappear. "So what good does that do?" you may wonder. Never fear; the selection you made is now stored as the *previous selection set,* and you can specify this selection later by typing **Previous** at the command line. The previously selected objects are then selected — and highlighted — again.

Although enteringthe SELECT command displays a bewildering number of options at the command line, the following options are its important ones:

- ✔ **Mouse picks.** This option enables you to use the mouse to pick objects to add to the selection set.

- ✔ **Windows.** This option enables you to use bounding or crossing windows (as described in the preceding section) to add objects to the selection set.

- ✔ **Group.** If you previously specified a group of objects, as described in the following sections, this option enables you to add the group to the selection by entering the group's name at the command line.

- ✔ **Polygon.** This option enables you to use a polygon, instead of a window, to enclose a group of objects. A *window polygon,* or *WPolygon,* selects all the objects surrounded by the polygon you create; a *crossing polygon,* or *CPolygon,* selects all objects surrounded by or crossing the polygon boundary.

- ✔ **Fence.** This option is the most fun. A *fence* is basically a *crossing polyline;* to use it, you just draw a polyline around the screen, through all the objects you want to select,clicking the mouse after every line segment; you thereby select every object the polyline touches. Neat, huh?

- ✔ **ALL.** This option just picks everything — even objects not visible on the drawing screen. If you want just slightly less than everything, use ALL, and then click the objects you don't want to remove them from the selection set.

You can use these options in combination or separately.

AutoCAD for Windows has been "cleaned up" in a kind of unfriendly way. Some of the command prompts, with all their options, were starting to look too complicated, so the program now just doesn't show all the options if too many of them are available. You're supposed to be able to find these missing options by pressing F1 and using Help, but this task can be time-consuming and distracting. Instead, just enter ? at the command prompt for these options. AutoCAD won't like the question mark one bit, however — in fact, it throws a nasty error message at you — but the program then offers the entire list of options that should have appeared in the first place.

Using the SELECT command from the command line

To use the SELECT command from the command line, start by typing **SELECT** at the command prompt and then pressing Enter. Then you type the appropriate designation for any option you want to use (the uppercase letters that appear in the option name on the prompt). The options for the SELECT command, which AutoCAD does not display unless you enter something wrong, such as **?** appear on the command line as follows:

```
Window/Last/Crossing/BOX/ALL/Fence/WPolygon/CPolygon/Group/
        Add/Remove/Multiple/Previous/Undo/AUto/SIngle
```

The important options to remember that are not available elsewhere are ALL, to select all objects, WPolygon and CPolygon, to create bounding and crossing polygons, and Fence, to draw a polyline through objects you want to select.

If you don't remember how to enter the option you want, type ? at the prompt; AutoCAD responds with an error message but then lists all the options on the command line.

Selecting from the toolbar

The standard toolbar in Windows uses a drop-down icon flyout to enable you to access different selection options, but this type of flyout can be pretty hard to use. No tool tips appear for the icons on the flyout, so determining exactly which icon does what is often difficult. Figure 8-5 has a guide you can use to decide which icon to pick as a shortcut for the selection option you want.

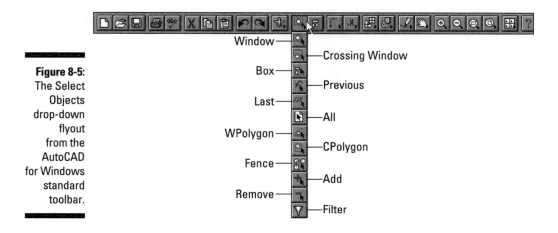

Figure 8-5:
The Select
Objects
drop-down
flyout
from the
AutoCAD
for Windows
standard
toolbar.

Window

Box

Last

WPolygon

Fence

Remove

Crossing Window

Previous

All

CPolygon

Add

Filter

Getting Editing

AutoCAD uses two styles of editing: *command-first editing,* and *selection-first editing.* Unfortunately, these editing styles do require some explanation.

With *command-first editing,* you enter a command and *then* pick the objects on which the command works. You're unlikely to be familiar with this style of editing for graphics work unless you're a long-time user of AutoCAD. But command-first editing is common in nongraphical environments such as DOS. Whenever you type **DEL *.*** in DOS, you're issuing a command — **DEL,** for *del*ete — and then choosing the objects on which the command works — ***.*,** meaning all the files in the current directory. Command-first editing is the default style of editing in AutoCAD.

In *selection-first editing,* you perform the same steps — in the same order — as you do in Windows-based applications, on the Macintosh, or if using a typical word processor, drawing program, and so on: You first select the object and *then* choose the command. To delete a line of text in a word processor, for example, you highlight (select) it and then press the Del (Delete) key. The text you highlight is the object you want to delete, and pressing the Del key is the command. Notice that whether you want to delete, underline, or copy the text, the first act is the same: You highlight the text to select it.

For most of its life, AutoCAD has been a command-driven, command-first program. The selection-first style of editing is a recent addition to the program — one that doesn't yet work in all circumstances. Newer yet is *direct manipulation.* Direct manipulation is a refinement of selection-first editing in which you perform most commands by using the mouse to actually grab the selected object and perform an action on it, such as moving it to a "trashcan" icon to delete it or to another on-screen location to reposition it.

AutoCAD supports direct manipulation through a powerful but somewhat complicated technique called *grip editing.* Grips, as you should know by now, are handles that appear on an object you select; you can then use grips to move, copy, rotate, or otherwise edit the object. The complications arise from the fact that you can do so many things with an object after you select it. (Look for more information on grips in the section "Grip editing," later in this chapter.)

Throughout this book, you use selection-first editing and direct manipulation wherever possible. This style of editing is the style nearly all other programs use and is becoming more and more the style AutoCAD uses. So try to learn and use this editing style in AutoCAD as well; you'll finish your work faster, better, and with less confusion as you move between AutoCAD and other programs. (Hey! — why delve into the strange and different when you can stick to the familiar? You'll find plenty of other odd challenges in AutoCAD to worry about. I promise.)

Command performances

(Okay, so I lied. I'm going to discuss *this* odd challenge after all.) As I explained in the preceding section, command-first editing is the venerable (no, *not* outmoded . . . at least, not *totally*) practice of first entering an editing command and then selecting what the command works on. Command-first editing is always available in AutoCAD; unlike selection-first editing, you can't turn off command-first editing.

You're usually better off getting in the habit of using one or the other style of editing most of the time. Command-first editing may actually be a good choice for you if you spend most of your time in AutoCAD, because AutoCAD implements this editing style more consistently throughout the program; command-first editing *always* works. Selection-first editing, on the other hand, is more natural for most people and is the style other programs use, so it's the best choice for many users.

Even if you try to stick with selection-first editing, however, you do need to use command-first editing occasionally. (Command-first editing may, in fact, seem like your only choice if you're an experienced AutoCAD user who doesn't want to switch back and forth from one style to another.) Certain commands tend to stubbornly ignore your previous selection and ask you for a new one. In this case, you need to tell AutoCAD to recover the previous selection by typing **Previous** at the command line to recover the previous selection, or you need to make a new selection — which means you're back to using command-first editing after all.

The following steps show you how to perform command-first editing using the CHAMFER command (which chops off a corner or intersection and replaces it with a line segment):

1. **Use the LINE command, as dscribed in Chapter 7, to create two lines that intersect or that would intersect if extended far enough.**

   After you finish your intersecting (or would-be intersecting) lines, you select the <u>Chamfer</u> command.

2. **Type** CHAMFER **at the command line and press Enter, or click the Chamfer icon from the Feature flyout on the Modify floating toolbar (Windows only) .**

3. **Pick a chamfer distance for the first line by typing the distance at the command line and pressing Enter.**

   The *chamfer distance* represents how much of the first line AutoCAD trims back from the corner. Enter any chamfer distance less than the length of the first line. (If the length of the first line is 2.0 units, for example, the chamfer distance you specify must be less than 2.0.)

4. **Enter a chamfer distance for the second line by typing the distance at the command line and pressing Enter.**

   Enter any chamfer distance less than the length of the second line.

5. **Select the first line to be chamfered by clicking the line.**

   If you select the lines to be chamfered *before* you start the CHAMFER command, AutoCAD ignores the selection, and you can't restore it.

6. **Select the second line to be chamfered byclicking the line.**

   AutoCAD chamfers the lines, as shown by the second example in Figure 8-6.

The CHAMFER command is flexible and offers a number of options. In addition to extending lines to their intersection point, the command can force lines to intersect without actually creating a chamfer, add a chamfer without trimming the existing lines, and run other options. Unless you're a more experienced AutoCad user, however, you probably won't use the CHAMFER command all that often. You can find more about the CHAMFER command in AutoCAD's on-line Help or reference manual.

Two lines that almost intersect   Similar lines chamfered

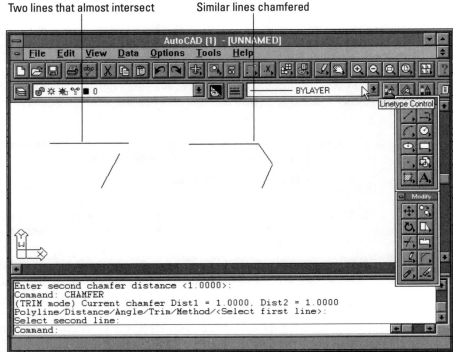

Figure 8-6:
Two sets of
almost
intersecting
lines, with
the second
set
chamfered.

Being manipulative

In spite of the ubiquitous nature of command-first editing, selection-first editing and direct manipulation are the preferred ways to edit in AutoCAD for most users. These related methods are closer to how most programs already work now anyway — and (mark my words!) how all programs will eventually work in the future. So from this point on, this book concentrates on these types of editing and simply lumps both selection-first editing and its direct manipulation offspring together under the term "direct manipulation" (to avoid being wordy, of course.)

Using direct manipulation to edit, however, may actually require more preparation and forethought than using command-first editing. This additional effort is partly because of the inconsistencies inherent in the way AutoCAD works and partly because of the complexity involved in using direct manipulation for such an exacting application as AutoCAD.

To use direct manipulation, you must engage in a bit of setup work to coax AutoCAD to work differently than it has in the past, stick in the mud that it is. (These setup steps are described in the section "The Selective Service," earlier in this chapter, as well as in Chapter 4.) You must make sure that the Noun/Verb Selection option in the Object Selection Setting dialog box is turned on to enable direct manipulation. The Use Shift to Add and Press and Drag options in this dialog box also support this style of editing, although these features don't work consistently throughout AutoCAD, even after you specify them.

Creating your selection first also may require extra work. To use way-cool selection techniques such as Fence with direct manipulation, you must type the SELECT command on the command line (and press Enter, of course) and then choose the Fence option at the prompt. After you make your selection and press Enter to exit the SELECT command, however, your selection disappears; but you can resurrect the selection for use with a subsequent command by entering the Previous option at the command line (it's alive — it's alive!). With some commands, however, not even this roundabout method works; so experiment to discover which of the commands you use demand that you make a selection only *after* the command is entered. (Yes, command-first editing rears its ugly head once again.)

Another difficulty of direct manipulation is that it's hard to use for exacting work such as CAD. You really need to set distances, offsets, and so on exactly right if the drawing you create is a template to be used for construction or manufacturing. You can't just drag a tangent up against a circle, for example; the tangent must touch the circle at one, and only one, point. And in this sort of work, a two-inch square simply *cannot* be $1^{63}/_{64}$ inches on one side and 2 inches on another. Such a glaring disparity just is not acceptable!

Your allies in getting your geometry exactly where you want it in selection-first editing are the *snap grid* and *object snaps.* As described in Chapter 4, the snap grid helps you create objects of just the right size; object snaps help you create objects with just the right relationship to one another. Adjusting the snap grid and using the correct object snaps, however, are extra steps that take some of the ease out of direct manipulation. If you use them enough, however, these features become second nature to you.

The following steps show you how to perform selection-first editing, using the ERASE command as an example:

1. **Select the objects you want to erase by using one of the following methods:**

   • Press and hold the Shift key as you click each object.

   • Use a bounding window (drag the mouse from left to right) to enclose the objects.

- Use a crossing window (drag the mouse from right to left) to enclose or connect with the objects.

- Type **SELECT** at the command line, press Enter, and choose at the following prompt an option such as ALL, Fence, WPolygon, or CPolygon.

2. **Type** ERASE **at the command line, or click the Erase icon on the Modify floating toolbar (Windows only).**

3. **Press Enter to erase the objects.**

   If you selected your objects by using the SELECT command, you must enter the Previous command to select them a second time.

Figure 8-7 shows several objects selected by using the fence option just before using the ERASE command to erase them. (Zap!)

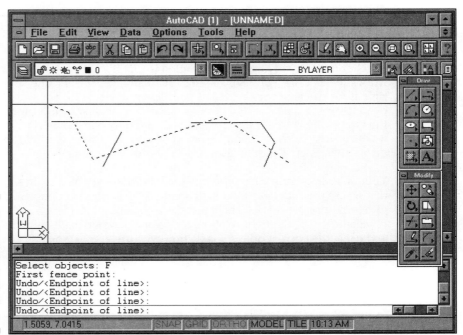

Figure 8-7:
Fence line
running
through (and
thereby
selecting)
objects to be
erased.

The Fence option of the SELECT command ignores whether you turned on the Press and Drag selection option; you must define the fence line by clicking and releasing at each vertex, or fence point.

Grip editing

Grip editing is familiar to almost anyone who has ever edited graphics on a computer — unless your only graphics experience, of course, is with a version of AutoCAD prior to Release 12. If you're an experienced user only of AutoCAD Release 11 or earlier, you've probably never seen grips. And even if you're an experienced user of other graphics programs, you've never seen grips in quite the way AutoCAD uses them. Either way, some explanation is in order.

Grips, as explained earlier in this chapter, are little handles that appear on an object after you select it. You use these handles in many programs for direct manipulation of the object. *Direct manipulation*, as used here, involves the following operations: To move an object, you grab the object's middle grip and drag that grip; to stretch an object, you grab a corner, or edge grip, and drag that grip; to move a copy of the object, you hold down a modifier key, such as Alt, while dragging the middle of the object. Even the little frames around the graphics you import into a word processing program are likely to work this way.

AutoCAD grips are much like the grips used in other programs, albeit with some major differences. First, grips require a little setup wizardry to get them to work just right. The DDGRIPS command, entered at the command line, opens the Grips dialog box, in which you can click the appropriate check box to enable grips. You can also enable or disable grips within *blocks*, change the grips' colors, and change the grips' size all by clicking the appropriate check boxes in the Grips dialog box. None of these options are as important as simply having grips turned on, however. (You can also turn grips on and off directly by typing the commands **GRIPS 1**, for on, and **GRIPS 0**, for off, directly at the command line.)

Another way in which AutoCAD grips are different from those of other programs is in when the AutoCAD grips appear (or, more accurately, fail to disappear). As in other drawing programs, AutoCAD displays grips on a selected object. But unlike the perfectly well-adjusted grips in those other programs, AutoCAD grips *don't go away* after the object they encircle no longer is selected. In fact, they seem to hang around *forever* (much like that annoying "Twilight Zone" theme music keeps running over and over again through your mind after you've heard it one time too many — do-do-do-do, do-do-do-do, do-do — arrrrrggghhh!).

Grips, in fact, remain visible both on *previously selected* and on *currently selected* objects. The persistence of these grips can become really confusing, too, especially if you're trying to figure out exactly what is currently selected on-screen. This persistance does, however, enable you to use the grips as targets for future editing chores, such as to make one object touch another.

Despite their persistence problem, AutoCAD grips *are* much better than the grips found in most other programs, because you can do so much more with them. You can, for example, use AutoCAD grips to move, stretch, or copy an object. You can also use them to rotate an object, scale it to a different size, or mirror an object — that is, create one or more copies. In conjunction with the snap grid, object snaps, and the cursor location display, you can use grips for some pretty complex editing chores. Options such as Ortho also affect the workings of grip editing in interesting ways. Finally, grips actually act as *temporary snaps* themselves. (This is undoubtedly the reason that grips remain on an object even after it's deselected — you may want to snap to it.)

AutoCAD grips are also better — but correspondingly more complicated — than grips in other programs in that there are three kinds of AutoCAD grips: hot, warm, and cold varieties. (I could compare these to the grip one person may have on a significant other, but that would just be causing trouble.) A *hot grip* is the grip that you use to actually perform an action, such as stretching an object. A *warm grip* is any grip on a selected object that isn't a hot grip (nothing's happening to its object at the moment). A *cold grip* is a grip on an unselected object that only acts as a snap target. Cold grips and warm grips both appear as empty, not-filled-in squares; their default color on-screen is blue. Hot grips, on the other hand, appear on-screen as red, filled-in squares.

What all these grip capabilities really mean to the beginning user, however, is that effectively using grips in AutoCAD requires a fair amount of practice. What can help you the most in learning to use grips is simply your determination to do so. If you set your mind to use grips as much and as frequently as possible in your drawings, the little buggers will slowly — but surely — yield their secrets to you.

Exercising your grip

The following steps show you all the different operations in which you can use grips:

(***Note:*** Make sure that the <u>P</u>ress and Drag and <u>U</u>se Shift to Add object selection settings are turned on in the Object Selection Settings dialog box *before* you start these steps! See Chapter 4 for details.)

1. Click an object on-screen to give it grips (if you don't already have one).

Warm grips appear around the object on-screen.

Cold grips and warm grips both are empty, not-filled-in, squares; their default color is blue. They are identical except that warm grips appear on selected objects, cold ones on nonselected objects.

2. Click one of the grips of your selected object to make it hot.

The blue, empty square turns to a red, filled-in square. This grip is now hot.

Grip editing options now appear on the command line. The first option to appear is STRETCH.

3. **Press the spacebar (or press Enter) to cycle through the grip editing options on the command line.**

   The displayed grip editing option changes as you press the spacebar or Enter. The options that appear are, in order, STRETCH, MOVE, ROTATE, SCALE, and MIRROR. The appearance of your selected object changes as you display each option. Choosing STRETCH, for example, causes a stretched version of the object to appear on-screen.

4. **Keep pressing the spacebar (or Enter) until STRETCH (or the option you want) reappears as the grip editing option.**

5. **Drag the hot grip in the direction in which you want to stretch (or otherwise manipulate) your object.**

Figure 8-8 shows a line being stretched by its midpoint. The Dotted line shows the new locationof the the line after the line command is completed by pressing Enter.

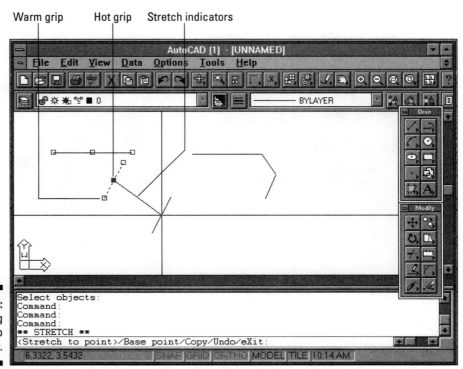

Warm grip   Hot grip   Stretch indicators

Figure 8-8:
Stretching
the hot grip
of an object.

You can experiment with all the grip editing options to learn exactly how they affect a selected object, including using all the options while holding down the Shift key (see the following tip).

If you want to see what a grip editing option does to your object without actually changing it, press and hold the Shift key while dragging the object's grip. Holding down the Shift key during grip editing causes the grip editing action to affect a copy of the object rather than the original; the original object remains in place, unchanged. (I guess you could consider this a Grip Tip.)

Chapter 9
A Zoom with a View

*O*ne of the advantages of AutoCAD is its useful capability to give you different ways to view your drawing. You can zoom in close, zoom out to a great distance, and pan around. There are different ways to do this in DOS and Windows, explained in some detail in this chapter.

Keeping the appearance of the screen in synch with the actual drawing file — having the screen reflect changes as you make them — is the biggest single challenge to the performance of AutoCAD. User frustration over having to wait for redraws of the screen, and for full *regenerations* (REGENs) of the screen image from the drawing database, has pushed an awful lot of AutoCAD-related hardware sales over the years. This chapter describes some of your options for getting more performance out of AutoCAD.

Degenerating and Regenerating

From AutoCAD's point of view, each drawing has two parts. The important part is the DWG drawing file, a highly precise database of objects stored on disk. AutoCAD uses high-precision numbers to describe the location of each object. The less important part is the part that you interact with — the on-screen display of the drawing. For the on-screen display, AutoCAD uses less precise integer numbers that are easy to calculate but less accurate than the numbers used in the DWG file.

As you modify the drawing, the on-screen display accumulates little dots, called *blips* (unless AutoCAD's Blip mode is off; see the section "Accelerate your software," later in this chapter). Blips can act as a record of where you picked objects with the mouse. For this and other minor problems with the display, using the REDRAW command clears up the screen. The REDRAW command actually clears the current *viewport* — described in Chapter 14 — and refreshes the display from the *integer display list,* a description of the on-screen display that AutoCAD uses to quickly update the screen's appearance. (You can also turn off blips by setting the Blip mode to a value of 0.)

The REGEN command (short for *regeneration*) does more than the REDRAW command. The REGEN command goes back to the DWG file for information on what objects have changed and need to be displayed with their new positions, colors, or linetypes. It then creates a new display list. The REGEN command also reorganizes the database that makes up the display for better performance and then redraws the current viewport from the new display list.

Some changes introduced in AutoCAD's Release 12 greatly reduced the need for redraws and regens. If you leave blips off, you may rarely need to use the REDRAW and REGEN commands. The performance of these commands is still a big topic for AutoCAD aficionados, however, so you may hear about them more than you would expect.

In AutoCAD for Windows, you can force a redraw in two quick ways. The first is to use the Redraw icon on the standard toolbar, which has a Redraw All icon on its flyout, too. The second uses a pair of commands, Redraw View and Redraw All, on the View menu. The keyboard shortcuts for these commands are Alt+V+V and Alt+V+A.

Safe at Any Speed

You can do a number of things inside AutoCAD to speed up performance. The most important ways to improve performance, however, probably involve changes outside AutoCAD. You can tune both hardware and software for optimum AutoCAD performance.

Get heartier hardware

The hardware you use has a very great effect on AutoCAD's performance. The following sections offer some basic guidelines.

RAM cram

The most important single factor is the amount of *RAM* (*random access memory*) in your machine. For DOS, Autodesk, the makers of AutoCAD, recommends 12MB; for Windows, 16MB is the recommendation. You should consider these numbers bare minimums. If you are working on large drawings (more than 500K in size), 16MB may be a better number for DOS and 24MB for Windows.

In AutoCAD for Windows, a number of other factors may increase your need for more RAM. If you have other programs running at the same time as AutoCAD, you will want 2–4MB of additional RAM for each program. If you are running multiple AutoCAD sessions (available only with the Windows NT version in Release 13), you will want 2–4MB per additional session as well. If you are using AutoCAD's render features to produce shaded renderings of your drawings, the sky is the limit on your RAM needs. (AutoCAD can do all these things using hard disk space to substitute for RAM, but performance will be much slower.)

In fact, the busy light on your hard disk drive is the best indicator of when you need more RAM. If the hard disk light is flashing often — indicating that AutoCAD is using the swap file on disk — the operation that's in progress will go much faster if you buy more RAM. The more you see the light flashing, the more performance will improve with additional RAM.

Bigger, faster, stronger . . .

A bigger, faster hard disk is another important performance optimization. (Luckily, and contrary to intuition, a bigger hard disk is faster than a smaller one.) First, a faster hard disk will load AutoCAD, other programs, and drawings quicker, which may save you only a couple of minutes per day but will have a surprisingly large effect on your perception of your system's performance. Second, during the inevitable times that AutoCAD swaps things in memory to disk, a faster hard disk reduces the performance gap between RAM speed and disk speed.

AutoCAD uses disk space as if it were extra RAM, a technique called "virtual memory." The more you use virtual memory, the more performance slows down. Buying more RAM reduces the need for AutoCAD to use virtual memory; buying a faster hard disk improves the performance of virtual memory when it is used.

Many systems have an extra drive bay and can easily have another hard disk installed. For maximum flexibility, however, consider adding SCSI — *S*mall *C*omputer *S*ystems *I*nterface, pronounced "scuzzy" — to your system and using it to support external devices. A single SCSI port can support not only disk drives but tape drives, CD-ROM drives, and so on.

You can add and remove external devices easily and take them with you from one SCSI-equipped machine to another. (Though asking a colleague, "Do you have a scuzzy machine?" may get you an odd look or two.) SCSI can be hard to install and configure, but after you get it working, you may wonder how you managed without it.

Big performance in small packages

The *microprocessor* in your computer is the computer's "brain," the place where it forms calculations and figures out what to do next. Swapping your current microprocessor for a faster one is a simple way to speed up your system. But a microprocessor swap may not work well for you. All the components in a system work together, and just switching the microprocessor may simply mean that other slow components become the reason for slow performance on your system. But the microprocessor has a big effect on AutoCAD performance, and a microprocessor swap — or even a new system with faster components throughout — may be worth considering.

AutoCAD depends on microprocessor performance, which varies sharply among x86 computers. The 386/387 combination is slowest. A 486DX is faster, but the Pentium has by far the best AutoCAD performance of all. Get a Pentium system, especially a 75 MHz or faster system, if at all possible. (Make sure that it's a version without known bugs, though.) Among compatible microprocessor manufacturers, both AMD and Cyrix have experience building reliable stand-alone math coprocessors, so you can expect to get good performance from their various chips and chip combinations. NexGen, however, is offering a supposedly Pentium-class chip with no built-in math coprocessing capability; ignore systems built around NexGen chips.

Don't get bored with graphics boards

There is a bewildering confusion of graphics options for AutoCAD users, with many confusing claims about performance. Read the AutoCAD monthly magazines for up-to-date, AutoCAD-specific reviews of graphics boards before buying. (Chapter 19 provides a listing of these magazines.) Don't depend on manufacturers' claims or reviews from magazines that don't test AutoCAD specifically. And don't buy a graphics card if your hard disk light is flashing all the time while you're using AutoCAD — go buy more RAM first.

Fast mice?

In worrying about performance, don't forget that the human doing the work is really the slowest part of the system. Different input devices may help you work faster and reduce the risk of repetitive stress injuries, such as carpal tunnel syndrome. Trackballs are a good alternative to the mouse; buy one and learn to use it at least some of the time; learn to use it both left- and right-handed. Taking advantage of this flexibility may prevent you from overstressing one wrist, elbow, or arm to the point that soreness or injury occurs.

Other input devices may also help you work faster. A bigger monitor may reduce the amount of time you spend panning around trying to find things in your drawing. A digitizer tablet may even be worth looking into; talk to someone who uses one and find out more.

Accelerate your software

You can do many simple things with your software to speed up AutoCAD's performance. Some of these changes are outside AutoCAD; others are inside it. The following sections offer a few tips in each area; for other tips, almost any source of information about AutoCAD — such as the documentation, on-line services, magazines, and so on — includes some speed tips.

Outside AutoCAD

A few operations you can perform outside AutoCAD to keep your system revved up include the following:

- **Defragment your hard disk.** The newest versions of DOS and Windows include utilities to defragment your hard disk, and third-party utilities may do an even better job. A defragmented hard disk, with files occupying contiguous (adjacent) areas and all free space in one area, should improve performance.

- **Keep subdirectories clean.** AutoCAD frequently scans the subdirectories with support files (those containing fonts, sample drawings, and so on) in them when it's looking for things. The more files in these subdirectories, the longer it takes AutoCAD to search them. So keeping extraneous files out of these subdirectories will improve performance.

- **Restart your computer.** Under DOS, the memory extension software that lets AutoCAD reach more memory can become cluttered with old information. Restarting your computer — shutting it on and off every few hours — is a drastic, but highly effective, way to free up memory.

General good ideas within AutoCAD

You can also do a few things inside AutoCAD to speed system performance. The following are just generally good ideas anyway:

- **Use layers.** The more you use layers, the more you can control performance when using the next couple of tips.

- **Put more complex objects on separate layers.** Even if you already have a layer for hatching, for example, consider putting complex hatches on their own layers away from less complicated ones.

✔ **Freeze unneeded layers.** By freezing layers you're not using, you prevent them from being redrawn, thus speeding performance. (You also prevent yourself from accidentally putting objects on these unneeded layers.) However, unfreezing layers usually requires a regen, so only freeze layers you know you won't need for a while.

Performance-specific acts within AutoCAD

You can do some things inside AutoCAD to speed system performance that cost accuracy or intelligibility but that may speed up performance to a degree that makes the changes worth it. Use the following tips only in drawings where performance is a concern:

✔ **Delay hatching.** Wait until near the end of the drawing to add hatching, especially complex hatches. Use simple hatches until the end of the drawing creation process. (See Chapter 12 for more information on hatching.)

✔ **Wait to add text.** Redrawing text can take a great deal of time; if you delay putting text in your drawing, you're less likely to spend time waiting for it to redraw. Use the QTEXT command to place empty boxes in place of text, or use simple, fast fonts, such as TXT or SIMPLEX, until near the end of the drawing creation process and then change to a more interesting font. (You can also put your text on a layer and freeze it.)

✔ **Turn blips off.** Blips are a performance concern mainly in that they clutter up the drawing, forcing redraws. You can turn blips off with the BLIPMODE command or the Blips option in the Drawing Aids dialog box.

✔ **Turn fill off.** Not filling in objects such as traces, polylines with width, and filled polygons increases performance, at the expense of drawing accuracy. You can turn fill off by using the FILL command, the FILLMODE system variable, the Solid Fill option on the Display menu, or the Solid Fill check box in the Drawing Aids dialog box.

✔ **Turn text off.** Not drawing text also speeds performance, but also at the expense of drawing accuracy. You can turn text display off by using the QTEXT command, the QTEXTMODE system variable, the Text Frame Only option on the Display menu, or the Quick Text option in the Drawing Aids dialog box.

✔ **Turn selection highlighting off.** This is a real last resort, because not having your selections highlighted may make it harder to do good work. You can turn selection highlighting off by using the Highlight option in the Drawing Aids dialog box.

Use the DDRMODES command or choose Options⇨Drawing Aids from the menu bar to open the Drawing Aids dialog box.

How to Zoom-Zoom-Zoom on Your Room-Room-Room

Moving your viewpoint in to get a closer view of your drawing data is called *zooming in;* moving your viewpoint back to get a more expansive view is called *zooming out.*

Zooming in and out of your drawing is one of the big advantages AutoCAD offers over manual drawing. You can work very closely on tiny little objects and then zoom out and move around rooms, houses, or neighborhoods from an Olympian perspective.

Panning is closely related to zooming. If you zoom in enough that some of your drawing no longer shows up on-screen, you're going to want to pan around — move left, right, up, and down in your drawing without zooming in and out. Panning is easy in AutoCAD for Windows, which has scrollbars and the built-in aerial view, but harder in the DOS version.

Both panning and zooming change what is known as the *view.* The view is simply the current location and magnification of AutoCAD's depiction of your drawing. Each time you zoom or pan, you establish a new view.

AutoCAD used to do a regen if you zoomed in and out too much, but Release 12 and its memory-hogging, 32-bit display list fixed that. (Regen is a set of instructions for updating the screen display of your drawing; in Release 12, AutoCAD was upgraded from 16 bits to 32 bits, making it more capable at the cost of requiring more memory.) Now you can zoom in from near Earth orbit to a close-up view of your living room without causing a regen.

Aerial view utilities are widely available for the DOS version of AutoCAD. Get one and try it to make panning and zooming easier.

Out of the frying pan . . .

Panning isn't complicated, but it is confusing to use until you're comfortable with it. If you have AutoCAD for Windows, use scrollbars or the built-in aerial view. If you own the DOS version, consider getting an add-on aerial view utility.

The basic idea of panning with AutoCAD is that you pan by a certain distance, called a *displacement.* You don't pan by a specific number of units left, right, up, or down, and you don't specify the center point of your new view of things. Rather, you enter a displacement, which is the *X* and *Y* (horizontal and then vertical) distance to move the on-screen view. Or you can enter two points: a starting point and then a second point. AutoCAD figures out the distance between the two points and then pans that amount. Neither the starting or finishing point actually has to appear on-screen at the start of the pan or at the finish.

The following steps show you how to pan in a simple drawing:

1. **Type** ZOOM EXTENTS **at the command prompt and press Enter to zoom to the outer limits of your drawing.**

2. **Type** ZOOM .5X **at the command prompt and press Enter to zoom in halfway.**

3. **Start the PAN command by using one of the following methods:**

   • Type **PAN** at the command prompt and press Enter.

   • Click the Pan icon (the hand) on the standard toolbar and then click the PanPoint icon (the hand with the black dot at the end of the index finger) from the Pan flyout (Windows only).

   • Choose View⇨Pan⇨PanPoint from the menu bar (DOS only).

4. **Type either a displacement or the first point and press Enter.**

   The displacement is the amount you want your viewpoint to move. For example, typing **-3,-4** and pressing Enter shifts your viewpoint three units to the left and four units down.

   If you used a displacement, your drawing is ready to pan; just press Enter again. If you entered the first point, continue with step 5.

5. **Type the second point, press Enter, and you're done.**

The following displays the command line with the commands for a displacement pan:

```
Command: PAN
Displacement: -3,2
Second point: <Enter>
```

You can also enter the first and second point of the displacement by selecting points on-screen. Although inexact, this process can become intuitive for you with experience. It may be a good alternative to scrolling, especially in DOS.

The ZOOM DYNAMIC command supports both panning and zooming; see the following section on zooming.

Time to zoom

Zooming is simpler than panning, and it has no alternative, such as scrolling, either. So you must learn how to zoom around, in, and out of your drawing.

The Zoom command has different options. The most important of these are:

- ✔ **All/Extents.** ZOOM ALL zooms out to the current limits of the drawing, or at least far enough out to display all the drawing if some of it is outside the limits. ZOOM EXTENTS zooms out to show everything in the current drawing.

- ✔ **Dynamic.** This option supports both panning and zooming with a view box that you position. It's the next best thing to the aerial view, it's free, and it doesn't take up screen space, either.

- ✔ **Window.** Great for zooming in — zooms to a section of your drawing that you specify by placing a window around the area you want to look at. You can also use it to zoom out, but then you have to enter the point coordinates at the command line.

- ✔ **Scale (X/XP).** Scales the drawing; values less than one cause you to zoom in, values greater than one cause you to zoom out. You can also think of the value as a scaling factor; .5X causes the screen image to shrink to half its apparent size, and 2X causes the screen image to double in apparent size. (Use XP after a number to scale relative to paper space; see Chapter 14.)

The zoom options take some getting used to. Experiment with all the options and the aerial view to find the approach that works best for you. (Occasionally, too, your drawing may seem to disappear. Learn how to use zoom and you can always discover where it went!)

Unfortunately, zooming to extents doesn't leave a margin of white space around the objects in the drawing. Follow a ZOOM EXTENTS command by typing **ZOOM .9X** at the command line (and pressing Enter) to get AutoCAD to zoom out just a little bit more.

The following steps show you how to use ZOOM DYNAMIC to handle both panning and zooming. Until you get used to it, however, ZOOM DYNAMIC is confusing to use. In AutoCAD for Windows, or if you have an aerial view feature in an add-on package, you may want to use the aerial view to do zooming and panning instead. For more on aerial view, see the following section.

1. **Type** VIEWRES Yes **at the command prompt to turn on Fast Zoom mode.**

   This mode is on by default; if Fast Zoom is off, changes made to the display always cause a regen, which is very slow and time-consuming.

2. **Start zoom dynamic by using one of the following methods:**

   • Type **ZOOM DYNAMIC** at the command prompt and press Enter.

   • Click zoom dynamic on the Zoom icon flyout on the standard toolbar (Windows only).

   • Choose View⇨Zoom⇨Dynamic from the Zoom secondary menu bar (DOS only).

   The drawing window automatically zooms out beyond its extents (the limits of the current drawing), and a box appears. If an X does not appear in the box, move the mouse pointer into the box so that the X appears. A dashed green box indicates the original view; a movable box with an X in it indicates a view you can pan and zoom; and a box around the edges of your drawing indicates its extents.

3. **To pan the drawing, use the mouse to move the box around on-screen and click after you finish.**

   Clicking anchors the left edge of the box and starts the zoom part of the command. Figure 9-1 shows a circle and several overlapping rectangles during execution of the ZOOM DYNAMIC command.

4. **To zoom, move the mouse left or right.**

   This action establishes the size of the new view.

5. **To pan while zooming, move the mouse up, down, left or right, or both.**

   This action establishes the up and down orientation of the new view. The left edge is anchored, but the right edge changes as you move the mouse left or right.

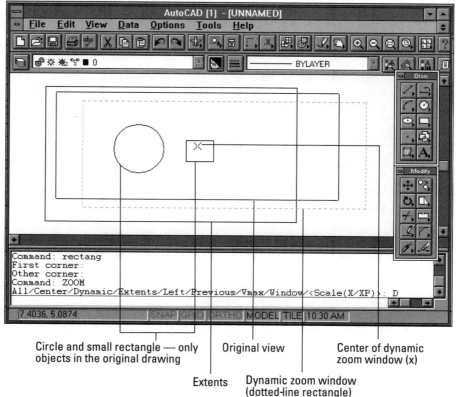

Figure 9-1:
The on-
screen look
during a
ZOOM
DYNAMIC
operation.

Circle and small rectangle — only   Original view   Center of dynamic
objects in the original drawing   zoom window (x)

                              Extents   Dynamic zoom window
                                           (dotted-line rectangle)

6. Click to return to pan mode.

Now that you've set the size of the view (by zooming), you get another
chance to pan.

**7. Repeat steps 3 through 6 until the new view is the right size and in the
right locations.**

At first, this procedure will take several tries, moving between panning and
zooming. With practice, you'll be able to do this quickly.

8. Press Enter to establish the new view.

The View from Above: Aerial View in AutoCAD for Windows

The aerial view feature offers a quick way to navigate around your drawing as well as a way to magnify parts of the drawing. Although the magnification part is occasionally useful, think of the aerial view primarily as a way to control zooming and panning around your drawing.

To open the Aerial View window, click the Aerial View icon on the standard toolbar. Figure 9-2 shows the location of the Aerial View icon and the Aerial View window. The tool tip says "Tool Windows" because the button is a flyout with several options; the Aerial View icon, with the little airplane, is the default choice.

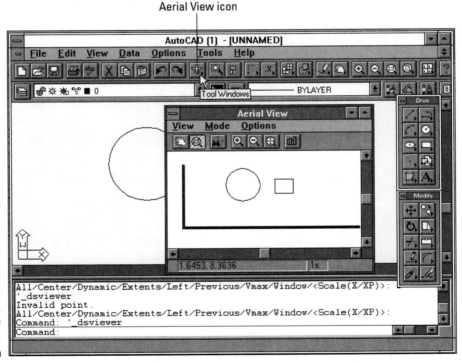

Figure 9-2:
Click the Aerial View icon on the standard toolbar to open the Aerial View window.

Zooming and panning with aerial view requires a little bit of finesse, because the actual proportions of your drawing window are fixed. If you want to both pan and zoom, it's best to zoom first, to define how big an area you want to see, and then pan. Follow these steps to zoom and pan with aerial view:

1. **Click the Aerial View icon from the Aerial View flyout on the standard toolbar to open the Aerial View window.**

2. **Click the Zoom icon in the Aerial View window.**

   The Zoom icon is the second button from the left, next to the hand, showing a magnifying glass with a rectangle in it.

3. **Click and drag on part of the image in the Aerial View window to create the zoom window.**

   AutoCAD updates the display in both the Aerial View window and the drawing area to show the result of the zoom. Keep clicking and dragging until you've set the zoom correctly and then pan.

   Figure 9-3 shows the Aerial View window and the drawing area behind it during a zoom. The dashed box is the zoom window.

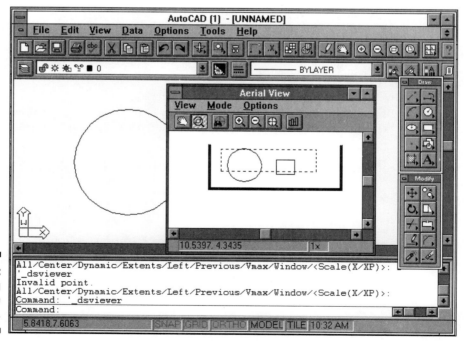

Figure 9-3:
Zooming
with the
aerial view.

Where you draw the zoom window determines where you pan the view as well. The left edge of the zoom window that you create by dragging becomes the left edge of the drawing window. If you drag correctly, you don't need to pan.

The Aerial View window doesn't clean up after itself very well, so the quality of the image in it may deteriorate as you pan and zoom around. Click the Aerial View button on the standard toolbar twice to make the Aerial View go away and then come back and redraw itself.

4. **To pan, click the Pan icon in the Aerial View window.**

   The Pan icon is the first button from the left, the one with the hand on it. As you move the cursor into the middle part of the Aerial View window, the cursor controls a box made up of a dotted line; this box is the panning window.

5. **To pan, move the panning window around.**

6. **Click to establish the new view.**

7. **Repeat steps 3 through 6 until the drawing area has the correct view.**

8. **Click the Aerial View icon on the standard toolbar to close the Aerial View window.**

Aerial View has other controls that you may want to experiment with. However, the controls are most useful if you leave Aerial View on-screen. In general, you should close the Aerial View window when not panning and zooming, because it takes up too much screen space.

If Aerial View is present but does not work, turn on Fast Zoom mode by typing **VIEWRES Yes** at the command prompt and pressing Enter.

Part III
Make Your Drawing Beautiful

The 5th Wave   By Rich Tennant

In this part...

Text, dimensions, and hatch patterns — mysterious embellishments to the uninitiated — have long been important elements in drawing and drafting. In AutoCAD, these elements are flexible, and you can instantly edit and update them as you change the geometry beneath them. After you get everything working, AutoCAD is definitely much better for almost all drawing purposes than pencil and paper could ever be — and far more versatile in enabling you to create a drawing that's truly beautiful. The purpose of such additions to your drawing as text or hatching is to prepare it for printing — or as CAD users say, for a plot. AutoCAD plotting is flexible, powerful, and a little harder to use than you may think, so pay attention. In this part, you can pull all the pieces together and create a drawing you can be truly proud of.

Chapter 10
Text with Character

- -

- -

*T*ext can be one of the most important parts of an AutoCAD drawing. Text can be an intrinsic part of the drawing, integrated with other drawing elements. Text in a drawing can be brief descriptive lines of text, or it can consist of long paragraphs that describe, annotate, or otherwise add to the drawing.

Dimensions — text that displays the measurements of objects — is a kind of text that AutoCAD handles especially well (although with a staggering number of options). You can find more about dimensions in Chapter 11.

For nondimension text, AutoCAD gives many more options to those who use Windows than to DOS users. You can enter lines of text characters with many style options on both AutoCAD for Windows and AutoCAD for DOS, so that the text serves either as an integral part of the drawing or as supplementary comments. But only AutoCAD for Windows has direct support for *paragraphs* of text with automatic line breaks, which are much easier to edit than *lines* of text. And only AutoCAD for Windows supports OLE (object linking and embedding), which enables you to edit text in one program easily and have the result show up in another program. Both AutoCAD for DOS and AutoCAD for Windows support text styles and include the new spell checker, finally added in Release 13 after years of protest from "por spellurs" like me.

Getting the Right Height

Both text and dimensions require that you specify a *height* for characters; this is a very important and difficult parameter. Because it's a different kind of animal — and one that can bite you in an uncomfortable spot if you treat it badly — even the detailed setup information earlier in this book didn't cover text height.

Text that looks good on-screen is unlikely to look good on your printout because the screen and the printout use text so differently. Most text in a drawing is not part of the drawing *per se,* but rather an attempt to communicate something about the drawing to the person using the printout. The text must be a height that the reader is used to. And physical and psychological factors have a big effect; for example, a reader tends to hold a small printout closer to his face than he does a large blueprint. Yet the larger blueprint may have more need for detail in text than the smaller drawing does.

Take note of the following tips for help in getting the height of your text right:

✔ **Use previous models.** Do you have existing drawings that resemble the one you're trying to create in AutoCAD? You want drawings that are not only on the same size paper but that also have similar purposes, similar fonts, and so on. Get out your trusty ruler and measure the text height on similar drawings that you like. Then use this height as the starting point for your own drawings.

✔ **Start with the defaults.** Start with AutoCAD's defaults for text height (.2), and don't try to get fancy with either text height or style until you complete the actual geometry of the drawing. Changing things from a known base is much easier than it is from a varying mélange of heights, styles, and so on.

✔ **Do it late.** I hate to suggest that anyone put off anything until the last minute, but putting in text, or at least prettying it up, may be a good candidate for this approach. By doing it late, you avoid messing with the text for endless hours when you should be getting the drawing's geometry right. And by putting in text late, you have an excellent idea of what the final document will look like, giving you a chance to get the text size right.

✔ **Use single lines.** Create all your text using as few lines as possible while doing your work and then break up the text into separate lines at the end of your project. (You will need to retype most of the text, but this is actually less trouble than editing and re-editing it while maintaining many line breaks.)

> ✔ **Prototype.** If at first you don't succeed . . . try your text out on check plots, determine if it's what you want, and modify from there. Prototypes are much easier to create early in the project rather than late. Then, as you actually add text at the end of the project, you have a solid idea of what you're doing.

The default text height is .2 for scientific and decimal units, $^3/_{16}$" for engineering and architectural units, and $^3/_{16}$ for fractional units. The measurements of .2 for scientific and decimal units and $^3/_{16}$ for fractional units are good starting points if you're working in inches; these measurements each yield about five lines per inch — slightly larger text than in this book.

But if you're working in feet, meters, or some other units, neither .2 nor $^3/_{16}$ is likely to be a good measurement. Text that is $^3/_{16}$ meter tall would be almost as tall as this page! If you're working with measurements other than inches, use a measurement that yields about five lines per inch (or two lines per centimeter), instead of the default to get text of a reasonable size. (After you enter a text height, it becomes the new default until you change it to something different again.) You can adjust from your new default to meet your specific needs.

The Same Old Line

The DTEXT command is the simplest form of text entry and editing, and you can access it in both AutoCAD for DOS and AutoCAD for Windows. The DTEXT command enables you to enter single lines of text, one at a time; it's quick and easy to use for short lines of text. And because it's the same in both DOS and Windows, the DTEXT command is good to use if you're passing drawings back and forth between versions.

The DTEXT command, however, causes problems if you need to enter multiple lines that look like part of a single paragraph. The problem is that, almost inevitably, you want to edit the text. If you cut a word or two in one line, the DTEXT command does not automatically adjust subsequent lines to make all lines the same width. Instead, you must change several lines so that all lines remain equal in width.

Suppose, for example, that you want the following text to appear on your drawing for a house:

```
Put the house number
at the same height as
the houses next door.
```

Now to add the words *and mailbox* to the items that should be at the same height as the houses next door, and keep the lines the same width, you must edit both the second and third lines, as well as add a fourth, as follows:

```
Put the house number
and mailbox at the
same height as the
houses next door.
```

And if space is tight and you can't add a fourth line, you need to rejigger the width of the lines to force everything into three lines, as follows:

```
Put the house number and
mailbox at the same height
as the houses next door.
```

Entering text

Despite its difficulties, the DTEXT command is useful. The following steps show you how to enter text by using AutoCAD's DTEXT command:

1. **Start the DTEXT command by using one of the following:**

   • Type **DTEXT** at the command prompt and press Enter.

   • Click the Dynamic Text icon from the Text icon flyout on the Draw floating toolbar (Windows only).

   • Choose Draw⇨Text⇨Dynamic Text from the menu bar (DOS only).

2. **Specify the insertion point for the first text character.**

   You can either enter the point from the command line, use the mouse to select a point on-screen, or press Enter to locate new text immediately following a previous text object.

3. **Specify the height for the text.**

   This prompt doesn't appear if you are using a text style that already has a defined height. You can find more details about text styles in the section "Text with Style," later in this chapter.

4. **Specify the text rotation angle by entering the rotation angle from the command line and pressing Enter or by rotating the line on-screen by using the mouse and grips.**

   Figure 10-1 shows the cursor box that appears after you select the options.

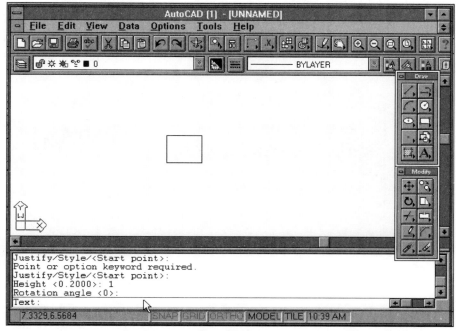

AutoCAD [1] - [UNNAMED]
File Edit View Data Options Tools Help

Figure 10-1:
With the DTEXT command already started on the command line, AutoCAD now waits for you to specify the text.

```
Justify/Style/<Start point>:
Point or option keyword required.
Justify/Style/<Start point>:
Height <0.2000>: 1
Rotation angle <0>:
Text:
```

5. Type the first line of text and press Enter.

6. Type additional lines of text, pressing Enter at the end of each line.

7. To complete the command, press Enter at the start of a blank line.

To align lines of text correctly, make sure that you type all the lines in just as you want them to appear, pressing Enter after each line to make the next line appear just after it. Otherwise, aligning different lines of text precisely is harder to do (unless you set your snap and grid just right and use the OSNAP command). If you are entering one and only one line of text, the TEXT command enables you to enter one line and then exit after you press Enter. The TEXT command is different from the DTEXT command, which keeps prompting you for additional lines of text. For many people, however, DTEXT is easier to use because you see the text on-screen as you type it.

Editing text

To edit text that's already on-screen, use the DDEDIT command. The DDEDIT command prompts you to select a text object and then opens a single-line text editor, as shown in Figure 10-2.

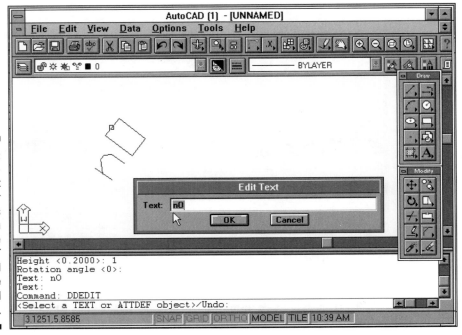

Figure 10-2:
The single-
line text
editor
appears
after you
enter the
DDEDIT
command
at the
command
line.

You can edit text in the single-line text editor, but you can't copy text within the line or paste text from elsewhere. To edit, you simply keep some of the characters, delete others, and type in new ones. Editing in the single-line text editor is a limited and frustrating way to work with text, so for text that is longer than a line or two, use the paragraph editing commands described in the following section.

Entering and Editing Paragraph Text

The limitations of working with the DTEXT command have led to a fairly desperate call for better text editors. In AutoCAD for DOS, you can use other text editors and even tie them into AutoCAD. The default choice is the DOS EDIT editor. But you can use any editor that works in ASCII text mode. One of my favorites is the text editor in Sidekick for DOS, from Borland International, Inc.

To set the external text editor, use the command SETVAR MTEXTED. This command controls the editor that you start. Make sure that you specify the text editor's path name.

AutoCAD for Windows incorporates a built-in text editor that should meet your needs. If you still want to use an external editor, however, set the MTEXTED variable appropriately.

Creating formatted text with any text editor other than the built-in text editor in AutoCAD for Windows requires that you insert formatting characters in the text. The characters \P, for example, represent a forced line break. For more information on such characters, see your AutoCAD documentation.

Using the paragraph editor in AutoCAD for Windows

In AutoCAD for Windows, the MTEXT command opens a built-in text editor that enables you to enter and edit text without going to an external editor. Using this feature is much better than editing single lines at a time by using the DTEXT command or entering complicated formatting commands in an external editor.

The following steps show you how to enter and edit text by using the Edit MText dialog box:

1. **Start the MTEXT command by using one of the following methods:**

   • Type **MTEXT** at the command prompt and press Enter.

   • Click the Text icon from the Text icon flyout on the Draw floating toolbar.

2. **Specify the insertion point for the first character.**

   You can either enter the coordinates of the point on the command line or use the mouse to select a point on-screen.

   Ignore the other options for the MTEXT command that appear after you start the command; you can access all of them more easily in the paragraph editor.

3. **Specify the other corner of the text box.**

   Enter the coordinates of the point on the command line or use the mouse to select a point on-screen.

   You aren't really specifying a box here, because the text just keeps spilling out of the box if you type too much. You're really specifying the right margin of the text.

After you specify the other corner, the Edit MText dialog box appears, as shown in Figure 10-3.

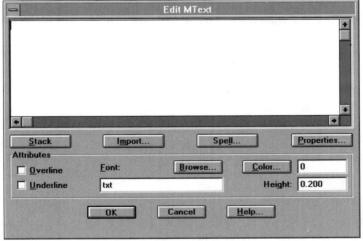

Figure 10-3:
The Edit
MText
dialog box in
AutoCAD for
Windows
includes a
built-in
paragraph
editor.

4. **Type the text you need in the text box at the top of the editor dialog box.**

The lines automatically wrap within the text box width specified in the previous steps, as shown in Figure 10- 4.

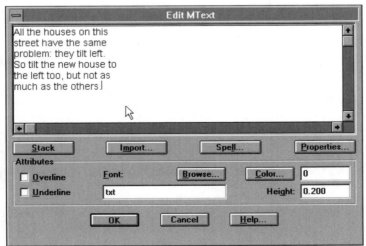

Figure 10-4:
As you enter
text in the
Edit MText
dialog box,
your text
lines wrap
automatically
according to
the width of
the text box
you specify.

Although the Edit MText dialog box has no Edit menu, you can use the following standard control keys in Windows for cutting, pasting, and so on:

- **Ctrl+X:** Cut selection to the Clipboard.
- **Ctrl+C:** Copy selection to the Clipboard.
- **Ctrl+V:** Paste Clipboard contents into selection.
- **Ctrl+Z:** Undo.
- **Ctrl+Shift+Spacebar:** Insert a nonbreaking space.
- **Enter:** Start a new paragraph.

5. **Modify the text's properties by using the dialog box's options.**

   The Edit MText dialog box includes a number of options, which are described in the following section. You can probably figure most of them out by experimentation.

6. **To complete the text, click OK.**

Windows text editor options

This section briefly describes the options in the AutoCAD for Windows text editor. You can do anything in the Windows text editor that you can do by using the MTEXT command directly, only much more easily:

- ✔ **Import:** Imports an external text file, which you can find by browsing through DOS subdirectories.
- ✔ **Spell:** Spell-checks text.
- ✔ **Overline, Underline:** Adds an overline or underline to text.
- ✔ **Font:** Enables you to enter a font name or browse through DOS subdirectories to find one. (Font, Browse, and the text entry box with the default entry txt are all part of the area for specifying the font.)
- ✔ **Color:** Enables you to enter a color number or pick a color from the color slide.
- ✔ **Height:** Enables you to specify the text height, using the units in your drawing.
- ✔ **Properties:** Opens the MText Properties dialog box so that you can specify overall properties for the text block (see Figure 10-5).

The MText Properties dialog box contains two groups of options. The first group of options, labeled *Contents*, affects the actual contents of the text box:

✔ **Text Style:** Sets the overall style for the text block (more information on text styles can be found in the following section).

✔ **Text Height:** Sets the overall text height, which you can override for specific blocks of text.

✔ **Direction:** Sets the direction in which text is written, either left to right or top to bottom.

The second group of options in the MText Properties dialog box, labeled *Object,* affects the text box as an overall object:

✔ **Attachment:** Sets the point at which the text starts and the direction in which it moves as it expands beyond the original text boundaries, combined with the justification.

✔ **Width:** Sets the width of the text boundaries.

✔ **Rotation:** Sets the rotation angle of the text.

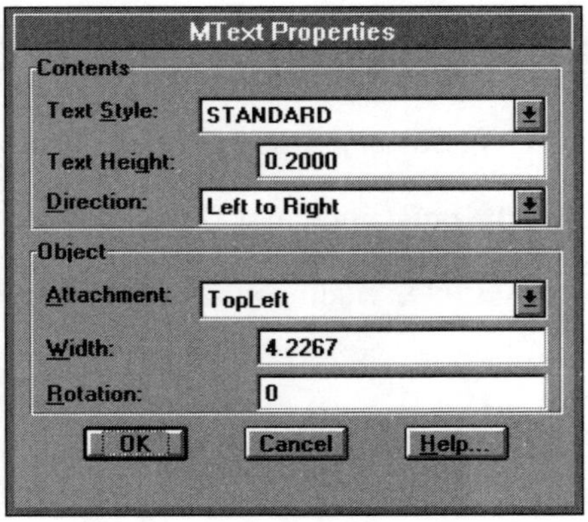

Figure 10-5:
The MText
Properties
dialog box.

MText Properties

Contents

Text Style: STANDARD

Text Height: 0.2000

Direction: Left to Right

Object

Attachment: TopLeft

Width: 4.2267

Rotation: 0

OK   Cancel   Help...

Text with Style

The following three factors determine the appearance of AutoCAD text:

✔ The formatting commands used

✔ The text font

✔ The text style

Text style actually includes the font, but the font is worth discussing separately, because of its effect on another vital concern: performance.

Fonts and performance

A *text font* actually consists of dozens, hundreds, or thousands of tiny lines. Drawing these lines is not a fast process, especially with the many characters that may exist in a really complicated font.

Imagine a drawing of an entire floor of a large building, with labels for each of the major parts of the floor. If you work on the whole drawing at once, AutoCAD may need to update thousands of characters each time you pan or zoom. The complexity of the task, and the time you must wait to complete the task, is greatly affected by the simplicity or complexity of the font you use.

AutoCAD includes a number of fonts. For the most effective performance, consider using the simpler fonts such as *TXT* or *ROMANS*. Figure 10-6 shows some of the simpler fonts available in AutoCAD. ROMANS is a good compromise between appearance and performance.

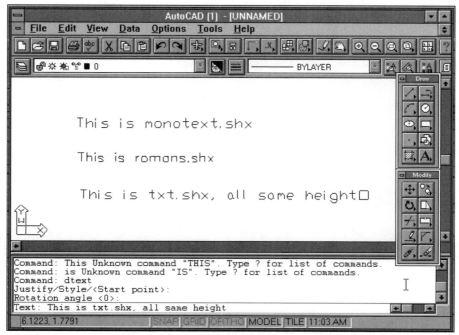

Figure 10-6: Some of AutoCAD's built-in fonts.

You can also use TrueType and PostScript Type 1 fonts if you want to take a real trip to Fontasy Island (ahem!); you can find instructions for using these fonts in the AutoCAD documentation. Performance speed is a concern in using these fonts, too, however; you must also load the fonts on each machine on which you intend to view or print the drawing.

Text styles

A *text style* is a description of the properties used in creating text. Text style gives you a running start on getting all the various text settings right, and it helps maintain consistency of text appearance within and across drawings.

AutoCAD comes with but a single text style: *STANDARD*. To create a new text style, or modify an existing one, follow these steps:

1. **To start the STYLE command, type** STYLE **at the command prompt and press Enter (or choose** <u>D</u>ata⇨<u>T</u>ext Style).

2. **Type the text style name at the prompt and then press Enter.**

    If you enter an existing style name, AutoCAD modifies that style; if you enter a new name, AutoCAD creates a new style.

    Enter **?** for the style name, and AutoCAD prompts you for what styles to list. Enter ***** for all names, **S*** to list all style names that start with *S,* and so on. AutoCAD lists the names and descriptions of all the text styles that match the letters you enter.

    The Select Font File dialog box appears.

3. **Select the font file from the dialog box.**

    Unfortunately, AutoCAD does not preview the font for you, so this task may involve some trial and error. (The AutoCAD reference manual shows all the fonts available to you.)

4. **Type the text height at the prompt and then press Enter.**

    If you enter **0**, the style definition does not determine the height of text; instead, AutoCAD prompts you for a text height each time you use this style. If you enter a value for the text height, you do not need to redefine it each time you use the style.

5. **Type the width factor at the prompt and then press Enter.**

    The width factor is a multiplier of the character width, from .75 (condensed text) through 1.0 (normal) to 4.0 (wide characters). The same font can look very different in different widths.

6. **Type the obliquing angle at the prompt and then press Enter.**

The angle range you can enter is from –80 degrees (tilted backward, almost horizontal) to 80 degrees (tilted forward, like normal italics but also almost horizontal). An angle between 15 and 30 degrees looks like normal italics.

7. **If you want the text displayed backward, type** Y **and then press Enter. Otherwise, just press Enter.**

   (This may seem silly, but it can be very useful for some applications. The same is true for upside-down text, as in the following step.)

8. **If you want the text displayed upside-down, type** Y **and then press Enter. Otherwise, just press Enter.**

9. **If you want the text displayed vertically rather than horizontally, type** Y **and then press Enter. Otherwise, just press Enter. (This feature is available only for certain fonts.)**

AutoCad ends the STYLE command; the style you just created or modified becomes the current text style.

The following example shows the commands you enter on the command line as well as all the prompts for the STYLE command:

```
Command: STYLE
Text style name (or ?) <STANDARD>: BUDSTYLE
New style.
Font style <txt>: ROMANS
Height <0.0000>:.2
Width factor <1.0000>:
Obliquing angle <0>: 30
Backwards? <N>
Upside-down? <N>
Vertical? <N>
BUDSTYLE is now the current text style.
```

Checking It Out

With Release 13, AutoCAD has finally added a feature that users have long wanted: a spell-checker. Although this may seem like a small deal given that most drawings contain few words, even one misspelling in a drawing for a $10 million proposal can be a major problem. So the spell-checker is a welcome addition to AutoCAD. Use it!

Because most computer users are by now pretty familiar with the general concept of a spell-checker, and because the one in AutoCAD is relatively simple, the following steps should be enough to get you started on checking your spelling in AutoCAD:

1. **Start the spell-checker by using one of the following methods:**

   • Type **SPELL** at the command prompt and press Enter.

   • Click the Spelling icon from the standard toolbar (Windows only).

   • Choose Tools⇨Spelling from the menu bar.

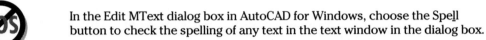 In the Edit MText dialog box in AutoCAD for Windows, choose the Spell button to check the spelling of any text in the text window in the dialog box.

2. **Select the objects you want to check by clicking them in the drawing area.**

   Entering **All** selects all text objects. Press Enter to initiate the check.

   If AutoCAD finds no misspellings, it displays a message on the command line, and the command terminates. If the program finds a misspelling, the Check Spelling dialog box appears with the misspelled or unrecognized word.

3. **Use one of the following options to tell AutoCAD how to handle the misspelling:**

   • **Ignore/Ignore All.** Ignores the current word and continues checking, or ignores the current word and any future instances of it as well.

   • **Change/Change All.** Changes the current word to the highlighted word and continues checking, or changes the current word and all other instances of it as well.

   • **Add.** Adds the misspelled word to the dictionary.

   • **Lookup.** Looks up the new word entered in the text entry area under Suggestions.

   • **Change Dictionaries.** Changes to a different dictionary.

   • **Context.** Displays the words among which AutoCAD found the misspelled word.

   AutoCAD then continues with spell checking until it has checked all the selected text objects. If it finds no more misspellings, AutoCAD displays a message on the command line, and the command terminates.

Using the spell-checker can save you a lot of trouble and embarrassment. As ads for spell-checking products have long pointed out, a boss or client who finds an error in your spelling is likely to be suspicious of the correctness of the rest of your drawing as well. So always spell-check your document before you make a final plot of it.

Chapter 11
Entering New Dimensions

. . . .

In This Chapter

▶ Dimension basics

▶ Linear, radial, angular, ordinate and other dimension types

▶ Creating dimensions

▶ Dimension styles

. . . .

*F*irst off, let me assure you that you have not actually entered the Twilight Zone in this chapter. (Though sometimes when working with dimensions in AutoCAD, it may *seem* like you have.) *Dimensions* are labels that AutoCAD puts on an object to show the object's length, width, diameter, and other important numbers. AutoCAD dimensions automatically update themselves as you change the objects they are associated with. If you have a dimension that shows the length of a gun barrel, for example, and you drag the barrel to lengthen it, AutoCAD automatically updates the dimension that shows the barrel length. Sounds easy, right? (Oh, you wish!)

Unfortunately, dimensioning is one of the most complicated features of AutoCAD. Marking dimensions with pencil and paper is so flexible that drafters have developed an enormous number of ways to show dimensions. And with the cramped nature of most drawings, both traditional and CAD drafters want many ways to force dimensions into small spaces in the drawing. A myriad of ways exists to depict dimensions, therefore, and AutoCAD offers dozens of dimensioning variables to support as many dimension styles as possible.

Dimensioning has improved a great deal in the last few versions of AutoCAD, including new changes in Release 13. *Associative dimensions* — dimensions that update automatically instead of needing to be manually updated as you change an object — are now the rule, not the exception. AutoCAD now groups dimension variables into dialog boxes, reorganized in Release 13, that enable you to easily change the variables by clicking an image of the dimension. Dialog boxes also remind you what your options are and show you how related variables may affect each other.

Dimension styles enable you to group options together and apply them as a group, and dimension style families make handling minor variations within a style easier than the task would otherwise be.

But even with all these changes, complexity abounds. Dimensioning in AutoCAD is just so powerful that learning it all takes time. To avoid being overwhelming (and very lengthy), this chapter covers only the basics of dimensioning. The chapter is very useful to the novice who wants to get a feel for dimensioning, as well as to the more advanced user who wants a quick look at the new dialog boxes for Release 13. For more information on the advanced features of dimensioning, however, you need to go to the AutoCAD documentation — and be ready to do a great deal of experimenting as well.

New Dimensions of Sight and Sound . . . and CAD

(Okay, so maybe we *have* entered the Twilight Zone. Rod Serling, where are you?) Although you may have drawn or even simply seen dimensions in your past work, you may not realize that a dimension actually consists of many parts. Figure 11-1 displays the following important parts of a dimension:

- **Dimension text.** Dimension text is the set of numbers that indicate the actual dimension. In AutoCAD, you can specify prefixes to appear before the dimension text, suffixes to appear after it, and tolerances to indicate the precision of the measurement.

- **Dimension line and arrowhead.** The dimension line goes from the dimension text outward, to indicate the size of the dimension. The arrowhead shows where the dimension line terminates.

- **Extension line.** The extension line extends from the end of the dimension line to the object that the dimension measures.

Imagine that you had to specify to a very young child — who was, of course, excellent at drafting — every aspect of every part of a dimension; only then can you start to realize the potential complexity of AutoCAD's dimensioning. To get the most out of the limited attention span most people have for dimensions, this section explains dimensions in general via the Dimension Styles dialog box and then describes specific types of dimensions only to the extent that they differ from linear dimensions.

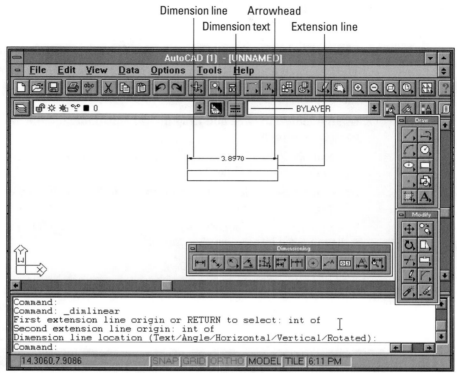

Figure 11-1:
The parts of
a dimension.

Setting up dimensions

To create even a simple dimension, you must do some setup work — in Windows, anyway — and then make an informed choice from many different options. This section includes what you need to know to start using dimensions.

In AutoCAD Release 13 for DOS, the major dimension types are available on a secondary menu of the Draw menu. But in AutoCAD Release 13 for Windows, different types of dimensions are available only from the command line — and who's going to remember all those commands anyway — or from the Dimensioning toolbar. The only trouble is that you'll want to put this toolbar away much of the time because it takes up so much screen space. So learn the command line commands for dimensioning that you use most.

The following steps show you how to make the Dimensioning toolbar appear and disappear on-screen:

1. **Choose Tools⊅Toolbars⊅Dimensioning from the menu bar.**

   The Dimensioning toolbar appears on-screen, as shown in Figure 11-2. (The keyboard shortcut for this entire operation, by the way, is Alt+T+T+D.)

2. **Use the mouse to click and drag the Dimensioning toolbar where you want it on-screen.**

   You can place the toolbar on any side of the screen or leave it floating somewhere in the middle.

3. **After you finish using it, close the Dimensioning toolbar by double-clicking the close box in the upper-left corner of the toolbar.**

   The Dimensioning toolbar vanishes from your screen — poof! (Almost like it disappeared into . . . *another dimension!*)

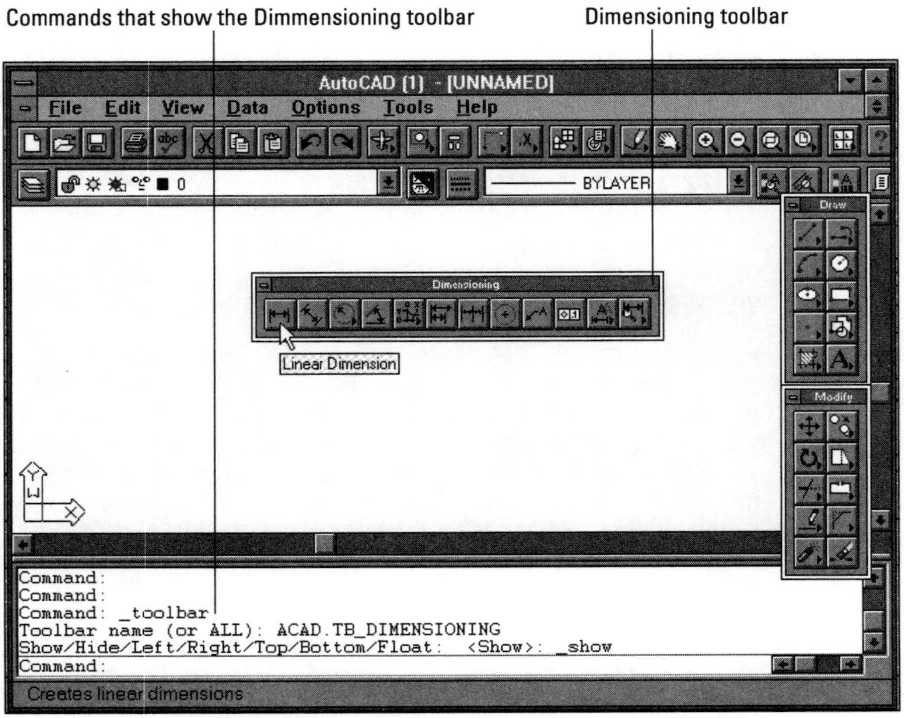

Commands that show the Dimmensioning toolbar   Dimensioning toolbar

Figure 11-2:
The Dimensioning toolbar and the command line commands that open it.

```
Command:
Command:
Command: _toolbar
Toolbar name (or ALL): ACAD.TB_DIMENSIONING
Show/Hide/Left/Right/Top/Bottom/Float:  <Show>: _show
Command:
```

Creates linear dimensions

What all these crazy dimensions mean

Several different types of dimensions are available from the Dimensioning toolbar in AutoCAD for Windows or from the Dimensioning secondary menu in AutoCAD for DOS. Not all the options are equally important to everyone, but knowing in general what these options are certainly helps you get to the actual work of creating a dimension sooner rather than later. The following options are represented by the icons, from left to right, on the Dimensioning Toolbar:

- ✔ **Linear Dimension** (also accessed by using the DIMLINEAR command). A *linear dimension* is a horizontal or vertical dimension with extension lines going vertically (for a horizontal linear dimension) or horizontally (for a vertical linear dimension) to the origins of the extension lines, which define the endpoint of the dimension.

- ✔ **Aligned Dimension** (also accessed by using the DIMALIGNED command). An *aligned dimension* is a linear dimension tilted to the same angle as a line drawn through the endpoints of its extension lines.

- ✔ **Radial Dimension** (also accessed by using the DIMRADIUS command). A *radial dimension* is a dimension from the center of an arc or circle, with one end of the dimension line at the center and an arrowhead at the curve.

- ✔ **Angular Dimension** (also accessed by using the DIMANGULAR command). An *angular dimension* is a dimension drawn inside an angle; the dimension line curves along an arc inside the measured angle. (When I first saw this command, I thought it was another name for a not-especially-bright fisherman. Duhhhh!)

- ✔ **Ordinate Dimension** (also accessed by using the DIMORDINATE command). An *ordinate dimension* is a leader (defined later in this section), followed by the *X* or *Y* coordinate of the point.

- ✔ **Baseline Dimension** (also accessed by using the DIMBASELINE command). A *baseline dimension* is actually a series of related dimensions drawn from a single baseline. Each dimension is incremented from the previous one by a value that you enter. Baseline dimensions can be angular, linear, or ordinate, depending on the type of the previous dimension. If the previous dimension isn't one of these three types, AutoCAD prompts you for a dimension of one of the types.

- ✔ **Continue Dimension** (also accessed by using the DIMCONTINUE command). This option continues a baseline dimension.

- ✔ **Center Mark** (also accessed by using the DIMCENTER command). The *center mark* is the central point of a diameter or radial dimension. It can have several different aspects that you specify. The Center Mark icon gives you direct access to this feature.

✔ **Leader** (also accessed by using the LEADER command). A *leader* is a single-line dimension that connects an annotation to a drawing feature. (So if you're asked by a spacey-looking stranger to "take me to your leader," just turn on AutoCAD. . . .)

✔ **Tolerance** (also accessed by using the TOLERANCE command). A *tolerance* is a specifically formatted description of the maximum allowable variation in a measurement. The TOLERANCE command enables you to specify the symbol and other aspects of the tolerance.

✔ **Align Dimension Text** (also accessed by using the DIMTEDIT command). This icon gives you direct access to text location and rotation angle.

✔ **Dimension Style** (also accessed by using the DDIM command). This icon enables you to specify the dimension style and modify its characteristics using the Dimension Styles dialog box.

AutoCAD does not require you to specify objects to dimension; it draws a dimension between any points you specify. Usually, however, the points for which you want to indicate a dimension are part of an object. To keep things general, though, the points that you attach the dimension to are simply referred to as the origins of the dimension's extension lines.

Creating a dimension

Although many types of dimensions exist, most dimensioning concerns the three most common types you encounter: *linear dimensions*, *radial dimensions*, and *angular dimensions*. This section describes how to create dimensions and about how easy dimensioning can be if you can use an existing dimension style. Look for more about the detailed options for different kinds of dimensions in the section "Doing Dimensions with Style(s)," later in this chapter.

The following steps show you how to create linear dimensions for both sides of a rectangle:

1. **Draw a rectangle by typing the RECTANG command at the command prompt and pressing Enter.**

   If you already have a rectangle in your drawing, you can use that instead. (If you want to apply dimensioning to another shape, use these steps as a general guideline, filling in the appropriate commands and data as applicable to your drawing.)

2. **Start the DIMLINEAR command by using one of the following methods:**

   • Type **DIMLINEAR** at the command prompt and press Enter.

- Click the Linear Dimension icon (the left-most icon) on the Dimensioning toolbar (Windows only).

- Choose Draw⇨Dimensioning⇨Linear from the menu bar (DOS only).

3. To specify the origin of the first extension line, snap to a corner on the left side of the rectangle by using the intersection snap.

Type **int** and then click the corner you want.

4. To specify the origin of the second extension line, snap to the other corner on the left side of the rectangle by using the intersection snap.

Type **int** and then click the corner you want.

AutoCAD automatically draws a *vertical* dimension— that is, it displays the length of the object in the vertical direction.

5. Click anywhere on-screen to indicate where you want to place the dimension, or type a location for the dimension on the command line and press Enter.

6. Repeat steps 2 through 5 to create a horizontal linear dimension.

This time, AutoCAD automatically draws a *horizontal* dimension — that is, it displays the length of the object in the horizontal direction (see Figure 11-3).

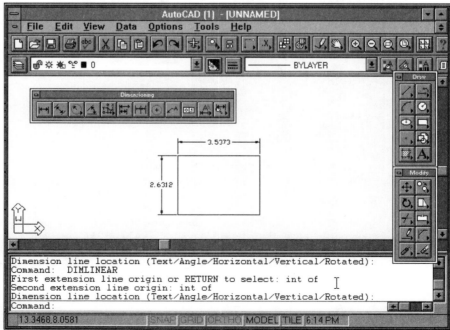

Figure 11-3:
A pair of linear dimensions for a rectangle.

Doing Dimensions with Style(s)

Probably the best way to understand dimensions in detail is by using the Dimension Styles dialog box. The Dimension Styles dialog box enables you to change just about any dimension variable and almost automatically groups the variables into a style you can use later. Though still no picnic, understanding dimensioning variables in terms of the Dimension Styles dialog box is probably not a bad idea, because it's likely to be the main way you'll interact with dimensions.

The Dimension Styles dialog box

Figure 11-4 shows the Dimension Styles dialog box, which is really the doorway to a number of related dialog boxes. The following sections explain the parts of this initial dialog box; descriptions of other, related dialog boxes follow. Type **DDIM** at the command line and press Enter to open the Dimension Styles dialog box.

Figure 11-4: The Dimension Styles dialog box.

```
                    Dimension Styles
  ┌Dimension Style──────────────────────────────┐
  │ Current:   STANDARD                      ▼   │
  │ Name:      STANDARD                          │
  │              Save        Rename              │
  ├─Family───────────────────────────────────────┤
  │  ◉ Parent                                    │
  │  ○ Linear      ○ Diameter     Geometry...    │
  │  ○ Radial      ○ Ordinate     Format...      │
  │  ○ Angular     ○ Leader       Annotation...  │
  │                                              │
  │       OK          Cancel       Help...       │
  └──────────────────────────────────────────────┘
```

The Dimension Style area

The Dimension Style area of the Dimension Styles dialog box dictates what style is currently in use. You should leave the STANDARD style unchanged so that you have a base from which to work and then create at least one style of your own for your dimensions. The name you create can be up to 31 characters long, so calling your version MYSTANDARD may be a good choice.

To create a new style, first use the Current drop-down list to select the existing style you want to use as a starting point and then type the name of the new style in the Name text box. Click Save to save the original definition of the style, and then you can modify options as described in the following sections. Click Save again to save your modifications.

Family area

If you assume that you use the Family area to specify what type of dimension the style applies to, you're wrong; this area doesn't work as you think. A dimension style applies to any kind of dimension. The Family area of the dialog box enables you to specify different values that apply to only a specific type of dimension within the overall style. Although the overall style for different types of dimensions, such as Parent, Linear, Radial, and so on, may use a certain font, a radial dimension within the style may use an entirely different one. This differentiation enables you to build up complex — and possibly hard to maintain — styles with many variations.

The Family area affects the options available in the Geometry, Format, and Annotation dialog boxes described in the following sections. If a given option doesn't make sense for the dimension family that's currently in force, AutoCAD dims the option in the dialog box, making it unavailable for use. If you choose a different family for which the option is pertinent, the option becomes available again.

The Geometry, Format, and Annotation buttons

These three buttons lead to dialog boxes that enable you to specify the major options for the dimension style.

One or more system variable controls each aspect of dimensions. In general, learning which of the dozens of dimensioning-related system variables control which aspect isn't worth your valuable time; just use dimension styles to control each parameter. If you frequently find yourself changing one or two specific aspects of a dimension, however, learning the name of the appropriate variable so that you can set it directly may actually be worth the effort. Check your AutoCAD documentation for information about which system variable controls which parameter.

The Geometry dialog box

Figure 11-5 shows the Geometry dialog box, which you can open from the Dimension Styles dialog box (by choosing the Geometry button, of course). The Geometry dialog box enables you to specify options that relate to the look of the dimension.

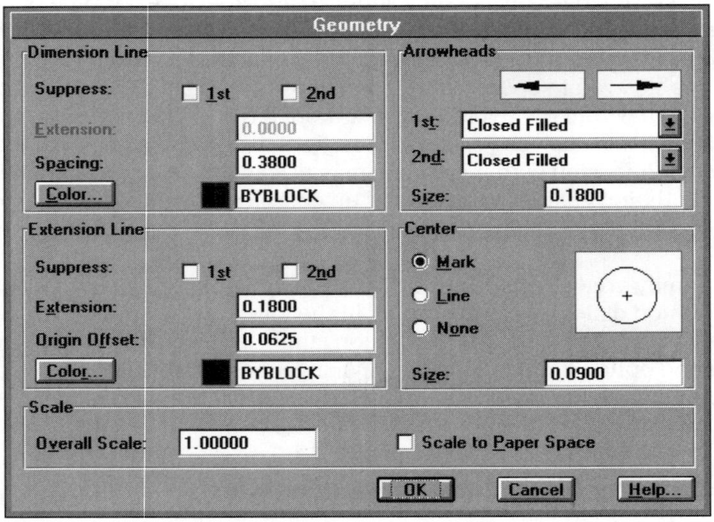

Figure 11-5:
The
Geometry
dialog box.

The following sections briefly explain the major areas of the Geometry dialog box.

Dimension Line

The Dimension Line area enables you to control the suppression of either the first (left) or second (right) dimension line if they're outside the extension lines. Extension specifies the length of a tick mark used as an arrowhead. You can also set the Spacing between dimension lines of a baseline dimension and the Color of the dimension line.

Extension Line

The Extension Line area enables you to control the suppression of the first or second extension line. You can also set the Extension distance beyond the dimension line for the extension lines, specify the gap by which the extension line is offset from its origin (Origin Offset), and choose the Color of the extension line.

Arrowheads

You can specify the look of first and second arrowheads and the arrowhead Size in this area.

Center

You can specify the appearance of the Center mark used in a radial dimension — as a small cross inside the circle (Mark), a small cross plus cross hairs (Line), or no mark at all (None) — as well as its Size.

Scale

You can set the Scale of the dimension here, either as an absolute scale or related to the paper space scale. See Chapter 4 for more information on dimension scales.

The Format dialog box

Figure 11-6 shows the Format dialog box, which you open from the Dimension Styles dialog box (by choosing — yes, the Format button). The Format dialog box enables you to specify options that relate to where you place a dimension, the origins of its extension lines, and how the dimension's aligned.

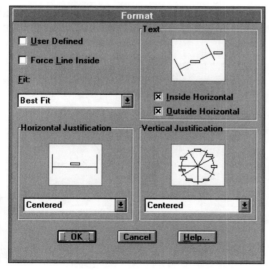

Figure 11-6:
The Format dialog box.

The following sections describe the major areas of this dialog box:

Fit

In this area, you can tell AutoCAD to prompt you, the user, as to where to put dimension text in a new dimension; you can instruct the program to add a line inside the dimension even if the arrowheads are outside the extension lines; and you can specify how to fit different parts of the dimension, even if the space between extension lines is too narrow for everything.

Text

You can indicate here how to place your dimension text: inside the extension lines or outside with a small leader pointing to the nearest arrowhead.

Horizontal Justification and Vertical Justification

You can choose from a number of options for the horizontal and vertical justification of text, including centered, justified to the first or second extension line, and over the first or second extension line.

The Annotation dialog box

Figure 11-7 shows the Annotation dialog box, which you open from the Dimension Styles dialog box (by choosing — that's right, you guessed it — the Annotation button!). The Annotation dialog box enables you to specify options that relate to the look of the text that displays the value of the dimension.

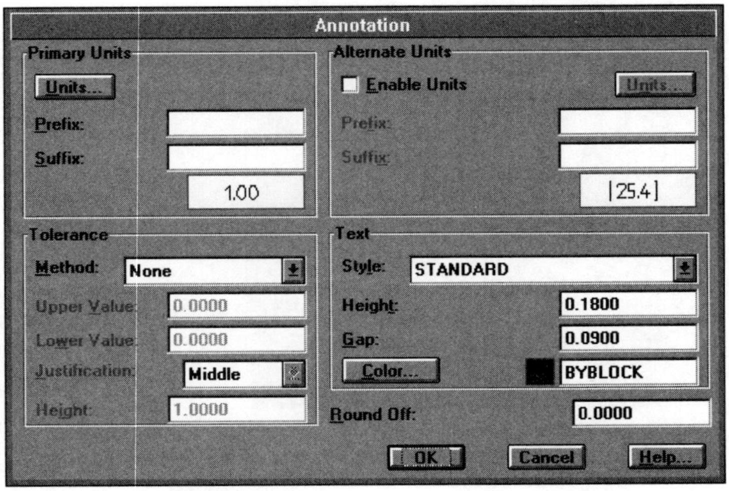

Figure 11-7: The Annotation dialog box.

The following sections describe the major areas of this dialog box (is that an echo I hear?):

Primary Units

Clicking Units opens a secondary dialog box, where you can specify a great number of things about the primary units used in your dimensions, including the type of units, type of angular units, precision and zero suppression for measurements, precision and zero suppression for tolerances, and scaling factor. You can also specify in the Primary Units area a Prefix or a Suffix for your units (such as "inches").

Alternate Units

You can use the options in this area to display alternative units in square brackets after your dimensioned text. If your primary units are decimal, for example, you may also want to display the measurements in fractions. All the options available for primary units are available for alternative units as well. Select Enable Units and click the Units button to choose the type of units you want

Tolerance

You can specify in this area a vast number of ways of displaying tolerances as well as the maximum and minimum allowable values for a dimension.

Text

You can specify in this area a text Style (including font), text Height, the Gap around text, and the Color of text.

Round off

This is the value to which AutoCAD rounds off all dimension distances. You should coordinate this value with the precision you specify for primary and alternate units. Displaying four digits beyond the decimal of precision and then rounding off to the nearest unit, for example, may not make much sense. (By now, of course, you may think that all too many things in AutoCAD don't make much sense; but this *really* doesn't. Trust me!)

The 5th Wave

By Rich Tennant

Chapter 12
Hatch...Hatch...Hatchoo!

In This Chapter

▶ What is a hatch?
▶ Creating a simple hatch
▶ Using the Boundary Hatch dialog box
▶ Hatch boundaries
▶ Hatch patterns
▶ Advanced hatching options

A *hatch* is a pattern that fills in an area of a drawing. Hatching is often used to convey the type of material represented by an object, such as insulation, metal, and so on. A hatch is similar to a linetype in that it conveys information about part of the drawing. But unlike with a linetype, you do not connect a hatch to an object. Instead, you connect a hatch to an empty space, surrounded by objects. (In many fields, showing empty space is important, as when an architect depicts a wall or grassy open space or an engineer shows a cutout.)

These details help explain why *hatch* is actually a short name for a longer idea. A hatch is a simple area that you define by using points. But the more useful, and common, kind of hatch is a *boundary hatch* — that is, a hatch pattern filling an area within a boundary. (*Boundaries* are the edges of objects.) If you apply a boundary hatch to an area, AutoCAD must engage in some guesswork about the exact nature of the boundary, as well as what areas you do and don't want hatched. If AutoCAD guesses wrong, you must tell it what to do.

Even *boundary hatch* is short for a longer term. The default type of boundary hatch is called an *associative boundary hatch*. This kind of hatch is new in Release 13. An associative boundary hatch remains *associated* — thus the name (clever, huh?) — with the objects that make up its boundary. If you modify the objects that make up the boundary, AutoCAD tries to adjust the hatch to fit. Of course, if the changes open up a hole in the boundary, AutoCAD may just have a hard time adjusting the hatch correctly.

If you use only simple hatches, you may not need to worry about modifying the objects of the hatch or whether AutoCAD can make the correct adjustments. You should, however, at least know what to do if you run into a situation that requires modification or adjustment. With this knowledge, you can avoid problems with the hatch and have some idea of how to go about making the hatch right if you do experience problems. The best way you can avoid problems related to a hatch is to avoid hatching until late in the drawing process. Creating the hatch near the end of your project benefits your program performance and can even help you avoid any need to rework your drawing.

Creating a Simple Hatch

Creating a simple hatch is easy if you use the HATCH command — as long as you stick to the default hatch pattern and other default options. Unfortunately, the HATCH command doesn't make changing hatching options at all easy. Furthermore, a hatch created by using the HATCH command is not associative; the hatch doesn't change even if you change its boundary. (Well, you can't have everything . . .)

The following steps show you how to use the HATCH command to create a simple hatch:

1. **Draw any closed shape.**

   A circle or rectangle is a good example. (If you already have a shape in your drawing that you want hatched, use these steps merely as a guide for finishing your own drawing.)

2. **To start the HATCH command, type** HATCH **at the command prompt and press Enter.**

3. **To specify the default values for the pattern, scale, and angle of the hatch, press Enter at each of these command line prompts.**

4. **Select the shape you drew as the boundary for the drawing.**

5. **Press Enter to indicate that you've finished selecting objects.**

AutoCAD hatches the inside of the shape similar to that of the rectangle shown in Figure 12-1.

You can create a boundary hatch without first selecting—or even creating—an object by picking out coordinates in your drawing area. The *direct hatch option* controls this feature. Instead of selecting an existing object as a boundary after entering the HATCH command and accepting its defaults, simply press Enter again and then type at the command line the coordinates of the points on-

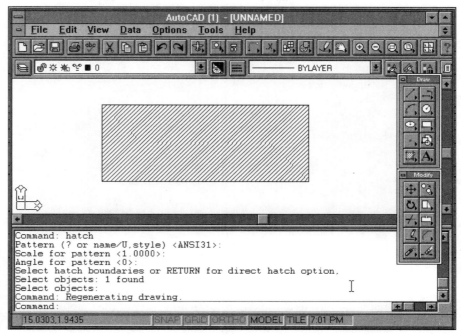

Figure 12-1:
A simple
hatch inside
a rectangle.

screen that are to serve as the hatch's boundary. (You can decide whether to keep as part of your drawing the polyline that these points define after you finish hatching.)

Unfortunately, AutoCAD's idea of what's inside this direct hatch boundary is kind of odd. And this kind of hatch also is a nonassociative hatch; to change its shape, you must redo it from scratch. To me, drawing some construction lines, creating a boundary hatch, and then hiding the construction lines is easier than predicting just what the direct hatch option may do. And, anyway, if you need to adjust the hatch later, you can just move the construction lines and the hatch changes to fit.

Using the Boundary Hatch Dialog Box

If you want a flexible hatch that's defined by its boundaries — that is, a hatch that updates if you update its boundaries — use boundary hatching. You can control boundary hatching by using the Boundary Hatch dialog box, which you access by clicking the Hatch icon on the Draw floating toolbar (Windows only) or by typing **BHATCH** on the command line and pressing Enter (both DOS and Windows). See Figure 12-2.

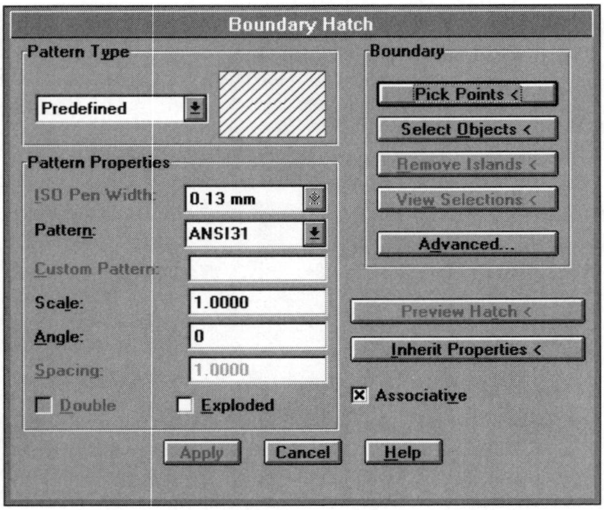

Figure 12-2:
The
Boundary
Hatch dialog
box.

The Boundary Hatch dialog box enables you to do two main things: specify the hatch pattern to use and define the boundary of the hatch area. Just about every option in the dialog box relates to one of these two tasks.

You can use predefined, user-defined, or custom hatch patterns. Most of the time, you're likely to find yourself using predefined hatch patterns, but the other hatch pattern options are nice to have. The next three sections describe the basics of creating a hatch pattern. You can find out how to create a boundary hatch in the section, "Create a boundary hatch," later in this chapter.

Predefined hatch patterns

To use *predefined hatch patterns,* select Predefined from the drop-down list box in the Pattern Type area of the Boundary Hatch dialog box. This selection sets the stage for choosing the hatch pattern.

You can scan through the hatch patterns in one of two ways:

- By selecting the name from the Pattern drop-down list box in the Pattern Properties area; this changes the hatch pattern shown in the preview square in the Pattern Type area.
- By clicking the preview square; this changes the hatch pattern shown and the Pattern name in the list box as well.

AutoCAD has about 70 predefined hatch patterns from which to choose, which is quite a long list. The list includes ANSI (American National Standards Institute) and ISO (International Standards Organization) standard hatch patterns. Figure 12-3 shows the ANSI hatch patterns to give you an idea of the kinds of hatch patterns available.

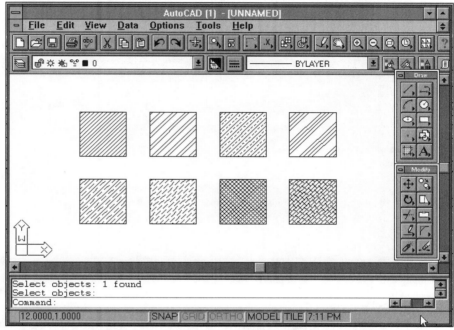

Figure 12-3: These ANSI hatch patterns, ANSI31 through ANSI38, are available from the list of predefined hatch patterns in the Boundary Hatch dialog box.

A good idea is to print out a small cheat sheet of hatch patterns that you commonly use and a larger one of all the hatch patterns available to you, whether predefined or custom, and then share it with others in your organization. These cheat sheets can save time and help you choose the right hatch pattern for your drawings instead of settling for one of the first hatch patterns you stumble on while clicking through the hatch patterns list.

User-defined hatch patterns

In addition to the predefined hatch patterns, you can use *user-defined hatch patterns* and *custom hatch patterns*. These two kinds of hatch patterns meet two different needs.

A *user-defined* hatch pattern makes a hatch pattern out of the currently selected linetype. Start by going back into your drawing and specifying the linetype you want to use. Then go back into the Boundary Hatch dialog box and specify User-defined hatch pattern in the Pattern Type area. You can specify the Angle and Spacing of the lines in Pattern Properties area. Figure 12-4 shows four user-defined hatch patterns with spacing increasing from one to four units and angles increasing from 20 degrees through 80 degrees. All the shapes are squares, aligned at right angles; the tilt in the third and fourth squares is an optical illusion.

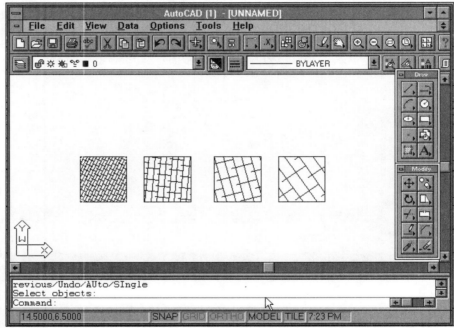

Figure 12-4:
User-defined hatch patterns with increasing spacing and angles.

Experiment with different options to determine what works well for you. Unfortunately, even after you find a hatch pattern that works well for a particular purpose, you can't save it. But you can write down how you created that pattern or create and update a drawing by using a master set of user-defined hatch patterns. Then you can reuse a hatch pattern by opening the drawing and using the Inherit Properties button in the Boundary Hatch dialog box, as described in the section "Inheriting properties," later in this chapter.

A *custom hatch pattern* is a hatch pattern that you can define and save in a file with a file extension of PAT. (No, football fans, I'm sorry. PAT doesn't stand for point after touchdown; it stands for *pat*tern.) This type of hatch pattern, however, falls out of the scope of a book such as *AutoCAD For Dummies*, but you can find out more about creating custom hatch patterns in your AutoCAD documentation (if you really want to).

Basic boundaries

After you define your hatch, you define the boundary in the Boundary section of the Boundary Hatch dialog box. (Makes sense.) You can define the boundaries of a hatch in two ways: by picking points in the area(s) you want hatched and by selecting objects that AutoCAD hatches for you. The actual operation involved in using either of these options is confusing to most people, and you'll probably need a little practice before you get used to it. (Not that you're simply "most people" — after all, you *did* buy this book. . . .)

The idea behind either definition option is simple, if applied to simple areas — that is, closed objects with no additional object inside them. To hatch such a simple area, you enter the HATCH command on the command line and then either pick points on the inside of the object or select the object or objects surrounding the area. AutoCAD then applies the hatch for you—and you're done.

This simple hatching gets a little more complicated if you have one closed object inside another. If you pick points inside the *enclosing* (outermost) object, but outside the *enclosed* (inner) one, you hatch only the area between the boundaries of the two objects. If you pick some points inside each object, you hatch the entire area within the outermost surrounding boundary, including the area within the inner boundary.

The results are somewhat reversed if you select objects instead of picking points. If you pick the outermost enclosing object(s) as well as the enclosed one(s), AutoCAD uses both boundaries and only hatches the area between them. In any event, after you finish picking or selecting, press Enter to return to the dialog box.

On the off-chance that all this is a bit confusing for you, Figure 12-5 shows how the different choices work applied to a series of donut-type figures (which are actually just two circles, one inside the other). You can hatch the ring with a single pick by picking points; you can hatch the entire enclosed area with a single pick by selecting objects (boundaries).

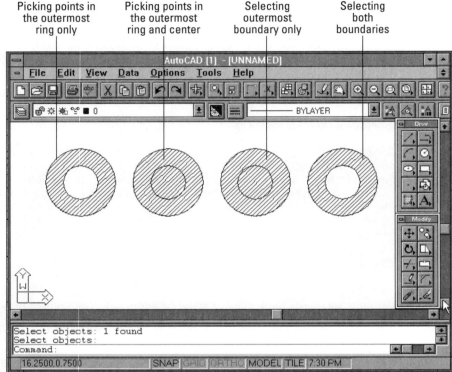

Picking points in the outermost ring only | Picking points in the outermost ring and center | Selecting outermost boundary only | Selecting both boundaries

Figure 12-5: Picking points and selecting object boundaries yield different results in hatching concentric circles.

Creating a boundary hatch

To demonstrate the workings of boundary hatches, the following steps show you how to hatch an object, such as the wheels of a (very) simple drawing of a car, by using the "picking-points" method of selecting the hatch area:

1. **Draw any object for use in creating a boundary hatch (or use an existing object that you want hatched).**

   You could, for example, draw an object such as a car. If you want to hatch an existing object in a drawing, you can do so, too, using these steps as a guideline.

2. **Open the Boundary Hatch dialog box by using one of the following methods:**

    - Type **BHATCH** at the command prompt and press Enter.
    - Click the Hatch icon from the Hatch flyout on the Draw toolbar (Windows only).
    - Choose Draw⇨Hatch⇨Hatch from the menu bar (DOS only).

    The Boundary Hatch dialog box appears.

3. **Choose any predefined hatch by selecting a hatch from the Pattern list box or by clicking the hatch pattern square in the Pattern Type area until the hatch pattern you want appears.**

4. **Click the Pick Points button.**

    The Boundary Hatch dialog box (temporarily) disappears, and your drawing reappears.

5. **Select a point inside the object you want to hatch by clicking it with the mouse.**

    On a sample drawing of a car, if using that, you'd select a point inside the left tire — that is, between the outermost and innermost circles, and below the side of the car.

    AutoCAD analyzes the drawing and decides what boundaries to use. Notice that this takes a few seconds, even on a simple drawing. On a larger drawing, this analysis can take quite a while.

6. **Press Enter to indicate that you have no more points you want to select.**

    The Boundary Hatch dialog box reappears.

7. **Click the Apply button.**

    AutoCAD hatches the part of the object you selected. (If you're using the tire example, it hatches only the part of the tire below the car; the central axle area is not hatched.) If you want to hatch another object in the drawing using the same hatch pattern (such as the other tire in the car example), you could continue on with step 8. If you had only one object to hatch, you're finished.

8. **Open the Boundary Hatch dialog box again if you want to hatch another object using the same hatch pattern, and repeat steps 3 through 7.**

    In our car wheels example, you repeat these steps for the second tire. Figure 12-6 shows how this drawing should appear midway through the hatching process for the second tire.

Inheriting properties

A neat option that can change the entire way you hatch objects is the Inherit Properties button on the Boundary Hatch dialog box. Despite its position in the Boundary Hatch dialog box (underneath the Boundary area), this feature works only with the Pattern Type and Pattern Properties areas and doesn't affect how boundaries are handled. Inherit Properties simply updates the pattern characteristics in the dialog box to make them the same as a hatch pattern you pick from the screen. So you can clone an existing hatch pattern simply by clicking Inherit Properties and then choosing the existing hatch pattern from the screen. You can use the copied hatch pattern as is or modify it by making changes in the Boundary Hatch dialog box.

If you use this Inherit Properties option, having a cheat sheet drawing of hatch patterns to clone really makes sense. Create such a drawing and share it with others.

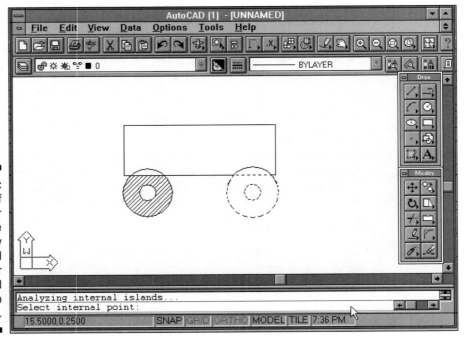

Figure 12-6:
A drawing of simple car with one tire already hatched and another selected and about to be hatched.

Advanced Hatching Options

AutoCAD has a number of advanced options for hatching, most of which you can ignore. This section covers two worthwhile options, however: defining boundary sets and styling. Figure 12-7 shows the Advanced Options dialog box, which you can open by clicking the A̲dvanced button in the Boundary Hatch dialog box. The Advanced Options dialog box contains the Define Boundary Set and Style areas that the following two sections describe.

Boundary sets

Hatching is "computationally expensive" — that is, it takes a *long* time! *Bound-ary sets* limit the area that AutoCAD considers when it determines where to hatch, thus saving you time. If you choose the Make N̲ew Boundary Set option in the Advanced Options dialog box, you temporarily return to your drawing, where you can create a bounding window (dragging left to right) or crossing window (dragging right to left) that specifies some of the objects on-screen. AutoCAD then considers only the areas within the objects you selected as it decides what to hatch.

To return to using the entire screen, click the From E̲verything on Screen radio button in the dialog box. All objects on-screen are again available for boundary selection.

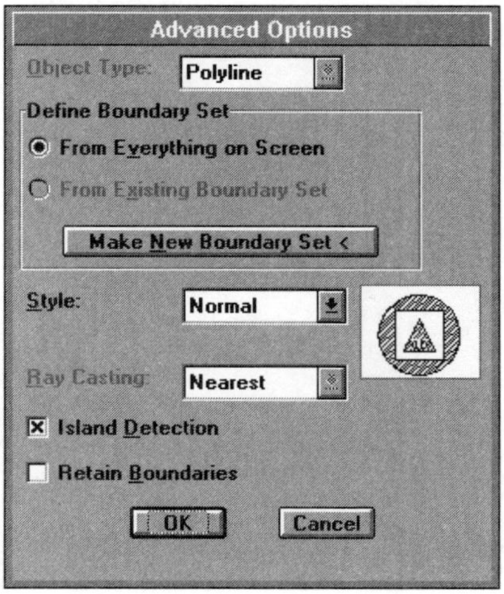

Figure 12-7:
The
Advanced
Options
dialog box.

Advanced Options

O̲bject Type: Polyline

Define Boundary Set
● From E̲verything on Screen
○ From E̲xisting Boundary Set

Make N̲ew Boundary Set <

S̲tyle: Normal

R̲ay Casting: Nearest

[X] Island D̲etection
[ ] Retain B̲oundaries

[OK]   [Cancel]

Styling

If you have several objects enclosing each other, knowing exactly which objects you hatch and which ones you don't can be very important. AutoCAD offers three style options in the Style drop-down list box of the Advanced Options dialog box to help you determine the hatch object: Normal, Outer, and Ignore. Each is described briefly in the following list. The example in the preview box to the right of the Style list box in Figure 12-7 shows the Normal style of hatching.

- ✔ **Normal.** This is the option that may seem strangest to non-AutoCAD users. The Normal option hatches the outermost ring between boundaries, skips the next ring in, hatches the next one, and so on, until alternating enclosed areas are hatched. This is the default style.

- ✔ **Outer.** This easy-to-understand option simply hatches the outermost area of an object and ignores the others.

- ✔ **Ignore.** This option is also easy to understand. It hatches everything within the outermost boundary of the object.

After you design your hatch and pick points or select objects to hatch, click the Apply button to close the Boundary Hatch dialog box and reveal your newly hatched drawing.

Well, I'll bet you're already hatching new ways to make your drawing beautiful. (Haven't I heard that somewhere before?) But before you get too deeply into your plotting, you may want to move on to the next chapter. Talk about *plots...* !

Chapter 13

The Plot Thickens

*P*lotting and printing are nothing new in AutoCAD, although in older versions of the program they weren't always easy to get right. (*Plotting* is simply printing to a different kind of printer device that uses pens instead of other types of print technologies. Because most AutoCAD drawings are eventually plotted, this book uses the term *plotting* to refer to both plotting and printing.)

Back in Release 12, AutoCAD added several features that make plotting much easier, including two of particular importance: the Plot Configuration dialog box and the Plot Preview feature. This chapter discusses all of AutoCAD's many plotting options to help you get the most out of them. You can then spend less time trying to figure out plotting and more time getting work done.

AutoCAD plotting is a big deal. Just the task of plotting a drawing is time-consuming and expensive. A *pen plotter*, the most common type of printer device used for serious work, costs a great deal of money to buy or lease and additional money to maintain. Pens jam and run out of ink, and the control software and hardware are vulnerable to bugs and problems. If everything *does* work, the resulting plot is expensive and time-consuming to produce. Even a small error forces a replot, which means more time and money. These difficulties are the main reason that setup is so important for AutoCAD; the cycle of plot, find problem, fix problem, replot is so costly and such a waste of time that you must avoid it if at all possible.

Until Release 12, AutoCAD was part of the problem rather than part of the solution. Plotting controls were hard to find and use, and AutoCAD did not show you in advance what the result of a plot would be. But with Release 12, and continuing into Release 13, AutoCAD plotting has improved greatly. The Plot Configuration dialog box, although it may appear to include too many functions, does enable you to control everything about plotting from one dialog box. The most valuable feature is Plot Preview, which basically enables you to check a plot on-screen. You can detect obvious problems quickly; you can even find problems in the details if you take the time to inspect the plot preview carefully.

This section covers the two most frequently used aspects of plotting: *plot previews* and *producing a plot*. You can also find more detailed information on plotter configuration and performance concerns.

Simple Plotting

Actually, creating a plot is easy, if you don't want to use any of the options. Just make sure that you have a drawing open on-screen and then follow these steps:

1. **Open the Plot Configuration dialog box by using one of the following methods:**

   - Type **PLOT** at the command prompt and press Enter.

   - Click the Print icon on the standard toolbar (Windows only).

   - Choose File➪Print from the menu bar (DOS and Windows).

   The Plot Configuration dialog box appears, as shown in Figure 13-1.

2. **Click OK.**

   AutoCAD plots your drawing.

You should usually do a plot preview before actually plotting your drawing so that you don't waste your time and money on a bad plot.

The following sections discuss the areas of the Plot Configuration dialog box in a different order than you may expect. The order matches the frequency with which you're likely to use and need information about the areas of the dialog box rather than the order in which the areas appear in the dialog box. Use the figures as a visual guide to find the section you want quickly.

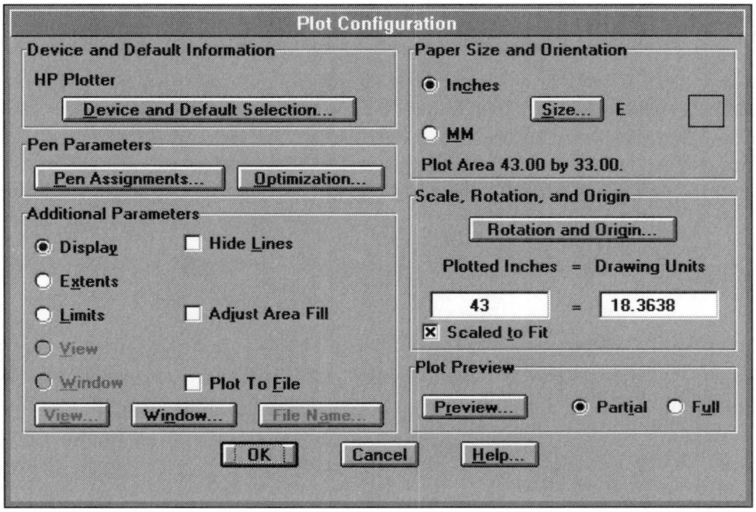

Figure 13-1:
The Plot
Configuration
dialog box.

Plot Preview

For every final plot you do, you should make several *check prints*. So what's a check print? A check print simply involves printing your drawing to a smaller, faster, cheaper device than the big, expensive, slow plotter on which you finally plot your drawing. Because they're cheap and fast, laser printers are being used more and more for this function. The only problem is that a laser print is small and monochrome, so not all problems are visible in the check print. But in terms of time and money, a check print is nearly free of charge compared to a plot, so detecting even an occasional problem this way makes check prints more than worthwhile.

And before every check print you do, you should do at least one *plot preview*. The on-screen plot preview is a nearly perfect complement to a check print. The plot preview is in color, which eliminates the drawback of a check print. And although the plot preview is small, you can use it to zoom in on possible trouble spots, possibly spotting — and eliminating — potential problems in your final plot.

Plot previews are also valuable early in the drawing process, just after you set up your drawing. Draw a few rectangles to represent roughly the objects you'll be drawing and then do a plot preview. The results may surprise you; if they do, you get a chance to fix problems early, saving hours of work and rework.

Doing a partial plot preview

A *partial plot preview* shows only a rectangle that represents the limits of the area you're plotting, overlaid on a rectangle that represents the paper you're plotting on. The following steps show you how to do a partial plot preview:

1. **Open the Plot Configuration dialog box by using one of the following methods:**

   - Type **PLOT** at the command prompt and press Enter.

   - Click the Print icon on the standard toolbar (Windows only).

   - Choose File⇨Print from the menu bar (DOS and Windows).

   The Plot Configuration dialog box appears.

2. **Click the Partial radio button.**

3. **Click the Preview button.**

   The Preview Effective Plotting Area dialog box appears, as shown in Figure 13-2. This dialog box appears only if you do a partial plot preview. Its only function is to show what the plotting area will look like.

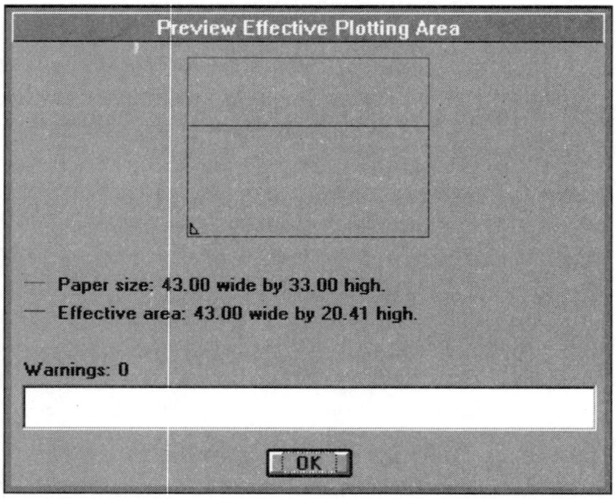

Figure 13-2:
The Preview Effective Plotting Area dialog box.

Preview Effective Plotting Area

Paper size: 43.00 wide by 33.00 high.
Effective area: 43.00 wide by 20.41 high.

Warnings: 0

OK

4. **Click OK to close the Preview Effective Plotting Area dialog box and then click OK again to close the Plot Configuration dialog box.**

So now you've done a partial plot preview. What good did it do you? Well . . .

An ineffective preview?

The Preview Effective Plotting Area dialog box leaves a little to be desired in terms of helping you preview your drawing. The image of the drawing at the top of the dialog box is a little hard to figure out. The image shows only the paper and the boundary of the drawing; none of the objects in the drawing appear in the image.

The *effective area,* that is, the boundary of the drawing area that you're plotting, appears in blue with a blue triangle. This blue triangle, the *Rotation icon,* represents the rotation of the drawing that you specify elsewhere in the Plot Configuration dialog box. (See the section "Scale, Rotation, and Origin," later in this chapter, for more information on your drawing's rotation.)

The paper size appears as a red rectangle. The paper size dimensions are the part of the paper that you can print on, not the actual paper size. (See the section "Paper Size and Orientation," later in this chapter, for more information on paper size.)

At the bottom of the dialog box, AutoCAD displays any warnings about problems that would otherwise occur if you plot the drawing. A warning may say, for example, that part of the area you're plotting lies outside the boundaries of the paper. AutoCAD's advance warning can save you time if you're actually ready to plot.

Doing a full plot preview

A *full preview* shows the entire plot on-screen. It takes more time than a partial plot preview but shows the actual objects that you plot and is quite a bit more useful. The following steps show you how to do a full plot preview:

1. **Open the Plot Configuration dialog box, as described in step 1 of the preceding section.**

2. **Click the F__u__ll radio button.**

3. **Click the P__r__eview button.**

   A preview of your drawing appears. If you're working on a complex drawing, AutoCAD may take some time creating the preview. A rectangle indicates the boundaries of the printable area. Along with the preview is a small Plot Preview dialog box containing the options P__a__n and Zoom and E__n__d Preview. Figure 13-3 shows a full plot preview.

4. **To inspect the drawing further, click P__a__n and Zoom in the Plot Preview dialog box.**

   This option opens a view box that works like the one in the Dynamic option of the ZOOM command (see Figure 13-4), as described in Chapter 9: Pan first; then move the box to establish the left edge of the area to zoom in on.

Next, click to move into zoom mode; grow and shrink the box, and slide it up and down to get the zoom area right. Click again to pan again. After you finally have the view you want, press the spacebar or Enter to zoom in.

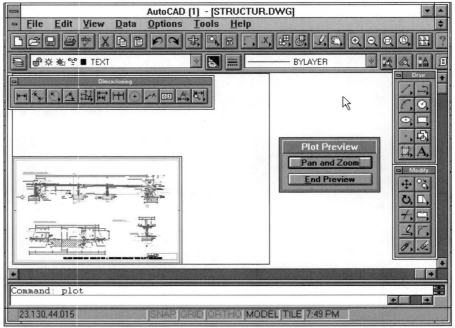

Figure 13-3:
A full plot preview showing the full plot in the lower left corner of the screen and a Plot Preview dialog box on the right side of the screen displaying additional options.

If your previous choice was Pan and Zoom, a new Plot Preview dialog box appears that enables you to return to the overall preview (by choosing the Zoom Preview option) or to end the preview (End Preview again). Choose one course or the other.

If you choose Zoom Previous, repeat step 4 until you've inspected as much of the drawing as you want. Then choose End Preview.

After you choose End Preview, you return to the Plot Configuration dialog box.

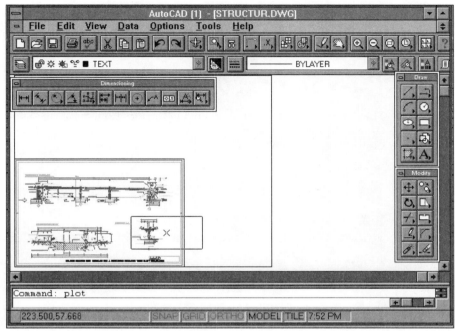

Figure 13-4:
Panning and
zooming on
the full plot
preview.

Configuring the Plot

You have many options to choose from when configuring your plot by using the Plot Configuration dialog box. In fact, you need to be careful to avoid the temptation of doing too little configuration.

Because you can rescale and reorient your drawing to fit it onto the paper you've chosen, you may be tempted to ignore the task of setting up your drawing and just fix the scale problems at plotting time. This temptation has two potential problems: First, linetype spacing needs to look right, and text must be readable in the final drawing. If you're rescaling your drawing image arbitrarily, linetypes or, especially, text are unlikely to come out right. Second, the geometry parts of your drawing need to fit a recognizable scale, such as 1" = 1 foot. Your scale is not likely to be recognizable if, at the last minute, you shrink your drawing by 74.36 percent to fit it onto the paper.

The options in the Plot Configuration dialog box are so numerous that you really must experiment with them to get a feel for how to use them well. This section just discusses the general areas of the dialog box so that you can quickly head to the part that you need to adjust.

You can do a preview of the plotting changes you make "free of charge" by using the Plot Preview option. In other words, don't waste time or paper on an incorrect plot — use plot preview.

Paper Size and Orientation

The Paper Size and Orientation area of the Plot Configuration dialog box, as shown in Figure 13-5, is where you should start the process of telling your drawing how to print itself.

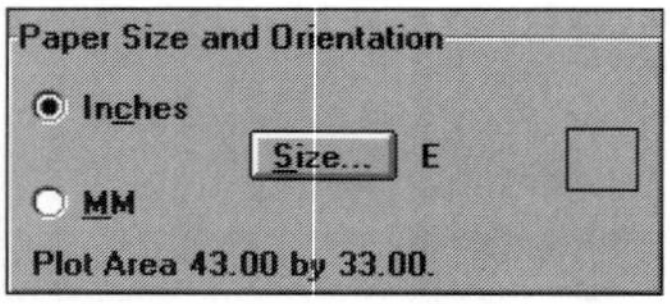

Figure 13-5:
The Paper Size and Orientation area of the Plot Configuration dialog box.

Paper Size and Orientation

◉ In**ch**es

○ **MM**

[Si**z**e...] E

Plot Area 43.00 by 33.00.

The first thing you should do is specify inches or millimeters as the plotting units, whichever is natural for the paper and drawing scale you're using. This specification affects how you set up the plot scale in the Scale, Rotation, and Origin area of the Plot Configuration dialog box.

Next to the Size button is a designation of the currently selected paper size—in this case, E. (You can find a review of some of the more common paper sizes in the sidebar "A few thoughts on paper," back in Chapter 5.) You can change the paper size by clicking the Size button. The Paper Size dialog box appears containing a list of all the standard paper sizes your plotter can handle (see Figure 13-6). You can also specify up to five user-defined paper sizes to appear in this list. (To add to the list, just enter a new width and height in one of the USER size areas.) Finish by selecting the paper size you want from the list and clicking OK. The Plot Configuration dialog box reappears.

Also next to the Size button is a pictoral representation of the plotter orientation. *Orientation* means that your plot can be either *portrait* (long axis on the vertical) or *landscape* (long axis on the horizonal). If the orientation isn't what you need it to be, you can change it in the next area of the dialog box.

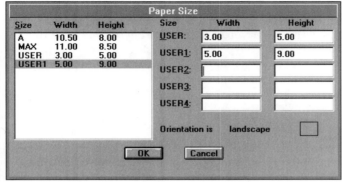

Figure 13-6:
The Paper
Size dialog
box of the
Plot
Configuration
dialog box.

Scale, Rotation, and Origin

The Scale, Rotation, and Origin area of the Plot Configuration dialog box, as shown in Figure 13-7, enables you to adjust the appearance of your drawing on the final plot. You can specify the scale you want your drawing plotted at, effectively zooming in or out; change the location of the drawing's origin (usually the lower left corner of your drawing), which has the same effect as panning; and change the rotation of the drawing so that the drawing is plotted at different orientations on the paper.

Figure 13-7:
The Scale,
Rotation,
and Origin
area of the
Plot
Configuration
dialog box.

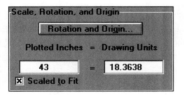

 If turned on, the Scaled to Fit option forces the plot area to fill the entire available paper size. This option also displays the ratio of plotted inches to units in the drawing. Each plotted inch, for example, may represent 20 drawing units; each drawing unit may be a foot, a kilometer, or any other measure, depending on how you set up and use your drawing. This is one of the great things about CAD: Your drawing can be huge or small, and you can plot it at any scale you want.

The Scaled to Fit option is especially valuable if you're printing on a different kind of paper than the paper you set up your drawing for, such as in making a check print. If the paper you're making the check print on is the same proportion and orientation as the paper you're using for the final plot, the relationship of the drawing to the paper should be the same in both cases.

If Scaled to Fit is turned off, the Plotted Inches = Drawing Units text boxes take on a new meaning, representing the scale you've created for your drawing. You can enter values in the text boxes to force a different scale for your drawing.

The Rotation and Origin button opens the Plot Rotation and Origin dialog box, as shown in Figure 13-8. This feature enables you to rotate your drawing on the plot and set the origin of the plot on the paper. You can specify where on the paper you want your drawing's lower left corner to be. (Some plotters can accept negative numbers so that the origin point is off the paper and some of the drawing is effectively cropped by the paper's edges.) If you use this dialog box, do a full plot preview to make sure that everything in your plot comes out the way you want it to.

Figure 13-8:
The Rotation and Origin dialog box, accessed by clicking the Rotation and Origin button in the Plot Configuration dialog box.

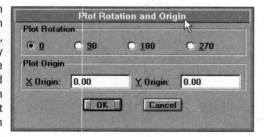

Additional Parameters

The Additional Parameters area of the Plot Configuration dialog box contains a number of loosely related options you can set (see Figure 13-9). Not all the options are available all the time; for example, the View parameter appears only if you've set up a view. The major purpose of this area, however, is to help describe which rectangular area of the drawing you're plotting. The radio buttons down the left edge of the Additional Parameters area control this function.

Figure 13-9:
The
Additional
Parameters
area of the
Plot
Configuration
dialog box.

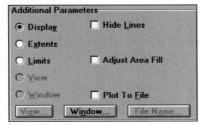

The Display, Extents, and Limits radio buttons are just about always available. Display plots the current viewport. (If you divide the drawing area into multiple viewpoints, as described in Chapter 14, the current one is simply the one you're working on right now.) Limits plots everything within the drawing limits, which you set by using the LIMITS command, as described in Chapter 5. Extents is tricky; it plots everything in the drawing extents, which is either the drawing limits or the rectangle that includes all objects in the drawing if one or more objects lie outside the current limits. But you can update the extents only by using a ZOOM ALL or ZOOM EXTENTS command. So enter one of these commands before clicking the Extents radio button.

To use the View radio button, first click the View button at the bottom of the area. (Remember, this button is available only if you've saved at least one view. Views are described in Chapter 14.) The View button opens the View Name dialog box, which enables you to select any named view (see Figure 13-10). After you select a view, the View radio button becomes available in the Additional Parameters area of the Plot Configuration dialog box.

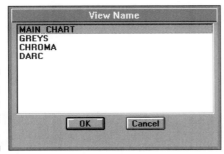

Figure 13-10:
The View
Name dialog
box.

To use the Window radio button, first click the Window button at the bottom of the area. This button opens the Window Selection dialog box, which enables you to specify any rectangular area on-screen that you want to plot (see Figure 13-11). You can use the Pick button to pick the corners if the area is completely visible on-screen; otherwise, you can enter the coordinates of the corners. After you specify a window, the Window radio button becomes available in the Plot Configuration dialog box.

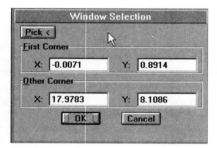

Figure 13-11:
The
Window
Selection
dialog box.

Other options in the Additional Parameters area of the Plot Configuration dialog box include Hide Lines, which removes hidden lines before plotting; Adjust Area Fill, which reduces boundaries of filled areas by one-half the pen width (to improve accuracy); and Plot to File, which enables you to plot to a disk file.

After you click the Plot to File check box, the File Name button becomes available to open a dialog box, in which you can enter a file name to plot to. If you don't enter a file name, the file name used is the current drawing name plus the extension PLT. Then you can copy the PLT file to the plotter or use it as a file to send to another AutoCAD user. AutoCAD PLT files are usually much smaller than AutoCAD DWG files. (To copy a file to the plotter, go to the DOS prompt and type **copy filename.plt prn**. Then press Enter.)

Configuring the Plotter

Configuring the plotter (or *device*, as it's called in several areas of the Plot Configuration dialog box) simply means, in this case, selecting the plotter or printer name (that of the one available to you) from the list that AutoCAD supplies and then setting up any pen-related options that are available. You actually configure a plotter during AutoCAD configuration; see the AutoCAD documentation for more information.

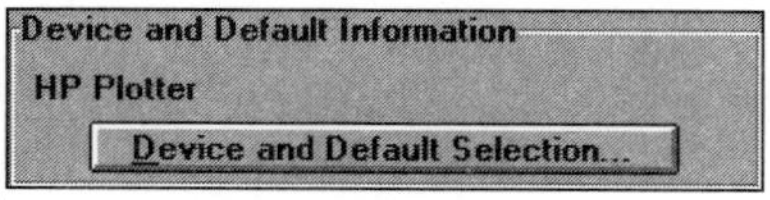

Figure 13-12:
The Device
and Default
Information
area of
the Plot
Configuration
dialog box.

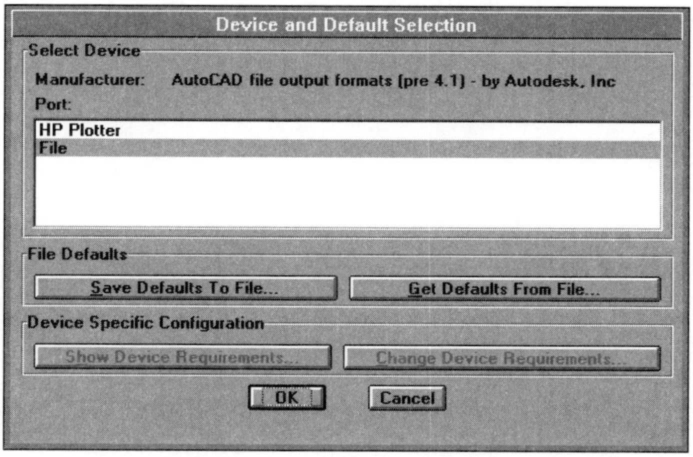

Figure 13-13:
The Device
and Default
Selection
dialog box.

The Device and Default Information area of the Plot Configuration dialog box, as shown in Figure 13-12, contains a single button: Device and Default Selection. This button opens, naturally enough, the Device and Default Selection dialog box , as shown in Figure 13-13. This dialog box enables you to save to and retrieve printer defaults from a file, as well as show and change the device requirements of your plotter. Although the options available vary greatly from one plotter or printer to another, this dialog box gives you considerable flexibility in managing them.

The Pen Parameters area of the Plot Configuration dialog box, as shown in Figure 13-14, contains two buttons: Pen Assignments and Optimization.

The Pen Assignments button is available only if a pen plotter is configured, and it opens the Pen Assignments dialog box, as shown in Figure 13-15. You can use this dialog box to specify the pen number assigned to each AutoCAD color, the linetype, the speed, and the pen width. (You can't edit all features on all plotters.) The Feature Legend button in the Pen Assignments dialog box displays information specific to the selected plotter. In the case of a specific Hewlett-Packard plotter, for example, the Feature Legend button opens a display of available linetypes.

Figure 13-14:
The Pen
Parameters
area of the
Plot
Configuration
dialog box.

Figure 13-15:
The Pen
Assignments
dialog box.

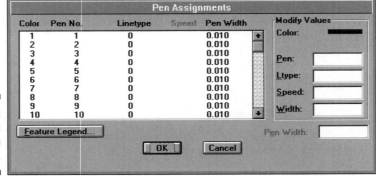

The Optimization button opens the Optimizing Pen Motion dialog box. You can find more about this feature in the following section.

Plotting and Performance

You can optimize plotting performance in AutoCAD a number of ways. Some of these optimizations are printer- or plotter-specific, and other users of the same device, or even the device's manufacturer, can be welcome sources of information about them.

You can also save time with a few general tips. Although it may seem obvious, plotting less stuff results in a faster plot. So turn off any layers that you don't need for the current plot before you start it. This is especially true if you have a border or a title block around your drawing. If you turn off the border, AutoCAD can plot the next line much quicker than if it must always draw a border line on the far right edge of the paper. You may even want to design your drawing so that areas along the right edge of the paper are empty where possible, enabling AutoCAD to do a carriage return that much more quickly.

You can also optimize pen motion by using the Optimizing Pen Motion dialog box, as shown in Figure 13-16. You open this dialog box by clicking the Optimization button in the Plot Configuration dialog box.

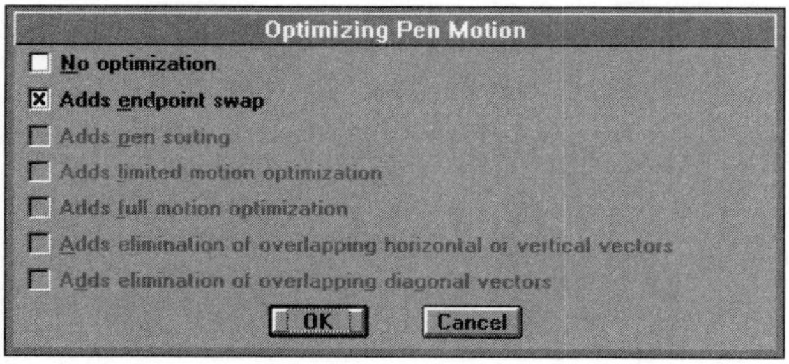

Optimizing Pen Motion

- ☐ No optimization
- ☒ Adds endpoint swap
- ☐ Adds pen sorting
- ☐ Adds limited motion optimization
- ☐ Adds full motion optimization
- ☐ Adds elimination of overlapping horizontal or vertical vectors
- ☐ Adds elimination of overlapping diagonal vectors

[OK] [Cancel]

Figure 13-16:
The Optimizing Pen Motion dialog box.

You will probably need to experiment with these options, or ask other users, to get the most out of them and their possibilities. In general, however, the default setting should be sufficient until you start plotting some really large AutoCAD drawings. The following chapter, in the meantime, shows you how to create some snazzy plots by using paper space.

Part IV
Having It Your Way

WHILE SEEKING HER PC-BASED RECIPE INDEX, DEBBY INADVERTENTLY LOADS A CAD PROGRAM. INSTEAD OF MAKING CHERRIES JUBILEE, SHE BUILDS A SUBOCEANIC DIVING PROBE.

In this part...

Setting up, drawing, dimensioning, hatching, and plotting are among the elements at the heart of AutoCAD. Becoming proficient at AutoCAD means mastering these basics until you can make AutoCAD work just the way you want it to work. But AutoCAD enables you to do so much more! Paper space turns AutoCAD into a kind of homegrown desktop publishing program for graphics. Blocks and external references help you manage data within drawings, between drawings, and even across a network. 3D commands enable you to do a whole new kind of work in AutoCAD, without buying any add-on packages or a different program. Together, these options extend AutoCAD's capabilities beyond anything possible without a computer — and even beyond those of just about any other drawing/ drafting program in existence.

Chapter 14

The Paper Space Chase

*O*ne of the biggest conceptual leaps in the development of AutoCAD was the addition of *paper space* in Release 11. Paper space enables you to create a set of windows to add to your drawing that you can then print, enabling you to rework the appearance of your printed drawing without changing the underlying geometry. Although much of CAD is an attempt to reproduce, or incrementally improve on, the pencil-and-paper work environment, paper space is a leap forward toward getting more out of the computer.

On the other hand, paper space is not strictly necessary for most work. Paper space is an "extra" that gives you a way to create many plotted views of your drawing efficiently.

This chapter discusses what paper space is and how to use it, how to set up paper space, and how to use the MVSETUP utlility.

Why Paper Space

Before moving forward, it is important to define paper space in more depth; many experienced AutoCAD users don't do much with it, and it's conceptually difficult for most novices to grasp.

Paper space is the opposite of *model space*. In model space, which is the only space discussed so far in this book, you draw objects, combine them into models — a circle is an object; a steering wheel is a model — and then print the result. Model space can print only one viewport at a time. In paper space, you can use previously drawn objects, combine different ways of looking at them, and then print the result. Paper space can print multiple viewports at a time. Figure 14-1 shows some work in progress in paper space. Notice that the "X-Y" icon that normally appears in the lower left corner of the drawing area—the UCS (User Coordinate System) icon—changes to a triangular shape. This change indicates that paper space is in effect.

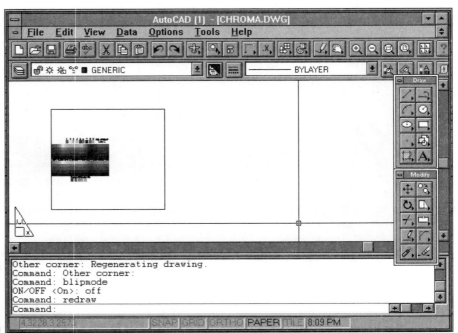

Figure 14-1:
Working in
paper space.

Using paper space is like creating a page in a magazine. You arrange text and graphics as needed to best communicate information to the person who will receive the printed output (though a drawing from AutoCAD tends to have more graphics than most magazine pages). You move around and resize each element freely to get the overall effect you want. And you don't need to choose from just one image of something that you want to show; you can take almost any view on it that you want.

In AutoCAD, the graphics come from views on your drawing. Each view is displayed in a rectangular area called a *viewport*. You can mix and match different sizes of viewports, and different kinds of views within the viewports, to achieve the desired overall effect. And you can do all this without changing anything in the underlying drawing.

When to launch paper space

Paper space adds some additional maintenance and work to your drawing. Paper space also has some performance concerns that limit its general usefulness. Making changes to your drawing in paper space, for example, causes time-consuming regenerations. And you can misunderstand paper space as a place to fix things that aren't right with the underlying drawing instead of fixing the drawing itself. Fixing problems in paper space is usually harder than fixing them in the underlying drawing and *much* harder than doing it right in the first place — which is why this book contains so much setup information. So use paper space sparingly, and when you do use it, take a gradual approach; otherwise, you may end up starting over again with a simpler drawing a couple hours before a deadline.

The main time you need paper space is when you want to place different views of the same objects on one sheet of paper. Without paper space, you would need to redraw the objects from every different point of view; with paper space, you can simply create multiple views of the same objects and combine them on the same sheet.

Think twice before using paper space, however, unless your needs are similar to those described in one of the following situations:

- **Different layers.** You want to show different groups of layers of a model so that different views of the model appear in different areas of the printout.

- **Different zooms.** You want to show different zoom resolutions of a model on the same printed sheet — for example, an overall plan and a zoomed-in detail of part of the plan.

- **See in 3D.** To show what a 3D (three-dimensional) object looks like, you usually need to show multiple views of the object from different points of view on the same printed sheet. Paper space is ideal for this kind of work.

Why not paper space?

Paper space creates a whole 'nother level of things to worry about, over and above the problems you encounter in model space. In AutoCAD, getting yourself into situations where you spend more time learning than you do drawing is easy enough to do in model space; with paper space, these situations can multiply. So try to stay out of paper space as much as you can, especially if you're still on the steep part of the learning curve for AutoCAD as a whole.

If that's not enough reason to avoid paper space, consider the following alternatives:

- ✔ **Regenerations.** No, this isn't the name of a new *Star Trek* movie (such as the one in which Captain Kirk comes back, dies, survives, dies again . . .); it's what happens every time you zoom or pan in paper space. Yes, *every time* you zoom or pan in paper space, AutoCAD regenerates the drawing. Switching between paper space and model space also requires a regen. Because you are more likely to use paper space for complex 2D or 3D models, this kind of recurring regeneration can be a daunting prospect.

- ✔ **Time sink.** Just as in any other program where appearances are the focus of your task, working in paper space can be a real time drain. Trying to get the viewports set up just right, changing the angle in the view, and other tasks can literally take hours. Fortunately, after you learn the right settings, you can apply them to any other drawing you do.

- ✔ **Other ways to do it.** Many times you can get a paper-spacelike effect without going into paper space. To combine views of pieces from several drawings, for example, you can create a new drawing in model space and then use external references (as described in Chapter 15) to pull in views of different pieces.

Safe space

Although paper space is very powerful, it's also kind of scary. Whenever it does make sense to use paper space, how can you avoid the dangers and get the most out of it?

The following tips may give you a few clues:

- ✔ **Try other approaches first.** Try doing in model space what you are trying to do in paper space. Use the VIEWPORT command in model space viewpoints, for example, to show your work at various viewing angles. Even if you then go into paper space, you'll have done some of the work already and should have a much better understanding of the rest of your task. You then can use in paper space what you've already done in model space.

✔ **Careful setup.** As in other areas of AutoCAD, you can maximize your chances of ending up with a useful drawing in a reasonable amount of time if you're careful about setup. Luckily, AutoCAD includes a setup program, called MVSETUP, that is a big help in setting up paper space. You can wade through more on MVSETUP later in this chapter.

✔ **Get incremental.** Try to create a simple, useful drawing in paper space first. Before trying more elaborate drawings, save the simple version someplace safe and then go on. This step leaves you with a fallback if you run out of time, patience, or the ability to deal with the more complex parts of AutoCAD.

✔ **Don't pan, zoom, or switch.** If working in a paper space viewport, minimize panning, zooming, and switching between paper space and model space, because all these tasks require regens. This lack of flexibility is another reason to take on simple tasks first when using paper space.

The following section describes how to use MVSETUP, which is certainly *not* flexible, but which does provide a structured way to help you get into using paper space. Use MVSETUP at least the first few times you try paper space and then experiment on your own as you glean a better understanding of what is and isn't easy— and possible.

Setting up Paper Space

You can set up paper space by using individual commands or through MVSETUP. Because MVSETUP takes you through the process in steps, you should use it first. You can then try individual commands on your later paper space efforts.

Using MVSETUP

The following steps are long, but they help you get paper space going effectively. (Imagine how many different things you'd need to remember if not for these steps!) From a high-level point of view, the parts of the process are as follows:

✔ Create a *title block*—an area of the drawing in which you enter the drawing name, the drafter's name, and any other relevant descriptive information you want to include.

✔ Create viewports.

✔ Get the model into the viewports.

The following 15 steps (Yikes! 15 steps? Isn't there a lite version?) show you how to set up paper space by using the MVSETUP program:

1. **Turn on paper space by double-clicking the MODEL button on the status bar to change to PAPER (Windows only) or by choosing View⇨Paper Space from the menu bar.**

   The UCS icon switches from its usual "X-Y" configuration to a triangular shape to indicate that paper space is on.

2. **Start MVSETUP by typing MVSETUP at the command prompt and pressing Enter or (but only with paper space on) by choosing View⇨FloatingViewpoints⇨MV Setup from the menu bar.**

   Note: If you start MVSETUP with paper space off, the program asks whether you want to turn on paper space. If you answer yes, MVSETUP works as described in these steps. But if you say no, MVSETUP works as a model space setup program, although you still need to complete some steps after it's finished.

3. **Type Options at the command line and press Enter.**

4. **Create a layer for the title block by typing Layer at the command line, followed by the name of the layer, and pressing Enter.**

   The layer name can be either an existing or a new layer name.

   You should put the paper space stuff — title block, viewports, and so on — on a separate layer or on a group of layers with names that start with the same character or two. You can create layers PSTITLE and PSVIEWS, for example, to hold the title block and viewports, respectively.

5. **To reset the drawing limits so that they enclose the paper space border, type Limits at the command line, press Enter, and then type Yes and press Enter again.**

6. **To specify how you want paper space units expressed, type Units and press Enter, then enter Feet, Inches, Meters, or Millimeters at the command prompt.**

   You can use the **Xref** option to attach or insert an external reference as a title block at this point. (Xrefs are explained in Chapter 15.)

7. **Press Enter to return to the original prompt that lists the options.**

8. **Type Title block at the original command prompt and press Enter.**

9. **Specify the origin of the border by entering Origin at the command prompt, and then press Enter.**

   This selects the Insert Title Block option, which is the default.

10. **Type the new location of the border, or click the new location in the drawing area, and press Enter.**

    AutoCAD opens a text window that lists the options for paper size. Figure 14-2 shows this text window.

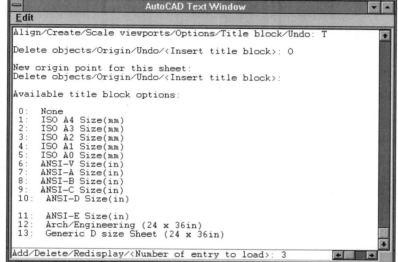

Figure 14-2: An AutoCAD Text Window displays the options for paper sizes.

```
                         AutoCAD Text Window
 Edit
Align/Create/Scale viewports/Options/Title block/Undo: T

Delete objects/Origin/Undo/<Insert title block>: O

New origin point for this sheet:
Delete objects/Origin/Undo/<Insert title block>:

Available title block options:

 0:   None
 1:   ISO A4 Size(mm)
 2:   ISO A3 Size(mm)
 3:   ISO A2 Size(mm)
 4:   ISO A1 Size(mm)
 5:   ISO A0 Size(mm)
 6:   ANSI-V Size(in)
 7:   ANSI-A Size(in)
 8:   ANSI-B Size(in)
 9:   ANSI-C Size(in)
10:   ANSI-D Size(in)

11:   ANSI-E Size(in)
12:   Arch/Engineering (24 x 36in)
13:   Generic D size Sheet (24 x 36in)

Add/Delete/Redisplay/<Number of entry to load>: 3
```

Be careful what you enter when choosing paper size; typing *A* for paper size *A*, for example, instead of the option number that AutoCAD lists, which is *7,* is all too easy an error to make.

11. **Type the number that corresponds to the paper size you want to use and press Enter.**

    AutoCAD closes the text window and then inserts the title block and border. Figure 14-3 shows the screen with title block and border.

12. **Insert the title block and border components as objects or save them separately.**

    Type **No** if you don't want to save the title block and border components; type **Yes** to save them separately. Then press Enter.

    After you finish MVSETUP, AutoCAD saves the current version of the title block and border and inserts it the next time you create the same title block and border with MVSETUP. You can modify the file and save it under the same name so that AutoCAD can load your custom file in the future.

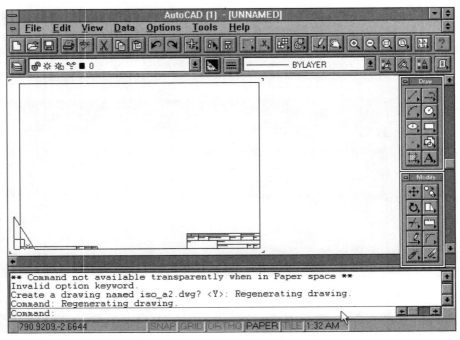

Figure 14-3:
The
AutoCAD
drawing
area with a
title block
and border
for ISO A2-
size paper.

13. **Type** Create **on the command line and press Enter to start the process of creating viewports.**

14. **Type** Create viewports **on the command line and press Enter to create the viewport(s).**

    AutoCAD opens a text window and lists the options for viewport creation. Figure 14-4 shows this text window.

15. **To specify the size and location of the viewport(s), enter the number corresponding to the option you want.**

    Notice that the size of the viewports is in paper units; for example, an 8-by-10-inch viewport fills a letter-sized sheet of paper.

    Use the following list as a guide in determining the viewport(s) you want:

    - **0** (None) creates no viewports.
    - **1** (Single) creates one viewport. You specify size by using the mouse or by typing in the locations of the viewport's corners.

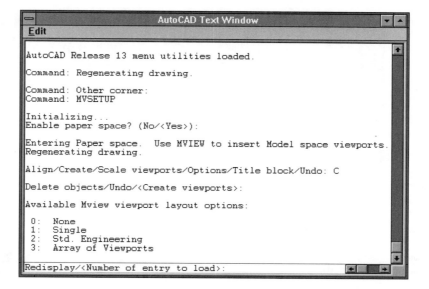

```
┌─────────────────────────────────────────────────────────┐
│ ─                    AutoCAD Text Window              ▼ ▲ │
│ E̲dit                                                      │
│ ┌─────────────────────────────────────────────────────┐▲│
│ │AutoCAD Release 13 menu utilities loaded.            │ │
│ │                                                      │ │
│ │Command: Regenerating drawing.                        │ │
│ │                                                      │ │
│ │Command: Other corner:                                │ │
│ │Command: MVSETUP                                      │ │
│ │                                                      │ │
│ │Initializing...                                       │ │
│ │Enable paper space? (No/<Yes>):                       │ │
│ │                                                      │ │
│ │Entering Paper space.  Use MVIEW to insert Model space│ │
│ │Regenerating drawing.                        viewports.│ │
│ │                                                      │ │
│ │Align/Create/Scale viewports/Options/Title block/Undo: C│ │
│ │                                                      │ │
│ │Delete objects/Undo/<Create viewports>:               │ │
│ │                                                      │ │
│ │Available Mview viewport layout options:              │ │
│ │                                                      │ │
│ │  0:  None                                            │ │
│ │  1:  Single                                          │ │
│ │  2:  Std. Engineering                                │ │
│ │  3:  Array of Viewports                             │▼│
│ │Redisplay/<Number of entry to load>:          ◄ ▮ ►   │ │
│ └─────────────────────────────────────────────────────┘ │
└─────────────────────────────────────────────────────────┘
```

Figure 14-4: An AutoCAD text window displays the options for viewport creation.

- **2** (Std. Engineering) creates a set of four equal-sized viewports. Specify the area that is to contain the four viewports and the X and Y distance between viewports.

- **3** (Array of Viewports) creates an array of as many columns and rows of viewports as you specify. Enter the number of columns of viewports (X), the number of rows of viewports (Y), the area into which you want to insert the viewports, and the X and Y distance between viewports. Figure 14-5 shows an array of three columns of viewports by two rows of viewports.

Congratulations! You just created a title block and several paper space viewports.

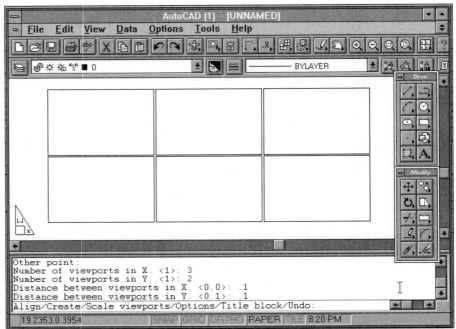

Figure 14-5:
An array
of six
viewports.

Using (paper) space(y) commands

You can also set up paper space by using commands entered on the command line. The important commands are as follows:

- ✔ TILEMODE. Moves back and forth between model space (SET TILEMODE = 1) and paper space (TILEMODE = 0).

- ✔ MVIEW. Controls the number and layout of paper space viewports. (MVSETUP uses the MVIEW command but doesn't enable you to see it directly.)

- ✔ MSPACE/PSPACE. Moves back and forth "inside" paper space viewports (the model space inside a viewport) and into paper space itself.

- ✔ VPLAYER. Turns layer visibility on and off in a specific viewport.

- ✔ ZOOM XP. The XP option of the ZOOM command zooms relative to paper space units rather than model space units. To show an entire drawing, use ZOOM 1XP; to show close-ups, use a value less than one. (To see your model correctly if it was drawn at $1/8' = 1'$sp, for example, use ZOOM 1/96XP.)

Using paper space viewports

After you have gone into paper space and created viewports, you can use the following three ways to access your drawing:

- ✔ **Paper space.** Working in paper space, you can change viewport sizes, arrange the viewport layout, add text to the title block, or add notes to the drawing. None of this activity affects the underlying model space drawing.

- ✔ **Model space viewports in paper space.** If in paper space, use the MSPACE command to work in model space within the viewports. Use PAN, ZOOM XP, and VPLAYER to change the appearance of your model and the displayed layer within each viewport. Limits, snap, and grid settings are kept in paper space, so you can change these settings in a viewport without affecting the underlying drawing.

- ✔ **Paper space off.** Turning off paper space returns you to your original model space drawing; all signs of paper space disappear. After you return to paper space, changes in the underlying drawing are reflected in the viewports.

To exit paper space completely, type **TILEMODE 1** on the command line and press Enter. To return, type **TILEMODE 0** and press Enter.

This information is enough for a good start, but you can learn many more things to get the most out of paper space. After you've used MVSETUP and created a drawing or two using paper space, see the AutoCAD documentation for more details.

Chapter 15

Playing with Blocks

. . . .

. . . .

A thing of beauty is a joy forever, as the old saying goes. But if you work and work on a drawing until it's a thing of beauty, you must be able to reuse it to make it a joy forever. Reusability is also a *huge* advantage of CAD over paper drafting. That's where AutoCAD's *blocks* and *external references* come in.

A *block* is a collection of objects grouped together to form a single object. A block can live within a specific drawing, or you can export a block so that multiple drawings can reference it. At any time, you can *explode* the block — that is, divide it back—into the objects that make it up and edit them.

An *external reference* is like an industrial strength block. An external reference is a pointer to a separate drawing outside the drawing you're working on. The referenced drawing then appears on-screen and in printouts as part of the original drawing so that you can use a whole drawing overlaid onto another drawing without increasing the size of the second drawing. But you can't explode the external reference; you can only change its appearance by editing the externally referenced drawing. If you do this, the appearance of the drawing changes in *all* the other drawings that reference it.

When should you use a block or an external reference? You should start with blocks; using blocks is what you'll do most often for individual work. Blocks save storage space within a drawing and make work more convenient. Writing out a block to a separate file by using the WBLOCK command is an intermediate step and makes the block more easily accessible to multiple drawings, while preserving the capability to explode the block. An external reference is for truly serious data sharing and is used most often in a networked environment, with multiple users sharing data files. Your own preferences and work style, however, as well as the standards in your organization if you work in a group, ultimately determine how you use blocks and external references.

This chapter describes how to use both blocks and external references. (What a coincidence, considering that's what I was just talking about! Wonder of wonders . . .) Try these features out and then use each as often as makes sense for your work.

Rock and Block

First, a little more block theory and then you can rock right into those blocks.

A block — formally called a *block definition* — is a collection of objects stored together under a single name. Convenience isn't the only reason for using blocks; blocks are also great file storage savers. Repeatedly using a block within the same drawing takes up only a little bit of storage space for each use, and AutoCAD stores only a single use of the block definition itself in each drawing.

Blocks are great for convenience and storage savings within a drawing. Blocks *aren't* great for drawing elements used in multiple drawings, however, especially in a multiuser environment. That's because blocks, after they get into multiple drawings, stay there; a later modification to the original block does not automatically modify all the drawings that use that block. So if you use a block with your company's name in a number of drawings and then decide to use fancier lettering on the name, you must make the change within each drawing that uses the block. External references, however, do enable you to modify multiple drawings from the original referenced drawing. (But you can learn more about external references in the section "Going External," later in this chapter.)

Still, blocks are important and convenient; they save file space and organize your drawing better. So take the time to learn about blocks and then use them as much as possible.

Creating and writing out blocks

To create a block, you can either use the BLOCK command to create a block for local use in the current drawing, or you can use the WBLOCK command to write the block out to its own file. (In other words, you can transform a block into a drawing simply by using the WBLOCK command.) The WBLOCK command enables you to access a block from other drawings but takes up more storage space and brings up maintenance concerns if, for example, you have different layer names in the main drawing and in the block. Use the BLOCK command first and the WBLOCK command if you need a block available to all your other drawings. (If, for example, you use a particular bolt in several drawings, you can write it out as a block and then reuse it elsewhere.)

To create a block for use within the current drawing, use the BLOCK command. The following steps show you how:

1. **Start the BLOCK command by using one of the following methods:**

   - Type **BLOCK** at the command prompt and press Enter.

   - Click the Block icon (the overlapping rectangle and circle) from the Block icon flyout on the Draw floating toolbar (Windows only).

   - Choose Construct⇨Block from the menu bar (DOS only).

   Whenever you create a block, notice what AutoCAD layer is current — that is, what layer you're working on. In AutoCAD, layer 0 is known as a *construction layer* for blocks. If you create a block on layer 0, it always inherits the color and linetype of the layer on which it is inserted. If you create a block on *any* other layer, it always retains the color and linetype in effect when it was created. Think of blocks created on layer 0 as chameleons. (And if you don't know what a chameleon is, ask a biology teacher.)

2. **Type the block name at the command prompt and press Enter.**

   You must name the block before you create it, so have a good name thought up in advance. (Hmmm — how 'bout "Frankenstein"? Oh, been used before . . .?)

   If you use the name of an existing block, AutoCAD redefines that block with the new group of objects you select. AutoCAD then updates all instances of the block in the current drawing to match the new block. This is a good reason to have all your blocks' names written down, along with a picture of what they look like. (You can store this information in a separate file— or a handwritten note.) Redefining all instances of a block just by using the same name for them can be a powerful feature. On the other hand, it can be an unintended mistake, too.

3. **Specify the insertion point by clicking a point on-screen or typing the coordinates of the point at the command line and pressing Enter.**

This is the point on the block where you insert the object after copies of the block are used elsewhere.

Try to use a consistent point on the group of objects for the insertion point, such as the upper left corner. This way you'll always know what to expect when you insert the block. (Some people mark the insertion point with a tiny cross or circle.)

4. **Select the objects that you want as part of the block.**

Figure 15-1 shows a group of selected objects that are part of a block. (The dashed linetype shows which objects are selected.) The figure also shows the commands that created this block.

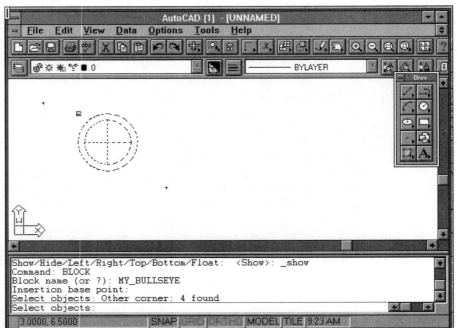

Figure 15-1:
Selecting objects for a block.

5. **Press Enter to complete the selection process.**

Your objects disappear! AutoCAD has stored the block, however, and the block is ready to use. If you want the objects to appear in the same spot they were in before you blocked them, you must reinsert them.

6. **Type** INSERT **or** DDINSERT **at the command line and press Enter to reinsert the block (see the following section); or type** OOPS **at the command line and press Enter to retrieve the individual objects and place them back where they were.**

   The block remains available in the drawing, whether visible or not. You can now use the original objects, add some new geometry, and create another block.

The following example shows the summary of commands you need to create a block:

```
Command: BLOCK
Block name (or ?): MY_BULLSEYE
Insertion base point: <Pick a point on or near the block>
Select objects: <Select objects
Select objects: <Press Enter>
```

To create a block and write it out for use with multiple drawings, use the WBLOCK command. The following steps show you how to do this:

1. **Type** WBLOCK **at the command prompt and press Enter to start the WBLOCK command.**

2. **Type the block name at the command prompt and press Enter.**

   You can type the name of an existing block and press Enter to write that block to a file; you can just press Enter to specify that the existing block and the output file have the same name; or you can type * to specify that the entire drawing be written to an output file.

3. **Select the objects to write out as a block.**

4. **Specify the insertion base point and press Enter.**

   Your objects disappear! AutoCAD stores the block as a file, however, just as before, and the block is ready to use. If you want the objects to appear in the same spot they were in before you blocked them, you must reinsert them.

5. **Type** INSERT **or** DDINSERT **at the command line and press Enter to reinsert the block (see the following section); or type** OOPS **at the command line and press Enter to retrieve the individual objects and place them back where they were.**

   The block remains available.

Put all the blocks you write into one subdirectory or set of subdirectories. AutoCAD's performance then improves whenever you browse for a block, because the program doesn't need to load extraneous file names. And *your* performance improves because you'll know where to look for a block. You also won't need to include the BLK extension in the filenames of block files so that you can find them later. You can do the same thing with external references.

Inserting blocks

AutoCAD provides you with four ways to insert a block into your drawing. The MINSERT command inserts blocks in a rectangular array. The INSERT command drives the insertion process from the command line. The DDINSERT command opens a dialog box for insertion and is the method you should use.

The fourth way to insert a block is available only in AutoCAD for Windows. You can minimize AutoCAD to an icon and then drag and drop a file's icon onto the AutoCAD icon. AutoCAD then opens and continues with the prompts for a block insert. This option is so different from most AutoCAD command interaction that it's more like a stupid pet trick; so show it to your friends, but don't bother using it unless you need some fun in your day.

To insert a block, follow these steps:

1. **Open the Insert dialog box by using one of the following methods:**

    • Type **DDINSERT** at the command prompt and press Enter.

    • Click the Insert Block icon from the Block icon flyout on the Draw floating toolbar (Windows only).

    • Choose Draw ➪ Insert from the menu bar (DOS only).

    The Insert dialog box appears, as shown in Figure 15-2.

2. **Enter the block or external filename by using one of the following methods:**

    • Enter the block name in the **B**lock text box or the filename in the **F**ile text box.

    • Click the **B**lock button to select from a list of blocks in the drawing.

    • Click the **F**ile button to select an external drawing.

    If you click **F**ile, you can modify the name in the Block text box so that the name of the block in your drawing is different from the filename.

    If you use the **F**ile button and enter the name of a block that's already in your drawing, AutoCAD updates the block in your drawing with the current contents of the file.

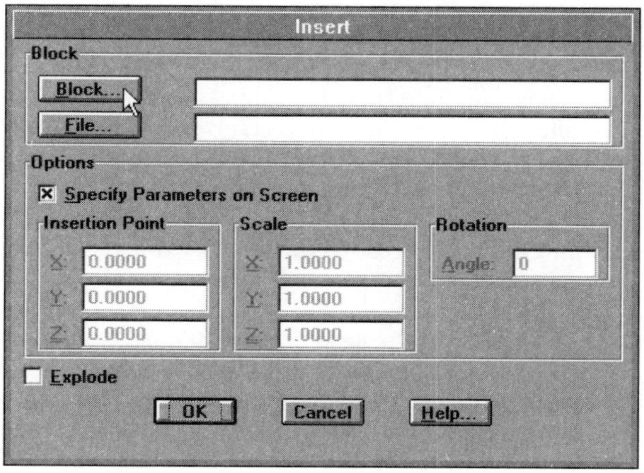

Figure 15-2:
The Insert
dialog box.

3. **Enter the insertion point, scale, and rotation angle of the block.**

   You can either click the Specify Parameters on Screen check box, to specify the parameters on-screen, or type the values you want in the Insertion Point, Scale, and Rotation text boxes.

4. **(Optional) Click the Explode check box if you want to insert the block as several individual objects rather than as a block.**

5. **Click OK.**

The GRIPBLOCK system variable controls the number of grips shown on each block. Normally, you should set GRIPBLOCK to 0, indicating that one grip is on the block (0 = 1; got that?). If you set GRIPBLOCK to 1, multiple grips appear on the block (1 = 2 or more; got that?). Drawing all those grips on each block can slow down performance. But if you use grips to snap to objects, and you want to snap to different points on a block, set GRIPBLOCK to 1 some of the time.

Exploding a block

This feature is important, but easy. Simply type the EXPLODE command at the command prompt and press Enter, click the Explode icon from the Modify floating toolbar (Windows only) or choose Modify➪Explode from the menu bar (DOS only). Then you can select the block. AutoCAD breaks down, or explodes, the block into its component objects. You can then add to the component objects to create another block or make changes to the component objects and use them to create yet another block.

Going External

In AutoCAD, an external reference (herein referred to as *Xref*) is not someone who used to be an official in a sporting contest. (Ex-ref—get it?) An Xref is a reference to another, *external* file —one outside the current drawing—that you can make act as if it's part of your drawing. Technically, a reference is simply a pointer from one file to another. The Xref is the actual pointer, but the combination of the pointer and file is often called the Xref. Drawings that you include in other drawings by means of an external reference are "Xref-ed in."

The big advantage of Xrefs over blocks is that if you change an original file, AutoCAD automatically copies the change into your drawing when you reload the Xref — that is, force an update — or when you save or reopen the drawing. This is both good and bad news.

If you improve the hatching on the screw drawing that you've Xref-ed in so that it looks better—voilá, your drawing also looks better.

But if you lengthen that screw $1/4$ inch and then decide that this isn't the change you wanted or that your plot no longer fits on a single sheet, you have problems. And if the layers in the Xref drawing and your original drawing conflict, the result is that you may just wind up with a few new layers in your drawing. (Great!) AutoCAD, fortunately, is smart enough to keep them all separate by giving the conflicting layers a new special name. You may, however, want to call your computer some of your own special —and unprintable names— if that happens.

So you need a certain amount of trust and organization to use Xrefs. If you don't have that feeling of trust (even if you simply doubt your own ability to remember what you can use an Xref for and how to update it correctly), don't use Xrefs.

The other major advantage of Xrefs over blocks is that they are not stored in your drawing even once. The storage space taken up by the original drawing you're Xref-ing in is not duplicated, no matter how many people refer to that file. (This is probably a much more efficient way than blocks to reuse other people's drawings.)

But Xrefs are basically good because they enable you to leverage your own or someone else's work easily and transparently, thereby increasing productivity.

Creating an external reference file

To create a file that you can use as an external reference, just create a drawing and save it. That's it. You can then start up a new drawing and create an external reference to the previous one. The Xref-ed drawing opens into your drawing as kind of an overlay. You can measure or object snap the Xref-ed geometry, but you can't modify or delete Xref-ed geometry until you "own" it. (More on that later in the chapter.) This is so simple that it takes a while to figure out all the opportunities Xrefs provide. But don't worry; if you've been setting up your files carefully and following some of the other suggestions in this book, you're at least mostly ready to use Xrefs.

Attaching an Xref

Attaching an external reference is easy. Just use the following steps:

1. **Start the XREF command by typing** XREF **at the command prompt and then pressing Enter to attach a file (or in DOS only, choose File ⇨ External Reference ⇨ Attach from the menu bar).**

   The Select File to Attach dialog box appears.

2. **Specify the drawing file you want from the dialog box and click OK.**

   If you use the name of an existing file, that file is redefined with the new group of objects you select. All instances of the file in the current drawing are then updated to match the new file.

3. **Specify the insertion point by clicking the mouse on-screen or typing the coordinates at the command prompt and pressing Enter.**

   The file's contents appear in monochrome on-screen.

4. **Specify the X scale factor.**

   The default factor is 1. (1 means the original scale of the file.)

5. **Specify the Y scale factor.**

   The default factor is whatever value you entered as the X scale factor.

6. **Specify the rotation angle.**

   The default is 0.

The externally referenced file appears in your file. Layers from that file also appear as layers in your file. Figure 15-3 shows an otherwise empty file, with the COLORWHeel drawing Xref-ed in, and the layers from that drawing added to it.

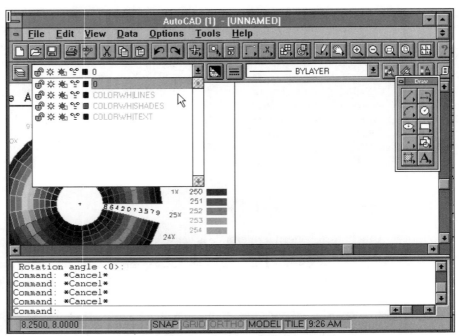

Figure 15-3:
Xref-ed
COLORWHeel
drawing and
its layers.

The following example shows the summary of commands you need to attach an Xref-ed file:

```
Command: XREF
?/Bind/Detach/Path/Reload/Overlay/<Attach>:
Attach Xref: <Select filename>
THEFILE loaded.
Block name (or ?): MY_BULLSEYE
Insertion point: <Specify the insertion point>
X scale factor <1> / Corner / XYZ:
Y scale factor (default=X):
Rotation angle <0>:
```

Detaching an Xref

If you decide you don't need an Xref in your drawing anymore, you *detach* it from your drawing. Detaching an Xref is simple, but not as easy as it could be. The following steps show you how:

1. **Start the XREF command by typing** XREF **at the command prompt and pressing Enter, and then type** Detach **and press Enter again to detach a file (or choose File ⇨ External Reference ⇨ Detach from the DOS menu bar).**

2. **Type the name of the Xref you want to detach at the command prompt and press Enter.**

   AutoCAD knows what Xrefs are in your drawing, so it *could* give you a scrolling list, just as it does for files to attach. Or it *could* have you pick a spot on-screen within the Xref-ed file that you want to get rid of. But *nooooo!* Instead, you must remember the filename and type it in yourself.

The externally referenced file disappears from your drawing. The file's layers and other data also disappear. The actual DWG file you used as an Xref, however, still exists outside your drawing.

More on Xrefs

You can do quite a bit more with Xrefs. You can permanently attach an Xref to a drawing, for example, by using the Bind option of the XREF command. You also need to watch out for people who may move your Xref-ed files out from under you, and you need to watch out for circular references, in which two or more files refer to one another in an overly intimate, if no doubt enjoyable, fashion. (Didn't know your AutoCAD files could be "X-rated," did you?) If you really have time on your hands between projects, you can even enable and monitor an Xref Log File and then use it to track your Xref history. See the AutoCAD documentation if you really want to know more about Xrefs.

Also beyond this chapter are other Xref concerns to think about: standard ways of maintaining Xref-ed files, who is in charge of changing them, and more. The information in this chapter, however, is at least enough to get you started and maybe enough to get you finished, too. If you start to use Xrefs extensively, find out what standards exist for their use in your organization; if none, make some up and publish and distribute them. The people who should have done it in the first place will be appropriately grateful.

Chapter 16

3D for Me, See?

Three-dimensional (3D) drafting and design capabilities — that is, adding height as well as length and width to your drawing — were once a high-end, extra-cost add-on to AutoCAD. Users who wanted to tackle 3D bought high-end machines and underwent additional training to be able to work in this new environment. Now 3D is part of the base AutoCAD package, But it has not suddenly become fast, easy-to-use, or trouble-free. This chapter offers a gentle introduction to the power and promise of 3D work in AutoCAD.

3D for Me . . .?

The concept of 3D would hardly seem to need introduction. We live in a three-dimensional world, and all the objects you can model in AutoCAD are actually three-dimensional.

But at a basic level, the way in which people see things is actually a two-dimensional (2D) representation of the three-dimensional world. The image that your eyes project onto the inside rear of your eyeballs is, after all, just as two-dimensional as a movie. (It's upside-down too, but that's another problem.)

Your mind uses a number of clues to generate a three-dimensional model from this two-dimensional image. These clues include depth cues from combining left-eye and right-eye images and inferences from the motion of objects, sounds, and previous experience. The mind puts all this together to help us perceive the world in 3D.

Similarly, drafting provides clues to help the mind construct a 3D model from the 2D image on paper. The use of multiple views and the experience of the viewer are probably the two most important clues to making 3D sense of 2D drawings. Design and drafting have succeeded pretty well for a long time by using 2D representations as the guide to creating 3D objects.

So what does using 3D in CAD mean? Basically, it means creating models instead of views. Instead of creating cross-sections of objects, or views of objects from certain perspectives, the designer or draftsperson creates a complete, accurate, 3D model of each object. This description or depiction of each object includes all the necessary information for AutoCAD to create a view from any perspective, without needing additional information for each view. With a 3D model, AutoCAD can even output commands to machines to create actual 3D objects, whether plastic prototypes carved from a tank of jelly by lasers, or an actual bolt, valve, or piston created by numerically controlled machine tools.

Why not 3D?

That sounds good; why not use 3D all the time? For several reasons, and you should take all of the following into account before you decide how much to use 3D on any given project:

- ✔ **2D input.** The mouse, keyboard, and drawing tablet are all 2D devices; they are not really suited for inputting 3D information. The more complex the 3D object you're trying to model, the more unsuitable these input devices are. And manipulating the 3D object with these devices after you've created it is extremely difficult.

- ✔ **2D output.** Almost all the output methods available to you are 2D; paper and the computer screen, output methods that every CAD user has access to, are the best examples. Getting the model right inside the computer is different when no easy way exists to get a 3D representation of that model to hold in your hands, measure, and test for fit with other 3D objects.

- ✔ **Performance.** Today's computers are barely up to the task of storing complex 2D models and rendering them on-screen and on the plotter; if the model is 3D, the difficulty increases geometrically. If you were to render a 2D view of a one-inch cube at 300 dots per inch, for example, you'd have 900,000 dots — just less than a million. Draw that same cube in 3D at 300 dots per inch, and you're up to 270 million dots. Processing the increased amount of information resulting from 3D can slow even the fastest computer to a crawl.

You can partially overcome each of these problems for simple models that use straightforward geometry. But the problems get worse and worse as your models get more and more realistic — and realism is the main reason for going to 3D in the first place. So why bother with 3D at all?

Why 3D?

Using 3D in AutoCAD does have its advantages, however. The following are the three key reasons why anyone in his right mind would bother with 3D:

✔ **Wave of the future.** As CAD pursues greater and greater realism, 3D becomes important in more and more areas. So any CAD user who wants to be competent a few years down the road needs to start becoming familiar with 3D now. But given the current performance problems, familiarity is all most people need at this point; expertise is too costly to develop unless your job, or the next job you want, requires it.

✔ **Sometimes it's nice.** Drawing in 3D is useful for a number of tasks. These include creating shaded renderings to help sell a design to a client, as well as fit-and-finish testing to find potential problems before a design is actually put into construction or manufacturing. These are tasks for which 3D is useful, however, but not strictly necessary; you can accomplish such tasks, although less elegantly, in 2D as well.

✔ **Sometimes it's needed.** Drawing in 3D is required for a small but growing number of tasks. Many mechanical designs are converted into 3D at some point in the design process. Models used for precise, computer-controlled numerical machining equipment or to drive a stereolithography machine (which creates a 3D plastic model by using lasers on a jellylike substance) must be 3D. And the shaded renderings used for both designing and selling are becoming a practical necessity in some fields.

How much work you should put into learning and using 3D depends on your needs. If your job doesn't require 3D, if using 3D is way in your future, or if it's nice to have but not necessary, ignore 3D until you've learned the rest of AutoCAD thoroughly and then start experimenting with it; at that point, you can consider taking a class or doing a small project in 3D. If 3D is required in your field, start experimenting now and consider learning it as a necessary function of AutoCAD.

3D prerequisites

You can do some experimentation with 3D on any computer system that can run AutoCAD. But if you want to pursue serious work in 3D AutoCAD, you should pay attention to the following prerequisites:

✔ **Thorough knowledge of AutoCAD.** You need to know the ins and outs of AutoCAD as a 2D tool thoroughly before doing much with 3D. Three-dimensional work is slow and complicated; if you're making avoidable errors at the 2D level, while at the same time trying to learn and use 3D, you'll never accomplish anything. So become expert in the rest of AutoCAD before making a serious effort in 3D.

✔ **A fast computer.** For serious work with 3D models, you need the fastest computer you can get. What does "fast" mean? A Pentium system that you can upgrade to dual Pentium, running Windows NT with 64MB of RAM and a one gigabyte hard disk would be in the ballpark. If you want to do shaded renderings of your 3D models, the sky's the limit.

✔ **Additional software.** Other, easier-to-use software may meet your 3D needs better than AutoCAD. But if you need the precision and power of AutoCAD for your 3D work, you'll also need other programs — either AutoCAD add-ons or separate packages — to do work that AutoCAD isn't as good at. Illustration packages, for example, can really help jazz up the appearance of your drawing.

✔ **A real project.** Developing the self-discipline and motivation necessary to learn 3D AutoCAD without a real project to motivate you is very difficult. If you don't have an actual work assignment, create a task for yourself. Something as "simple" as creating a 3D model of your living room and its furniture can make the difference between really learning something useful about 3D and just reading about it in the manuals.

Starting with 3D

The best way to get started with 3D is to take an existing 2D drawing that you already have in good shape and extend it into the third dimension. This usually means taking something flat such as a floor plan and extending it straight up into the third dimension. This modification gives you exposure to a number of 3D commands without having to go into all the details; it can also deliver some immediate benefit by helping you get more information out of a drawing you've already done.

Don't let this approach give you a false sense of security, though. To use 3D effectively, you basically must relearn how to enter coordinates, create and manipulate objects, and more. The rest of this chapter skips all that relearning in favor of getting a quick 3D bang for your buck with AutoCAD features most users already know. For a more thorough approach to using 3D with AutoCAD, see the AutoCAD documentation and check out the reliable AutoCAD sources in Chapter 19.

A simple room plan with furniture

To demonstrate 3D, this chapter uses a simple 2D drawing extended into the third dimension— that of the living room mentioned in the preceding section.

Figure 16-1 shows a simple floor plan for a living room. In 3D, you can extrude the walls upward and shade them to help visualize the final appearance of objects created from 2D drawings. You should create a similar drawing or use a 2D drawing you already have as the base for your experiments with 3D.

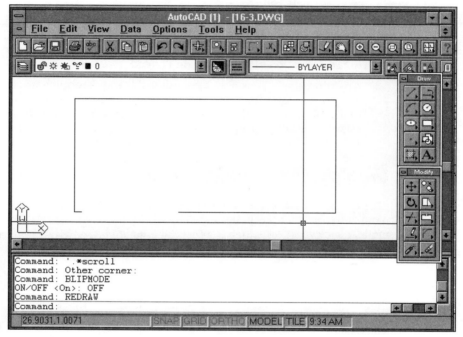

Figure 16-1:
A simple
floor plan
for a living
room.

Cleaning up your drawing

Unnecessary complexity or simple mistakes in your 2D drawing can cost you many minutes of manipulation, redrawing, and rendering time when you take your drawing into the third dimension. Make use of the following suggestions to clean up your drawing before you start:

✔ **Make needed fixes.** You can put off many tasks until late in the process of creating a drawing. You should, however, fix them all before starting to work in 3D. Add necessary text, dimensions, or annotations. Adjust for that quarter-inch discrepancy in the meeting of two walls. Change the layer names to your company's standard set. Generally, finish any task you've been putting off.

✔ **Xrefs and blocks.** This is a good time to implement some of the suggestions from Chapter 15 about subdividing your drawings into blocks and Xrefs. Building a 3D model out of parts is much easier than dealing with an entire scene at once. Consider dividing your drawing into blocks and Xrefs as much as possible.

✔ **Freeze layers.** Freeze any and all layers that contain text, dimensions, and even plumbing and other drawing elements that don't need to show up in the 3D version of your drawing. No sense in taking a performance hit for the regeneration of layers you don't need.

✔ **Anything else?** Think about your drawing and determine whether it has any other loose ends that you can tidy up. Consider creating a drawing that's just a subset of the data that you can experiment on before going to 3D with the entire drawing.

Viewports in model space

Chapter 14 discussed viewports in paper space, which are useful for laying out plots and presentations in both 2D and 3D. A cousin of paper space viewports, model space viewports are less powerful but simpler, and they impose less of a performance hit on AutoCAD.

Unlike paper space viewports, model space viewports divide the screen into separate rectangles with no gap between them, and you can't move or stretch them. You can't plot multiple model space viewports; that's what paper space is for. And a layer that's visible in one model space viewport is visible in all of them.

Model space viewports enable you to see several views of your model at once, each from a different angle. Although the different views subdivide the screen, it can have performance advantages. Shading a single viewport, for example, is much quicker than shading a full-screen image. After you get everything the way you really want it, you can change your drawing back to full-screen and shade the whole thing. Model space viewports are also very helpful when working in 3D. If you have different viewpoints in three or four viewports, creating 3D models is much easier. An object that looks correct in one viewport can be "double-checked" in another viewport for accuracy.

To set up model space viewports, use the VPORTS command. You can start VPORTS from the command line or by choosing View⇨Tiled Viewports from the menu bar. The VPORTS command enables you to create, save, and restore viewport layouts. To use VPORTS, you tell AutoCAD how many viewports to create and then specify the style.

If you specify two viewports, AutoCAD creates the viewports either one on top of each other or next to each other. If you specify four viewports, AutoCAD divides the drawing area into four parts. If you specify three viewports, AutoCAD asks you to specify where you want the largest viewport, and it takes up half the drawing area; you specify which half: above, below, to the left, or to the right. AutoCAD then squeezes the other two viewports into the remaining space.

Watch out; AutoCAD will continue to divide your screen each time you use the VPORTS command. You can have up to 16 viewports at a time on a PC — 32 on UNIX! Of course, they're too small to see anything on them . . . .

AutoCAD inserts a UCS (User Coordinate System) icon into the lower left corner of each viewport — the little X-Y icon you usually see in the same position in the drawing area. This icon helps you know what angle you're viewing the viewport from.

The options for the VPORTS command are as follows:

✔ **Save.** This option saves the current viewport configuration under a specific name.

✔ **Restore.** This option brings back a saved viewport configuration.

✔ **Delete.** This option deletes a named viewport configuration.

✔ **Join.** This option combines two viewports into one new viewport. The new viewport has the same view as the initial viewport from which it was created.

✔ **Single.** This option returns the drawing area to a single viewport with the view of the currently active viewport. Consider using Save to save the current viewport configuration before using Single.

✔ **?.** This option lists named viewports; use this option with Save, Restore, and Delete.

✔ **2.** This option subdivides the screen, or the currently active viewport, into two viewports, either on top of or next to each other.

✔ **3.** This option subdivides the screen, or the currently active viewport, into three viewports: a large one on the left, right, top, or bottom, and two smaller ones that split the remaining space.

✔ **4.** This option subdivides the screen, or the currently active viewport, into four equal viewports.

If you run the VPORTS command while model space viewports are already active, AutoCAD further subdivides the current viewport into more and smaller viewports. You can also join viewports, save a viewport configuration under a name, restore a named configuration, or return to a single viewport. Figure 16-2 shows the top viewport configuration of the 3 option— that is, the three-viewport configuration with the largest viewport in the top position, applied to the living room floor plan.

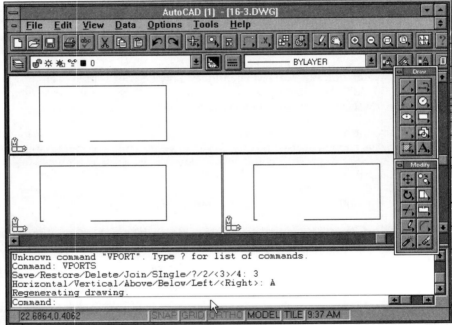

Figure 16-2:
Three viewports of the living room floor plan; this configuration displays the largest viewport in the top position.

Changing the viewpoint in your viewports

Figure 16-2 shows you that AutoCAD initializes all your viewports with the same point of view. You can change the viewpoints of your various viewports so that your viewports all have different points of view — or else, what good are they?

To change the viewpoint in a viewport, type the DDVPORT command at the command prompt and press Enter or choose View⇨3D Viewpoint⇨Rotate from the menu bar to open the Viewpoint Presets dialog box, as shown in Figure 16-3. Unfortunately, this dialog box is one of those things that you must ponder over for a while before it makes sense.

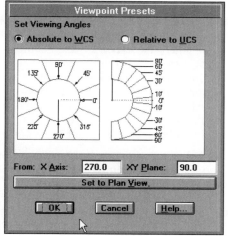

Figure 16-3:
The
Viewpoint
Presets
dialog box.

To help you make sense of the Viewpoint Presets dialog box, review the following description of its parts (the next few paragraphs assume that you have your angular units set to architectural defaults; see Chapter 5 to review angular units):

- ✔ **Set Viewing Angles.** This option tells the dialog box whether to set the viewing angle Absolute to <u>W</u>CS, in relation to the World Coordinate System (WCS), or Relative to <u>U</u>CS, in relation to the current User Coordinate System. If you choose the first option and then change the UCS, nothing happens in the viewport; if you choose the second option and then change the UCS, everything changes. (*Note:* The WCS is the standard XYZ coordinate system, where X is horizontal, Y is vertical, and Z extends out into the third dimension.)

- ✔ **From X <u>A</u>xis.** This text box and the square area above it set the viewing angle relative to the horizontal, or X, axis.

    Changing this angle on a typical house plan, for example, would be similar to strolling around the house to look at the house from different horizontal vantage points. You can set the viewing angle in one of three ways: by entering a value in the text entry box; by clicking one of the numbers at 45-degree increments around the circle, but within the square area; or by clicking a spot on the circumference of the circle. The first and last options enable you to move the viewpoint to any angle you choose; the middle option moves to exact 45-degree increments.

- ✔ **XY <u>P</u>lane.** This text box and the curved area above it set the viewing angle relative to the flat, 2D XY plane — the "floor" of the living room.

Changing this angle on a typical house plan, for example, would be similar to floating from one side of the house, over the center of it, and back down on the other side, taking in different vantage points along the way. You could consider the half circle an arched catwalk over the house that you can climb up on to take in the view. As with the X Axis choice, you can set the viewing angle in one of three ways: by entering a value in the text entry box; by clicking one of the numbers at various increments around the semicircle; or by clicking a spot on the inner circumference of the semi-circle. The first and last options enable you to move the viewpoint to any angle you choose; the middle option moves to exact increments.

✔ **Set to Plan View.** This option resets the X axis and XY plane views to 270 degrees from the X axis and 90 degrees from the XY plane, which is AutoCAD's default, top-down plan view.

By using the Viewpoint Presets dialog box, you can change the viewpoint in a viewport. (Say "viewpoint in a viewport" three times fast and notice the funny looks you get.) This even works on a single 2D viewport.

Figure 16-4 shows the result of setting the viewpoint to 315 degrees from the X axis and 60 degrees from the XY plane. Notice the change to the UCS icon.

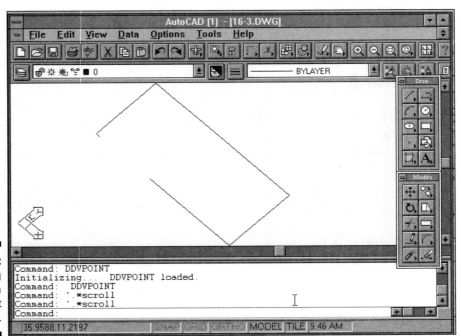

Figure 16-4:
The living
room from a
different
viewpoint.

The results of using the Viewpoint Presets dialog box can be surprising at first. Carefully compare the current settings indicated in the dialog box to the new settings you want to make sure that you're doing the right thing. Accidentally changing the XY plane angle so that you're looking at your plan from underground, for example, is all too easy to do. You may not even notice this until you use a HIDE or SHADE command; get in the habit of checking yourself by using the HIDE command whenever you use 3D objects.

Going to the Third Dimension

AutoCAD doesn't do a good job of handling some conversions of 2D objects to 3D. In fact, the way in which AutoCAD handles these conversions is often counterintuitive. So this section takes some extra steps to try to relate the 2D world to the 3D world as much as possible.

After you have your drawing set up in model space viewports and angled correctly, you can start extending into the third dimension. (You could do that anyway, but this way you can see the result.) This section presents some simple changes to make so that you can add the third dimension to a 2D drawing.

The methods used in this section are very introductory and are not suitable for "true" 3D work, such as that used in presentations, for checking fit between objects, and so on. But these methods, which some call "2.5D" (ha, ha!), are a good start to getting some value out of the 3D capabilities of AutoCAD, short of getting a master's degree in the subject.

Extruding walls

Extruding a wall just means pushing it up into the third dimension. Remember that scene in the movie *Fantasia* where the mountains and volcanoes push up through the earth? That's extrusion.

Unfortunately, extruding doesn't work well on objects that have no enclosed area, such as a typical line. If a line does enclose an area, AutoCAD extrudes the area, not the line. If you were to extrude a floor plan, for example, the extrusion either would not do anything (if the area was not completely enclosed) or it would create a solid block the size and height of the building. Pretty hard to rearrange furniture within a solid block.

So to extrude, you need to start with closed areas such as circles and polylines. This example starts with a simple floor plan made of polylines instead of lines. (AutoCAD used to have a DLINE command that was great for this stuff, but it was dropped in Release 13.)

The process starts by using the VPORTS and DDVPOINT commands to set up a group of model space views that show the drawing in plan view, from ground level, and from an offset view above. Just getting this set up takes a great deal of panning and zooming.

Use the following steps to extrude the walls of the living room plan to a height of eight feet:

1. **Type** EXTRUDE **at the command prompt and press Enter to start the EXTRUDE command.**

2. **Select the objects that you want to extrude by using a bounding or crossing window; in this case, select all the walls.**

3. **Press Enter after you finish selecting objects.**

4. **Type** 8', **for the height of the extrusion and then press Enter.**

   Make sure that you specify feet, not inches.

   You can also specify an extrusion path, but for now just use the default path, which is to extrude at right angles to the plane the object is in.

5. **Press Enter to specify the default (0) as the extrusion taper angle.**

AutoCAD extrudes the walls. Figure 16-5 shows the living room with its walls extruded to a height of eight feet. Notice that the plan view is unchanged, and the ground-level view is incomprehensible; only the offset view from above shows what the room really looks like.

Shading

Shading a figure is a quick way to make the figure's "3D-ness" apparent. Shading has almost none of the complications of rendering, a feature not covered in this book, but it does help make a drawing look solid. (Rendering creates a more realistically shaded image.) The SHADE command obscures hidden lines and then "paints" surfaces. The SHADE command also has a simple lighting scheme that doesn't do much but is simple to use. Notice that you can't print the shaded image, so shading is really useful only for quick on-screen views and presentations.

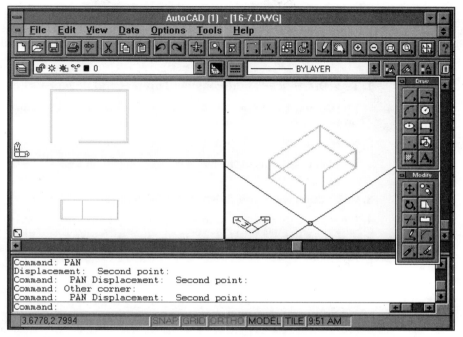

Figure 16-5:
The living
room with
extruded
walls in
multiple
viewports.

Before shading, you may want to adjust the SHADEDGE and SHADEDIF system variables. The SHADEDGE system variable has four values: 0 uses a simple light source, but doesn't highlight the edges of your objects; 1, the most useful setting, uses a simple light source and highlights edges; 2 simply performs a simulated hidden line removal; and 3 doesn't use lighting effects, but does highlight edges. You may want to experiment with all these settings, but 1 is the setting that you'll likely use most.

The SHADEDIF system variable controls the kind of lighting that AutoCAD uses. The higher the value, from the low of 0 up to a high of 100, the "sharper" and more contrasted the light. However, a high value makes the entire drawing appear dark. A value of 50 is a good compromise in many cases.

Unfortunately, the SHADEDGE and SHADEDIF system variables are command-line entries that you must set before you shade, so experimenting with them is a bit of work. The following steps show you how to change the drawing's color, set the shading variables to new values and then shade:

1. **Type DDCHPROP at the command prompt and then press Enter.**

   The Change Properties dialog box opens. This dialog box changes the properties of objects, including object color.

2. **Select the objects you want to change.**

   To select the walls of the living room, you can pick each one or use a crossing or bounding window in any of the model space viewports.

3. **Press Enter after you finish selecting objects.**

4. **Click the Color button in the dialog box to select the color.**

5. **Select the color you want to change the objects to.**

6. **Click OK.**

7. **Click OK to exit the Change Properties dialog box.**

   AutoCAD redraws the objects, such as the walls of the living room, in the color you've selected.

8. **Type SHADEDGE 1 at the command prompt and then press Enter.**

   This command sets the shading to use lighting effects and highlighted edges.

9. **Type SHADEDIF 50 at the command prompt and then press Enter.**

   This command sets an equal balance between ambient and direct light.

10. **Click the viewport you want to shade.**

11. **Type SHADE and then press Enter.**

12. **Repeat Steps 10 and 11 for any other viewports you want to shade.**

Figure 16-6 shows the results of shading all viewports. Notice that shading the ground-level view and the plan view didn't do much good. Shading works best on 3D objects with mass (not wireframe) when seen at an angle.

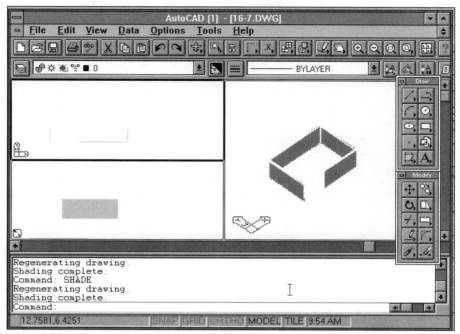

Figure 16-6:
The living
room is
shaded.

More 3D Stuff You Won't Find in This Book

This chapter only touches on what 3D can do — and on what you need to learn
to use it effectively. The tops of the walls in Figure 16-6, for example, are not
shaded. To shade the tops of the walls, you need to use the 3DFACE command
to stretch a "skin" over them. Or you could use the BOX command to create the
walls as solid objects in the first place. And rendering the walls would produce
a much better result than shading — and you could print it, too! But these
topics are worth a book of their own. (And it's not this one, I'm afraid.)

If you want to continue to experiment with 3D, take a course or two and buy
one or more books on the topic. Your reading and training time will be quickly
repaid in fewer mistakes and REDRAW commands—and better results.

Part V
The Part of Tens

The 5th Wave   By Rich Tennant

Larry The Balloon Man, employs a CAD software package in his balloon animal act.

LARRY the BALLOON MAN

In this part...

"Tens" sounds a lot like "tense," and tense is how AutoCAD for DOS and AutoCAD for Windows may make you feel sometimes. But never fear — help is on the way! Checklists are always a big help in getting things right and fixing things that are wrong. And a Top Ten list is a good way to quickly spot the best — or the worst — of almost anything, AutoCAD included. This Part of Tens features several lists — not all of which have exactly ten items (but, hey, who's counting?) — designed to help you get right into AutoCAD, get right out of trouble, and maybe have a chuckle or two in the meantime.

Chapter 17

Ten Keyboard Shortcuts for AutoCAD for Windows

In This Chapter

▶ What are keyboard shortcuts?
▶ More than ten good keyboard shortcuts

One of the best features of the Windows operating system is its keyboard shortcuts for menu entries. Each menu in most programs is coded with an underlined letter that you can use to open that menu. Just press and hold the Alt key, press the menu's shortcut key, and the menu opens. At this point, you can let go of the Alt key if you want. (Really. It won't go away.) Now look at the menu and find the command that you want; that command has a code letter that's underlined, too. Press that letter and — shazzam! — the command executes.

These keyboard shortcuts are especially valuable in AutoCAD for Windows. Opening menus and choosing commands can be very slow and arduous work, especially if you're performing a complicated task. You can even get a sore shoulder or elbow from all the mousing around that AutoCAD requires. Keyboard shortcuts avoid much of this work. Another good thing is that many of these keyboard shortcuts are standards from one Windows-based program to another.

Table 17-1 shows my favorite keyboard shortcuts for AutoCAD for Windows. I strongly suggest that you learn these and then memorize more on your own. Learning these shortcuts eliminates most of the need to use the mouse to select menus — and speeds up your work tremendously.

That little arrow (⇨) that you see connecting the menu commands in the table's third column simply means that you first open the menu listed on the left side of the arrow (open the File menu, for example) and then choose the menu command listed to the right of the arrow (the Save command, for example.)

**Table 17-1   Ten (or So) Useful Keyboard Shortcuts
for AutoCAD for Windows**

Shortcut	Ctrl+Key Equivalent	Menu Items	Action
Alt+F+S	Ctrl+S	File➪Save	Saves the currently open file
Alt+F+P	Ctrl+P	File➪Print	Prints the currently open file
Alt+E+U	Ctrl+Z	Edit➪Undo	Undoes the last action
Alt+E+R		Edit➪Redo	Redoes what you just undid
Alt+E+T	Ctrl+X	Edit➪Cut	Cuts
Alt+E+C	Ctrl+C	Edit➪Copy	Copies
Alt+E+P	Ctrl+V	Edit➪Paste	Pastes
Alt+V+V		View➪Redraw View	Redraws the current view
Alt+V+A		View➪Redraw All	Redraws all views
Alt+D+L		Data➪Layers	Opens the Layer Control dialog box
Alt+D+A		Data➪Drawing Limits	Changes the drawing limits
Alt+O+D		Options➪Drawing Aids	Opens Drawing Aids dialog box
Alt+O+O		Options➪Running Osnap	Opens Running Object Snap dialog box
Alt+T+T		Tools➪Toolbars	Turns toolbars on and off
Alt+T+A		Tools➪Aerial View	Turns Aerial View on and off
Alt+H+S		Help➪Search for Help on	Looks up something in Help

If you remember nothing else from this fluffy ol' Part of Tens, remember that Alt+F+S, or Ctrl+S, saves your file in almost any application. Get used to hitting Alt+F+S or Ctrl+S every few minutes, no matter what else you're doing, until it becomes a habit. Next time you make a big mistake, or a power outage occurs, you'll be glad you learned this shortcut.

Unlike in AutoCAD for DOS, AutoCAD for Windows puts its drawing commands into icons, not into menus. So, unfortunately, you can't use keyboard shortcuts for drawing commands.

In AutoCAD for Windows, you can use either menu shortcuts or Ctrl+key shortcuts for many functions. Use the Ctrl+key shortcuts you already know, but for learning something new, I recommend learning the menu shortcuts. Why? Menu shortcuts get you to almost all the program's functions; they're short and simple; they're similar between programs; and if you forget part or all of the shortcut, you always have the alternative of finding the command in the menus.

Chapter 18

Ten Plusses and Minuses of AutoCAD LT

*W*hat's AutoCAD LT? It's a lower-cost version of AutoCAD that many people call AutoCAD *Light*. AutoCAD LT does most of what AutoCAD does and costs a little more than one-tenth as much.

So why are you and others using AutoCAD Release 13 instead of AutoCAD LT? It's a bit complicated. This chapter shares the plusses and minuses of AutoCAD LT. Read all about it if you're interested. (*Hint:* The plusses are nice, but don't get too excited about them until you see the minuses.)

Plus: AutoCAD LT's Cheap

AutoCAD LT is cheap. Last I heard, its list price was $595 in the U.S., and street prices were as low as $300. That's *much* less than AutoCAD Release 13, which lists for $3,750 for a version containing code for both DOS and Windows. That's not the whole story, however; AutoCAD is often discounted, even to a price of less than $2,500, and most users are upgrading from a previous release and so are paying much less anyway (but still more than a brand-new copy of AutoCAD LT).

Plus: AutoCAD LT's Easy

AutoCAD LT is easier to learn and use than AutoCAD. AutoCAD LT is available only for Windows, so it involves fewer setup and configuration hassles. Some advanced features are missing, so you have less to learn. AutoCAD LT offers no customizability, so the program always looks and works the same, and again, that means less to learn. Compared to AutoCAD Release 12 for either DOS or for Windows, AutoCAD LT is easier by far both to learn and to use.

Plus: AutoCAD LT Opens Any DWG File through Release 12

The whole point of AutoCAD LT is that it's a less expensive program that looks and works like AutoCAD and that can open drawing files from AutoCAD without translating them to and from some other format. This is true up through Release 12, so users, departments, and companies that hold off on moving to Release 13 can transparently share files among AutoCAD users and AutoCAD LT users.

Plus: AutoCAD LT Uses Less Machine Horsepower

AutoCAD LT uses much less hardware power than does either version of regular AutoCAD. AutoCAD LT can run on a machine with only a 386 micropro-cessor, a 387 math coprocessor, and 4MB of RAM. (But I personally think a 486DX with 8MB of RAM is a more appropriate configuration, especially as you're going to want to multitask with other programs for Windows.) You can run AutoCAD LT comfortably on much less of a machine than you can AutoCAD "heavy."

Plus: Autodesk Listens to Users

Before the release of AutoCAD LT, users, dealers, and third-party vendors were starting to wonder whether Autodesk was flexible enough to respond to customer requirements. The need for a program that could do most of what AutoCAD could, with fewer hassles and at less cost, was so obvious that some hoped or feared that a competitor would come into the CAD market and significantly hurt AutoCAD as the market leader. Although the company backed off some on AutoCAD LT's customizability at the last minute, Autodesk basically filled a big hole in its product line by introducing AutoCAD LT and showed skeptics that it could respond effectively to market pressure. The longevity of AutoCAD as a market leader and as a CAD program in which people can comfortably invest their time and money is more secure as a result.

Minus: Missing Features

AutoCAD LT is missing a number of features that are included in AutoCAD, mostly at the high end of the 3D feature set. More important, however, is that AutoCAD LT is missing AutoCAD's huge number of customization options. You are extremely limited in how you can customize AutoCAD LT, and third parties aren't likely to devote much time to what add-ons could be developed for the program either. This lack of customization means that many users who depend on third-party add-ons simply cannot consider AutoCAD LT; this is probably the single biggest reason why AutoCAD LT is not a bigger hit in the marketplace.

Minus: Not the Current Interface

AutoCAD LT is intended to be an easier-to-use version of AutoCAD, but unfortunately, it's lagging well behind AutoCAD in moving to new versions. So when Release 13 for Windows arrived, with its many new ease-of-use features and more consistent interface, AutoCAD LT was no longer the easiest-to-use version of AutoCAD — Release 13 for Windows was. Although AutoCAD LT will probably be brought up to current standards with a Release 13 version of its own before too much time passes, the fact that it currently lags behind AutoCAD in upgrading to new interface features undermines the claim that AutoCAD LT is the easiest-to-use AutoCAD version around.

Minus: Not Current DWG File Format

The single biggest selling point of AutoCAD LT is that it's the only affordable CAD program that has complete access to drawings stored in AutoCAD's famous DWG drawing format. (Other programs must translate back and forth from DWG to other formats, which introduces overhead steps and translation bugs.) But because AutoCAD LT is not updated at the same time as AutoCAD,

AutoCAD LT still uses the file format shared by Releases 11 and 12 and *not* the new file format used by Release 13. So AutoCAD LT users can't share files with Release 13 users, unless the Release 13 user condescends to save the drawing in Release 12 format. This extra hassle undermines the biggest selling point of AutoCAD LT.

As with its user interface, AutoCAD LT will probably be brought up to speed with the new file format soon. But in the meantime, AutoCAD LT users are somewhat out in the cold, and offices with AutoCAD LT users in them may need to wait to upgrade any other workers to Release 13 until the AutoCAD LT users can access the new file format. This just makes AutoCAD LT seem like an impediment to the "power users" running AutoCAD — one that you can remove by the simple, but expensive, expedient of upgrading everyone to Release 13.

Minus: Dealers Got Mad

Dealers became very worried and, in some cases, angry about AutoCAD LT. This pressure was effective in getting Autodesk to remove almost all customizability features from AutoCAD LT just before its release. If third-party vendors had been able to customize AutoCAD LT more, they would have been much more of a threat to AutoCAD. But along with being angry, many dealers recognized that their future profitability — based simply on selling AutoCAD at high prices — was threatened. So the dealers started charging less for AutoCAD, providing less free support, and doing more consulting and software development and less sales work. Life after purchase is a little harder and a little more expensive for AutoCAD users, especially new ones, and Autodesk dealers are perhaps less motivated to develop new markets for AutoCAD than they used to be.

So what does this all have to do with AutoCAD LT? Once burned, twice cautious, as the saying goes, and Autodesk may be very careful in the future about doing anything to further alienate dealers. To the extent that this means doing less to improve and market AutoCAD LT, the product is bound to suffer as a result.

Minus: No More Generic CADD

Another CAD product, called Generic CADD, was once upon a time a growing, vital, low-end competitor to AutoCAD — exactly the kind of threat Autodesk feared. So after years of putting down Generic CADD as not ready for prime time, Autodesk suddenly decided that they liked it so much they bought the company. Generic CADD then became Autodesk's DOS-only, lower-cost alternative to AutoCAD, but it worked so differently from AutoCAD itself that the products didn't really form a product line. After AutoCAD LT came out (and after Generic CADD stopped moving forward quickly with new features), further development of Generic CADD ceased — a sad end to a once-exciting product. Although this doesn't have a direct or immediate effect on AutoCAD LT, the example that Autodesk set by stopping development of Generic CADD, its former low-end product, isn't particularly encouraging to AutoCAD LT users.

The 5th Wave   By Rich Tennant

"WE SHOULD HAVE THIS FIXED IN RELEASE 13."

Chapter 19

Ten Great AutoCAD Resources

*I*f you don't have time to read this entire chapter, I recommend the following resources as the minimum survival kit for an AutoCAD user:

- ✔ **A registered copy of AutoCAD.** AutoCAD may be expensive, but it's worth it; otherwise, it wouldn't have more than a million paid users. (In fact, if you're a professional, and AutoCAD doesn't pay for itself within a year, you're probably not using it right.)

- ✔ **A CompuServe account.** This is the second-best companion to your AutoCAD software, after this book, of course. You'll need a modem and access software, too. And hardly necessary to mention (though I will) is *CompuServe for Dummies*, also available wherever this fine volume is sold. (Do I smell another shameless plug lurking about?)

- ✔ **Subscriptions to *CADENCE* and *CADalyst* magazines.** Get both magazines for a year and then you can cut down to one or the other if you like.

- ✔ **Membership in a local users' group.** The AutoCAD world really is a community, and local users' groups are the town halls. Go to a few meetings of your local users' group at least to get your feet wet and find out whether you like it. (A national organization called NAAUG offers benefits too, as described later in this chapter.)

> ✔ **Your dealer's phone number.** The dealer who sold you AutoCAD is your main contact point for sales and support. Keep your dealer's contact information handy.

A short list of great AutoCAD resources, with contact information, can be found right here in Table 19-1.

Table 19-1	The AutoCAD Resources Short List
Resource	*Contact*
CompuServe	Customer Service, 800-848-8990
Autodesk Global Village	Autodesk's bulletin board system, 415-289-2270
North American AutoCAD User Group (NAAUG)	Send $25 to: Membership NAAUG San Rafael, CA 94912
CADENCE magazine	800-486-4995
CADalyst magazine	800-949-6525
AutoCAD Resource Guide, Local users' groups, Autodesk Training Centers	Autodesk, 415-332-2344 or 800-964-6432

Now here, in no particular order, are ten great AutoCAD resources for you to use.

GO ACAD

This section is brief, hoping that you'll read it and follow its suggestions. CompuServe is the #1 hangout on the Information Highway for AutoCAD users. After you're on CompuServe, GO ACAD is the command you use to get to the AutoCAD forum. You can learn more about how to use AutoCAD here than in any one class or book, except this book, of course. And CompuServe is interactive; if you post a question, whether a detailed technical question or a more general one, you'll likely have an answer within the hour. (Remember when I mentioned in the Introduction those expert users for whom this book wasn't written? Most of them hang out on CompuServe.)

CompuServe also has dozens of data libraries with information about setting up plotters or networks or configuring your system. Most often you can "browse" on a keyword or topic and find several pieces of information available. Then you can read a brief description of the information and decide whether you want to download the whole piece.

Introductory CompuServe memberships are included with many hardware and software purchases, and you can purchase a CompuServe starter kit in many stores. You can also order a kit by calling CompuServe's customer service at 800-848-8990. You can call this number to find out about membership fees, log-in numbers, and more.

I hate to tell anyone who's trying to learn AutoCAD that they need to add to their troubles, and getting on-line is not an easy task if you haven't done it before. You need to set up a modem to your computer's serial port and then run a phone line to the modem. You can then install your access software and connect to CompuServe. (Whew!) But for AutoCAD users, CompuServe is worth it.

 Other on-line services are great for many different things, and some even offer AutoCAD-specific forums. You can also hook up to forums for PC, printer, plotter, and graphics card support, often from the manufacturers themselves, via many such services. Unless you're already on CompuServe and looking for more on-line action, however, forget about it; CompuServe is *the* place for AutoCAD users to be.

The Internet

A great deal of talk these days revolves around the Information Superhighway, and the Internet is usually the main topic of these conversations. Although CompuServe is really where the on-line action is for AutoCAD users, a substantial number of users who won't pay for a CompuServe account *will* post messages on the Internet. CompuServe and other on-line services offer front ends to the Internet, but they charge for the service, so that's kind of beside the point. The best Internet connections (that is, those free of charge) are provided by schools — for their students — and businesses — for their employees. Try to get on the Internet through this kind of connection; you probably know someone at work or school who'd be glad to help you get started. If you can't get a fast, free Internet connection through your school or business however, I recommend that you start with CompuServe and its AutoCAD forums and then branch out to the Internet and elsewhere from there.

Autodesk Global Village

The Autodesk Global Village is both a CD-ROM and a network of local BBSs (computerized bulletin board systems) that put the CD-ROM on-line so that you can download from it. Get your own CD-ROM drive, though, and access both the CD-ROM version of the AutoCAD software and Global Village locally.

The CD-ROM, manufactured by Autodesk, includes AutoLISP programs, sample drawings, a BBS software program, and more. You can even use the CD-ROM to start other small AutoCAD bulletin boards of your own, if you're so inclined.

To get started, have your modem call Autodesk's BBS in Sausalito, California, at 415-289-2270. You can quickly discover what the number is for the Global Village BBS nearest you. The local BBS may offer discussion forums and other features in addition to the Global Village CD-ROM. (Like users' groups, the Global Village is also a good way to make local contacts that can lead to customers for your business and jobs for you.)

AutoCAD Resource Guide

This handy little manual includes an overview of the different AutoCAD versions and supporting computer platforms, third-party add-on applications and their developers, peripheral devices, books and training products, a directory of users' groups, and Autodesk Training Centers (ATCs). The book also contains a CD-ROM version with additional product information, device drivers, and more. To get either the book or the disk, call Autodesk customer information, 800-964-6432.

Local Users' Groups

Local users' groups are the heart and soul of the AutoCAD community. Find out where the one nearest to you meets and go to a few meetings. Call Autodesk at 800-964-6432 to locate the one nearest you, or look in the AutoCAD Resource Guide.

The biggest, most exciting users' group meeting of any sort that I've attended is the South Bay AutoCAD User Group, in San Jose, California. Personally, I am a member of the San Francisco AutoCAD User Group.

NAAUG

No, this isn't what you yell after a basketball hits you in the wrong spot. The North American AutoCAD User Group, or NAAUG, is administered by Autodesk, but it's a real users' group made up of real users, dealers, and other concerned individuals. NAAUG sponsors an annual three-day learning conference (Autodesk University), a newsletter, software, and more. The $25 annual dues include a T-shirt, software, the newsletter, and information about Autodesk University. The address to write to is:

NAAUG Membership
Post Office Box 3394
San Rafael, CA 94912

CADalyst and CADENCE Magazines

Although it's no doubt responsible for the sale of billions of dollars of PC hardware and related software, most of the computer press often ignores AutoCAD. *CADalyst* and *CADENCE* are the leading magazines devoted exclusively to AutoCAD. Both magazines provide tips and tricks, tutorials, technical columns, and hardware and software reviews, all specifically for CAD users. They have very similar circulation figures, heading toward 100,000 each, and somewhat different layouts and editorial focus. Get them both for a year while you're on the AutoCAD learning curve, and then, when renewal time comes, drop the one you like the least.

To subscribe to *CADalyst,* call 800-949-6525. To subscribe to *CADENCE,* call 800-486-4995.

If you'd rather not subscribe yourself, you can often find free copies at AutoCAD Training Centers and dealers. If not, see if you can get your company to pay for a subscription.

AutoCAD Training Centers

AutoCAD Training Centers, or ATCs, are the only authorized deliverers of AutoCAD training. Courses are expensive, so try to figure out the basics on your own and then take courses at the local ATC only to fill in gaps where you need more knowledge. Check the AutoCAD Resource Guide or call Autodesk for the number of the ATC nearest you.

Autodesk

In my experience, Autodesk is much more accessible than most big companies. Their main numbers are 415-332-2344 or 800-964-6432. Call and tell them what you're looking for; you're pretty likely to contact a friendly and helpful reception person who will connect you to another friendly and helpful person who will give you the information you need or tell you where to find it.

The big exception to Autodesk's accessibility is technical support. AutoCAD depends on its dealers to provide technical support, so don't call Autodesk with technical questions.

Your Dealer

The first and foremost line of support for AutoCAD users is the dealer from whom you bought AutoCAD. Dealer support policies and areas of expertise differ, but the dealer is your starting point for AutoCAD support and information.

If you are using AutoCAD within a multiuser, networked setup, though, find out whether someone in your company has been designated as the first line of defense for technical support and other information.

Part VI
Appendixes

"WAIT A MINUTE! THE MONSTER SEEMS CONFUSED, DISORIENTED. I THINK HE'S GONNA PASS OUT! GET THE NETS READY!!"

In this part...

1 n your body, an appendix is something that's unnecessary at best and hazardous to your health at worst. The appendixes in this book, however, are meant to be more helpful — and certainly less harmful — than that other kind. Installation is one of the trickiest parts of using AutoCAD; if you install AutoCAD yourself, you're going to need a few of the tips in you find in Appendix A before you get started. You find, too, as you get into the program that AutoCAD has a vocabulary all its own; the glossary in Appendix B should help you cross the bridge from English to this strange new language. And, of course, as you soon discover, getting your drawing to print at just the right size and scale is tricky; ah, but the tables in Appendix C make setting everything up for optimal printing. . . well, a *snap*.

Appendix A

AutoCAD Installation Survival Tactics

*I*nstalling AutoCAD can be anything from a stroll in the park to one of the biggest disasters ever to befall your computer. Although luck has something to do with how installation turns out, so does preparation.

I don't presume to take over the role of dealers who normally install AutoCAD, nor the voluminous AutoCAD documentation on the subject. But I do offer a few suggestions for making AutoCAD installation easier. Notice that most of the following tips, except the necessity of backing up, apply most strongly to AutoCAD for DOS. AutoCAD for Windows is easy enough that you are less likely to experience problems installing it, and the problems you do encounter are not as likely to be serious.

Buy a New Machine

Whoa! Did he just say *buy a new machine*? This must be some kind of joke, right?

Well, no. First, most of the installation problems that crop up in AutoCAD for DOS (or AutoCAD for Windows, for that matter) involve either memory conflicts or device driver conflicts. With a brand new system, you're somewhat less likely to suffer memory conflicts and *much* less likely to be hanging onto a bunch of old, oddball devices that don't work well with each other anyway and *really* descend into full-fledged armed conflict if installed together with AutoCAD.

Second, many AutoCAD users upgrade frequently to get the most out of their systems anyway. With more AutoCAD users moving to AutoCAD for Windows, and with Windows 95 in the future of many users, a hardware upgrade looms even more likely. Heck, Windows NT, with its prodigious hardware requirements, may even be in your future. Why not just go ahead and upgrade your system while you're getting ready to install AutoCAD? If you do the installation yourself, you're less likely to have problems; if you don't do the installation yourself, a dealer will also have an easier time installing the program on a new computer. (The dealer may also be a hardware reseller who can give you a good price for installation and ongoing support on a hardware/software bundle.)

Finally, the cost issue. Buying a whole new computer system sounds like a Big Deal. But remember, the U.S. list price of AutoCAD is approaching $4,000; that's more than any but the most bulked-up PC. The dozens of hours you can put in trying to install AutoCAD so that it works on old equipment, contrasted to the thousands of hours that you'll spend being more productive with a faster system, make this worth thinking about.

Get a Dealer to Do It

Take it from someone who has recently completely messed up a PC software configuration: Software installation problems are no fun. One of the main functions in the life of an AutoCAD dealer is to install the software for you. A dealer may charge you a bit, but it's probably less than your time is worth. Look at it this way: Installing AutoCAD often means learning a number of software and hardware details that you do not otherwise need to know before installing AutoCAD and will *never* need to know again after installing AutoCAD. Why not leave these problems to an expert?

If you try it yourself and then run into problems during installation, call a dealer before things get too bad. You can all too easily start deleting files to get more disk space or try to reconfigure — and before you know it, you're in a *real* jam. You needn't be embarrassed about requiring help in installing AutoCAD. So don't be afraid to call; the sanity you save may be your own.

Back up Vital Files

If you're the type of person who backs up your system regularly, good for you! Do it again before you install AutoCAD. Now!

But if you're not the type of person to perform a regular system backup — and I'm not, either — I doubt you'll start now. At least back up your key data files before installing AutoCAD. Make a "boot disk" using DOS's SYS command, or use the File Manager in Windows to choose Disk⇨Make System Disk. Also back up CONFIG.SYS and AUTOEXEC.BAT. Back up WIN.INI and SYSTEM.INI if you run Windows. This way, if your computer has a configuration meltdown and you can't use it until you get someone in to straighten out the mess, you'll at least have your key files to take to another system and work on in the meantime. And if you really have problems and end up reformatting your hard disk, at least you'll have something saved to start rebuilding from.

Get It All Together

Most AutoCAD users have pretty complex hardware and software setups, with several add-on devices, a plotter, and one or more third-party applications and utilities for AutoCAD. Add Windows to the mix, and you get an even more explosive brew.

Pick up and install all the latest upgrades and updates to your system before you start the AutoCAD installation. That means checking to see if new drivers are available for your hardware, as well as upgrades to your third-party applications and new versions of your utilities. Get all these pieces together and, if possible, get 'em installed and working before attempting the AutoCAD installation. The odds of quick success will increase greatly if you do.

Build It One Piece at a Time

You can make the process of installing AutoCAD much easier on yourself if you try for a series of small successes instead of going for the big score all at once. Uh, but what does that mean? It means that you start by installing just AutoCAD, with no third-party applications, utilities, or drivers. Make sure that AutoCAD works with a plain VGA monitor and the mouse before installing the drivers for your 24-inch monitor, accelerator card for Windows, and trusty, ten-year-old drawing tablet. Then you can add on the add-on software one piece at a time and test that, too. This way, if you run into a problem, you have a much better chance of being able to identify its source. You also have a much better chance of continuing to get at least some work done until you can figure out how to solve the problem. (And because a new software driver, for example, may take several days to arrive, this is a *big* help.)

One last note on this step-by-step installation: Fixing a working system is much easier than fixing a nonworking one. If a given step in the upgrading process fails — such as using your new plotter — you can diagnose your system, access CompuServe to download a new driver, and so on. If you just throw everything together and flip the switch, and things don't work, recovering can be much harder. A gradual approach is more likely to get the job done fairly quickly than a big rush.

If you already own a working version of AutoCAD and have enough hard disk space, install the new AutoCAD in its own directory and then find out if it works with all your stuff *before* deleting the old AutoCAD.

Take Your Time

Set aside a solid chunk of time to perform an AutoCAD installation or upgrade; half a day is a good starting point. Don't try to install the program if you have a deadline or are otherwise in a hurry. If you do run into a problem, you're more likely to solve it, and less likely to compound it, if you have some time set aside to think things through, call technical support, or do whatever else is needed. Everyone depends on their computers so much these days that you don't want yours to be unusable; so set aside the time to do the job correctly now and avoid problems later.

In the AutoCAD for DOS configuration process, choosing "no system pointing device" is a little too easy if you're not careful. If you're a Microsoft or compatible mouse user, make sure that you choose the Microsoft Mouse option — or you won't have a pointing device.

Glossary of AutoCAD Terms

The definitions that appear in this appendix are mine only; they are informal and describe the term in the way that this book uses it. For more complete and general definitions, see the AutoCAD on-line or printed documentation.

Aerial View: Windows only. The Aerial View is a separate window that displays a separate, Aerial View of your drawing. As you pan and zoom within the Aerial View window, the main drawing area also pans and zooms.

Angle 0 Direction: Specifies the direction that AutoCAD regards as 0 degrees. The Angle 0 Direction is measured relative to the following coordinate system: north is up, south is down, west is left, and east is right. So an Angle 0 Direction of 100 means that the direction slightly south of east is considered 0 degrees in your drawing until you change this setting again.

ANSI: American Standards Institute, a leading standards body.

AutoLISP: A programming language for AutoCAD. AutoLISP is an AutoCAD-specific version of LISP, a computer language used mostly in artificial intelligence programming.

blips: Little marks that show spots you've "picked" on-screen with the cursor. Turn the BLIPMODE system variable ON if you want the screen to show blips, OFF if you want to get rid of them.

bounding rectangle, bounding window: A rectangle surrounding objects. You can select objects with a bounding window, but only objects that are fully enclosed within the window. See also *crossing window*.

CAD: *C*omputer-*A*ided *D*esign. Also known as *CADD*, or *C*omputer *A*ided *D*esign and *D*rafting.

chamfer: A chamfer is a straight line that connects two other lines short of the point where they would otherwise intersect.

command line: A specific area of the AutoCAD screen, usually at the bottom, in which you enter commands and options. Many menu choices in AutoCAD also cause commands to appear on the command line.

command-first editing: Modifying the current drawing by entering a command on the command line and then selecting the objects that the command affects. The opposite of *selection-first editing.* See also *Noun/Verb Selection.*

coordinate entry: Locating a point in the drawing area by entering numbers on the command line that represent the point's cursor coordinates. See also *cursor coordinates.*

crossing window: A selection window that includes objects that are enclosed within it or that cross the window's boundaries. See also *bounding window.*

cursor coordinates: The location of the cursor as represented by its horizontal, or *X,* coordinate and its vertical, or *Y,* coordinate.

dialog box: A set of related options that are displayed on-screen in a rectangular window, or box, for you to specify or change.

DIESEL: DOS only. *D*irect *I*nterpretively *E*valuated *S*tring *E*xpression *L*anguage. A simplified version of AutoLISP for modifying the command line in AutoCAD for DOS. Because this is a simplified language, rumor has it that the original meaning of the first letter in DIESEL was "Dumb." See also *AutoLISP.*

digitizer: A drawing tablet. The name comes from the fact that the tablet converts lines and curves that are entered by drawing into a series of numbers, or digits.

dimension: A set of drawn objects including lines, numbers, and additional symbols and text to indicate the distance between two points.

dimension line: The line that shows the extent of a dimension.

dimension scale factor: The number by which the size of the text in a dimension should be scaled in order to appear correctly in the final printout of a drawing.

dimension text: The text that denotes the length of a dimension.

direct manipulation: Entering or modifying data by using the mouse to move or change an on-screen representation. Dragging a file icon into a trash can icon to discard it, for example, is direct manipulation.

displacement: Fancy word for distance.

display list: A set of directions for displaying the current open drawing and viewport on-screen. The display list is simpler and faster to draw, but less accurate than the underlying database that stores the drawing.

docked: Windows only. A docked toolbar is a toolbar that you can drag to any edge of the screen until its appearance changes. A docked toolbar has no title, and the area around the title has no color, so it takes up less space. See also *toolbar.*

donut: Two concentric circles that you can enter and edit as a single object. (The favorite concentric circle pastry of police officers.)

drawing area: The part of the AutoCAD screen that you can actually draw on. Usually located in the middle of the screen, below the menu bar and toolbars, and above the command line.

end point: A point at which a line or other nonclosed object has only one other point on the object adjacent to it.

extension line: In dimensioning, a line connecting one end of the dimension line to one of the objects that determines the size of the dimension.

fill: Filling is placing a pattern in the interior of an object. A fill is the pattern used in filling. See also *hatch, boundary hatch, associative boundary hatch.*

 floating toolbars: Windows only. Floating toolbars are groups of icons that you can drag around on-screen and that always appear — or float — over the drawing. Each icon represents an AutoCAD command.

floating-point numbers: Numbers that can indicate an extremely wide range of mathematical values. Floating-point numbers take longer to process than integer numbers and may take up more storage space in the computer.

floating-point performance: The speed at which a computer processes floating-point numbers.

 flyout: Windows only. A group of icons that appears, or "flies out," after you click an icon. The flyout expands your choices from one icon to a choice among several icons. The DOS equivalent of a flyout is a secondary menu.

freehand sketch: An object entered as a smooth series of pen strokes. AutoCAD converts it into a polyline made up of relatively short line segments.

geometry: The drawn objects that make up a drawing, not including additional elements such as dimensions and text.

grid interval: The distance between grid points. See also *grid, grid mode.*

grid, grid mode: A grid is a visible array of dots used to indicate distances on-screen. The grid is intended to serve as a kind of flexible graph paper in which the user can at any time redefine the size of the grid.

grip editing: Editing an object by dragging one of the "handles," or grips, that appear on an object after you select it. See also *grips — hot, warm, cold.*

grips — hot, warm, cold: A hot grip is the grip that you can directly manipulate; it appears on-screen in red. A warm grip is any other grip on a currently selected object. A cold grip is a grip on an unselected object.

ISO: International Standards Organization, a leading standards body.

hatch, boundary hatch, associative boundary hatch: A hatch is a pattern placed in the interior of an area enclosed by objects. A boundary hatch is a hatch that is begun by calculating the boundary from among the objects surrounding an empty space. An associative boundary hatch is a hatch that updates automatically if one or more of the objects that make up its boundary is modified.

layer: A group of objects that are associated for purposes of displaying and updating.

leader: A single line that connects a dimension or note to an object.

linetype: The pattern of dashes and dots used to draw a line.

menu bar: The list of menu names displayed across the top of the AutoCAD screen. In AutoCAD for DOS, the menu bar is displayed across the top of the screen only after you move the cursor to the status line at the top of the screen. See also *status line.*

model space: The mode in which most AutoCAD work takes place; where you create and edit objects. See also *paper space.*

multiline: A line that displays and prints as two or more parallel lines; you create and edit a multiline in the same way as a regular line.

Noun/Verb Selection: An option that runs most commands on an existing selection. With Noun/Verb Selection turned off, the commands that you enter ignore any existing selection, and you must select an object after entering the command.

Object Grouping: An option that enables you to place objects into named groups. You can then use the group name for quickly selecting the objects in the group.

object: A single item that you can select and edit separately. In previous versions of AutoCAD, objects were called *entities.*

object snap: Makes certain points on an object act like magnets so that if you click near that point, this action is the same as clicking the point itself.

ortho, ortho mode: A setting that forces lines to be drawn horizontally or vertically only.

pan: Panning is moving the drawing around so that a different part of the drawing appears on-screen in the current viewport.

paper space: A different mode for working with your drawing that enables you to change the view of a drawing, but not what's in the drawing itself. Paper space is best used to create a printout that combines multiple views of the same object. See also *model space.*

pickbox: The little box that appears at the cursor position after you select objects. The size of the pickbox determines what object you can select or snap to.

polygon: What your three-year-old says when your parrot dies. (Groan!) Seriously, any closed shape made up of three or more line segments. Triangles, rectangles, pentagons, hexagons, and other multisided shapes are examples of polygons.

polyline: A single object made up of multiple line or arc segments.

Press and Drag: Specifies that you can create a selection rectangle by pressing the right mouse button at one point, holding the button down while moving the mouse, and then releasing the button at a second point. (Moving the mouse with the button held down is called *dragging.*)

Object: A single item of geometry; part of a drawing that can be selected independently of any other part.

Object properties bar: Windows only. A toolbar that enables you to view and specify object properties, such as layer and linetype, with little or no keyboard entry.

RAM: *R*andom-*A*ccess *M*emory. The memory that your computer can access quickly and use as a "scratch pad" while working. Typical computers sold today have 4MB (MB is for *megabytes,* or million characters) of RAM. AutoCAD Release 13 works best with at least 12MB for AutoCAD for DOS or 16MB for AutoCAD for Windows.

redraw: Clears the screen and redraws the drawing by using the current display list. Redraws can take several seconds to perform on moderately complex drawings. See also *display list.*

regeneration (REGEN): Clears the screen and uses the drawing database to create a new display list and then redraws the drawing with the new display list. A *regen,* as it is referred to, can take from several seconds on simple drawings to many minutes on complex drawings.

SCSI: Small Computer System Interface. Affectionately known as "scuzzy," a method for connecting peripheral devices, such as hard disks and tape drives, to the computer. SCSI is relatively fast and enables several devices to be connected to a single port by plugging each new device into the previously connected one.

selection set: A set, or group, of objects that you have selected.

selection settings: Options that affect how selections are made and treated, such as Press and Drag and Noun/Verb Selection.

selection window: A window used to create a selection. Bounding windows and crossing windows are the types of windows used to create a selection. See also *bounding window* and *crossing window.*

selection-first editing: Editing by first creating a selection and then entering a command that affects the selected objects. Opposite of *command-first editing.*

side-screen menu: A menu of options that appears on-screen, usually in a strip down the right-hand side of the screen.

snap grid: If snap mode is on, the snap grid is the array of points that the cursor snaps to, based on the snap interval.

snap interval: The distance between snap points if snap mode is on.

snap, snap mode: A mode that causes the cursor to be attracted to points on-screen that are a specified distance apart.

spline: A flexible type of curve that has a shape defined by control points.

standard toolbar: Windows only. A toolbar with icons for commonly used functions such as opening a file. Usually found near the top of the screen, between the menu bar and the properties bar.

status bar: Windows only. A "toolbar" that displays information about the current AutoCAD session, such as the current coordinates of the cursor and whether ortho mode is in effect. You can also change some options (such as model space versus paper space) at the status bar. Usually found at the bottom of the screen.

status line: DOS only. A strip across the top of the screen that displays information about the current AutoCAD session, such as the current coordinates of the cursor and the current layer name. The status line appears at the top of the screen unless you move the cursor over it, at which point the menu bar replaces the status line.

system variable: A setting that controls the way that a particular aspect of AutoCAD works. You can change system variables from the command line by using the SETVAR command.

tangent: A line that approaches a circle and touches it at a single point. A tangent point on a circle is the only point at which a line at a specific angle to and direction from the circle can be tangent.

text height: The height of text, in the same units that are currently in effect for the drawing.

third-party application: A program from a vendor other than Autodesk (the manufacturer of AutoCAD) that works with or within AutoCAD.

title bar: Windows only. The strip across the top of the screen that displays the name of the currently active drawing.

title block: An area on a drawing that is set aside for descriptive information about the drawing, such as the company name, drafter's name, and so on.

tool tip: Windows only. A descriptive word or phrase that appears on-screen if you hold the cursor over an icon for a brief period of time.

UCS: User Coordinate System. The current set of coordinates used to describe the location of objects.

UCS icon: The "X-Y" icon that appears in the lower left-hand corner of the drawing area to indicate the angle of the User Coordinate System.

Use Shift to Add: An option that determines what happens if a selection is already made and you click an object. If Use Shift to Add is turned on, you must press and hold the Shift key to add an additional item to the selection set; if this option is turned off, you must hold down the Shift key to remove a currently selected item from the selection.

viewport: A rectangle that displays part of a drawing.

zoom: Zooming is moving the viewpoint closer to or farther from the drawing so that more or less of the drawing appears on-screen.

zoom dynamic: An option of the zoom command that places a zoom window that you can resize on-screen, which enables zoom to be specified interactively and combined with panning.

Appendix C

Paper Size and Scale

● ●

The standard paper sizes are called *A, B, C, D,* and *E.* The measurements of the sizes are described in the following list:

- ✔ *A* = 8½ x 11" (standard letter size in U.S.)
- ✔ *B* = 11 x 17"
- ✔ *C* = 17 x 22"
- ✔ *D* = 22 x 34"
- ✔ *E* = 34 x 44"

Figure **C-1** shows how the various standard paper sizes relate to each other.

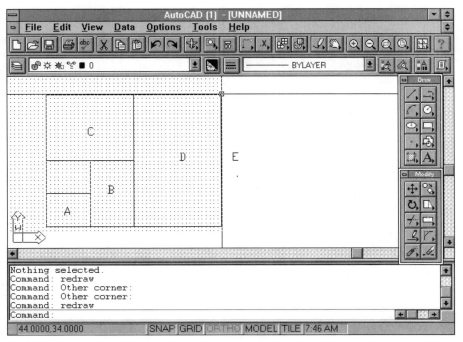

Figure C-1: Relationships between standard paper sizes.

For using the tables in this appendix, or for switching among paper sizes, knowing the relationships between the paper sizes is most worthwhile. Each successive size has its larger dimension double the smaller dimension of the previous size and has twice the total area. To make a small check plot and to maintain the same paper orientation, for landscape or portrait, use a paper size that is half the length and half the width of the final output. Such paper has one-fourth the total area of the larger paper. The paper sizes that maintain the same orientation are as described in the following list:

- ✔ *A* paper is half the length and width of *C* paper.
- ✔ *A* paper is one-fourth the length and width of *E* paper.
- ✔ *B* paper is half the length and width of *D* paper.
- ✔ *C* paper is half the length and width of *E* paper.

You can, for example, perform a check plot with correct proportions and layout for either *C* or *E* paper on plain old letter-sized *A* paper on a standard laser printer. (Your check plot will, of course, lack the color and detail that appears on the full-sized plot.) You can do a check plot for *D* paper on *B* paper; you can also do a check plot for *D* paper on *A* paper, but you must use the opposite orientation — that is, either landscape or portrait. (Just don't do a check plot; take it down to the bank and try to cash it.)

The paper size and the real-world size of the objects you want to represent in your drawing are the determining factors in setting up the parameters for your drawing. Another limitation is the use of certain standard drawing scales. You can't usually pick an unusual drawing scale such as $3/16$" = 1' just because it makes the drawing fit on the paper nicely; you generally must use an even multiple of two in the drawing scale denominator — that is, $1/2$", $1/4$", $1/8$", $1/16$", $1/32$", $1/64$", and so on. (Hope this doesn't become "2" confusing.) After you know the real-world sizes of the objects, the paper size, and the drawing scale, you can choose the limits you want to use.

Of course, in real life, you may have some flexibility in the paper size and drawing scale, depending on what enables you to fit a given set of objects conveniently. So knowing all the possibilities is *very* helpful. That's what the tables in this chapter are for.

The tables show you most of the likely combinations of paper size, drawing scale, and limits that you're likely to want to use. You can review the tables and discover what works for your drawing. Table C-1 is for units in feet and inches; Table C-2 is for any unit of measurement that works by powers of ten.

In addition to columns for paper size, drawing scale, and limits, the tables include columns for grid distance, snap distance, and linetype and dimension scale. These columns can help you set up your drawing so that everything works together. The grid distance and snap distance aren't too important, because you can easily change them as your needs change during the drawing process. But linetype and dimension scale do matter. Getting these settings correct from the start can greatly ease the process of printing a usable drawing. Use the values listed in these tables as a handy guide.

Table C-1 Picking Limits — Architectural Units, Horizontal Orientation

Paper Size	Drawing Scale	Limits	Grid	Snap	Linetype & Dimension Scale
8 ¹/₂ x 11"	¹/₆₄" = 1'	704 x 544'	100'	10'	768
8 ¹/₂ x 11"	¹/₃₂" = 1'	352 x 272'	10'	10'	384
8 ¹/₂ x 11"	¹/₁₆" = 1'	176 x 136'	10'	10'	192
8 ¹/₂ x 11"	¹/₈" = 1'	88 x 68'	10'	10'	96
8 ¹/₂ x 11"	¹/₄" = 1'	44 x 34'	4'	1'	48
8 ¹/₂ x 11"	¹/₂" = 1'	22 x 17'	2'	1'	24
8 ¹/₂ x 11"	1" = 1'	11 x 8 ¹/₂'	1'	6"	12
11 x 17"	¹/₆₄" = 1'	704 x 1088'	100'	100'	768
11 x 17"	¹/₃₂" = 1'	352 x 544'	100'	10'	384
11 x 17"	¹/₁₆" = 1'	176 x 272'	10'	10'	192
11 x 17"	¹/₈" = 1'	88 x 136'	10'	10'	96
11 x 17"	¹/₄" = 1'	44 x 68'	10'	1'	48
11 x 17"	¹/₂" = 1'	22 x 34'	2'	1'	24
11 x 17"	1" = 1'	11 x 17'	1'	6"	12
17 x 22"	¹/₆₄" = 1'	1408 x 1088'	100'	100'	768
17 x 22"	¹/₃₂" = 1'	704 x 544'	100'	10'	384
17 x 22"	¹/₁₆" = 1'	352 x 272'	10'	10'	192
17 x 22"	¹/₈" = 1'	176 x 136'	10'	10'	96
17 x 22"	¹/₄" = 1'	88 x 68'	10'	1'	48
17 x 22"	¹/₂" = 1'	44 x 34'	10'	1'	24
17 x 22"	1" = 1'	22 x 17'	1'	1'	12
22 x 34"	¹/₆₄" = 1'	1408 x 2176'	100'	100'	768
22 x 34"	¹/₃₂" = 1'	704 x 1088'	100'	100'	384
22 x 34"	¹/₁₆" = 1'	352 x 544'	100'	10'	192
22 x 34"	¹/₈" = 1'	176 x 272'	10'	10'	96
22 x 34"	¹/₄" = 1'	88 x 136'	10'	1'	48
22 x 34"	¹/₂" = 1'	44 x 68'	10'	1'	24
22 x 34"	1" = 1'	22 x 34'	1'	1'	12
34 x 44"	¹/₆₄" = 1'	2816 x 4352'	100'	100'	768
34 x 44"	¹/₃₂" = 1'	1408 x 2176'	100'	100'	384
34 x 44"	¹/₁₆" = 1'	704 x 544'	100'	10'	192

(continued)

Table C-1 *(continued)*

Paper Size	Drawing Scale	Limits	Grid	Snap	Linetype & Dimension Scale
34 x 44"	$^1/_8$" = 1'	352 x 272'	10'	10'	96
34 x 44"	$^1/_4$" = 1'	176 x 136'	10'	10'	48
34 x 44"	$^1/_2$" = 1'	88 x 68'	10'	1'	24
34 x 44"	1" = 1'	44 x 34'	10'	1'	12

Table C-2   Picking Limits — Mechanical and Other Units, Horizontal Orientation

Paper Size	Drawing Scale	Limits	Grid	Snap	Linetype & Dimension Scale
8 $^1/_2$ x 11"	$^1/_{1000}$ = 1	11000 x 8500	1000	100	1000
8 $^1/_2$ x 11"	$^1/_{500}$ = 1	5500 x 4250	100	100	500
8 $^1/_2$ x 11"	$^1/_{100}$ = 1	1100 x 850	100	100	100
8 $^1/_2$ x 11"	$^1/_{50}$ = 1	550 x 425	10	10	50
8 $^1/_2$ x 11"	$^1/_{10}$ = 1	110 x 85	10	10	10
8 $^1/_2$ x 11"	$^1/_5$ = 1	55 x 42.5	10	1	5
11 x 17"	$^1/_{1000}$ = 1	17000 x 11000	1000	1000	1000
11 x 17"	$^1/_{500}$ = 1	8500 x 5500	1000	100	500
11 x 17"	$^1/_{100}$ = 1	1700 x 1100	100	100	100
11 x 17"	$^1/_{50}$ = 1	850 x 550	100	10	50
11 x 17"	$^1/_{10}$ = 1	170 x 110	10	10	10
11 x 17"	$^1/_5$ = 1	85 x 55	10	10	5
17 x 22"	$^1/_{1000}$ = 1	22000 x 17000	1000	100	1000
17 x 22"	$^1/_{500}$ = 1	11000 x 8500	1000	100	500
17 x 22"	$^1/_{100}$ = 1	2200 x 1700	100	100	100
17 x 22"	$^1/_{50}$ = 1	1100 x 850	100	10	50
17 x 22"	$^1/_{10}$ = 1	220 x 170	10	10	10
17 x 22"	$^1/_5$ = 1	110 x 85	10	1	5
22 x 34"	$^1/_{1000}$ = 1	34000 x 22000	1000	1000	1000
22 x 34"	$^1/_{500}$ = 1	17000 x 11000	1000	1000	500
22 x 34"	$^1/_{100}$ = 1	3400 x 2200	100	100	100
22 x 34"	$^1/_{50}$ = 1	1700 x 1100	100	10	50
22 x 34"	$^1/_{10}$ = 1	340 x 220	10	10	10
22 x 34"	$^1/_5$ = 1	170 x 110	10	10	5

Paper Size	Drawing Scale	Limits	Grid	Snap	Linetype & Dimension Scale
34 x 44"	$^1/_{1000} = 1$	44000 x 34000	1000	1000	1000
34 x 44"	$^1/_{500} = 1$	22000 x 17000	1000	1000	500
34 x 44"	$^1/_{100} = 1$	4400 x 3400	100	100	100
34 x 44"	$^1/_{50} = 1$	2200 x 1700	100	100	50
34 x 44"	$^1/_{10} = 1$	440 x 340	100	10	10
34 x 44"	$^1/_{5} = 1$	220 x 170	10	10	5

Index

• X •

• Y •

• Z •

Title	Author	ISBN	Price
INTERNET / COMMUNICATIONS / NETWORKING			12/20/94
CompuServe For Dummies™	by Wallace Wang	1-56884-181-7	$19.95 USA/$26.95 Canada
Modems For Dummies™, 2nd Edition	by Tina Rathbone	1-56884-223-6	$19.99 USA/$26.99 Canada
Modems For Dummies™	by Tina Rathbone	1-56884-001-2	$19.95 USA/$26.95 Canada
MORE Internet For Dummies™	by John R. Levine & Margaret Levine Young	1-56884-164-7	$19.95 USA/$26.95 Canada
NetWare For Dummies™	by Ed Tittel & Deni Connor	1-56884-003-9	$19.95 USA/$26.95 Canada
Networking For Dummies™	by Doug Lowe	1-56884-079-9	$19.95 USA/$26.95 Canada
ProComm Plus 2 For Windows For Dummies™	by Wallace Wang	1-56884-219-8	$19.99 USA/$26.99 Canada
The Internet For Dummies™, 2nd Edition	by John R. Levine & Carol Baroudi	1-56884-222-8	$19.99 USA/$26.99 Canada
The Internet For Macs For Dummies™	by Charles Seiter	1-56884-184-1	$19.95 USA/$26.95 Canada
MACINTOSH			
Macs For Dummies®	by David Pogue	1-56884-173-6	$19.95 USA/$26.95 Canada
Macintosh System 7.5 For Dummies™	by Bob LeVitus	1-56884-197-3	$19.95 USA/$26.95 Canada
MORE Macs For Dummies™	by David Pogue	1-56884-087-X	$19.95 USA/$26.95 Canada
PageMaker 5 For Macs For Dummies™	by Galen Gruman	1-56884-178-7	$19.95 USA/$26.95 Canada
QuarkXPress 3.3 For Dummies™	by Galen Gruman & Barbara Assadi	1-56884-217-1	$19.99 USA/$26.99 Canada
Upgrading and Fixing Macs For Dummies™	by Kearney Rietmann & Frank Higgins	1-56884-189-2	$19.95 USA/$26.95 Canada
MULTIMEDIA			
Multimedia & CD-ROMs For Dummies™, Interactive Multimedia Value Pack	by Andy Rathbone	1-56884-225-2	$29.95 USA/$39.95 Canada
Multimedia & CD-ROMs For Dummies™	by Andy Rathbone	1-56884-089-6	$19.95 USA/$26.95 Canada
OPERATING SYSTEMS / DOS			
MORE DOS For Dummies™	by Dan Gookin	1-56884-046-2	$19.95 USA/$26.95 Canada
S.O.S. For DOS™	by Katherine Murray	1-56884-043-8	$12.95 USA/$16.95 Canada
OS/2 For Dummies™	by Andy Rathbone	1-878058-76-2	$19.95 USA/$26.95 Canada
UNIX			
UNIX For Dummies™	by John R. Levine & Margaret Levine Young	1-878058-58-4	$19.95 USA/$26.95 Canada
WINDOWS			
S.O.S. For Windows™	by Katherine Murray	1-56884-045-4	$12.95 USA/$16.95 Canada
MORE Windows 3.1 For Dummies™, 3rd Edition	by Andy Rathbone	1-56884-240-6	$19.99 USA/$26.99 Canada
PCs / HARDWARE			
Illustrated Computer Dictionary For Dummies™	by Dan Gookin, Wally Wang, & Chris Van Buren	1-56884-004-7	$12.95 USA/$16.95 Canada
Upgrading and Fixing PCs For Dummies™	by Andy Rathbone	1-56884-002-0	$19.95 USA/$26.95 Canada
PRESENTATION / AUTOCAD			
AutoCAD For Dummies™	by Bud Smith	1-56884-191-4	$19.95 USA/$26.95 Canada
PowerPoint 4 For Windows For Dummies™	by Doug Lowe	1-56884-161-2	$16.95 USA/$22.95 Canada
PROGRAMMING			
Borland C++ For Dummies™	by Michael Hyman	1-56884-162-0	$19.95 USA/$26.95 Canada
"Borland's New Language Product" For Dummies™	by Neil Rubenking	1-56884-200-7	$19.95 USA/$26.95 Canada
C For Dummies™	by Dan Gookin	1-878058-78-9	$19.95 USA/$26.95 Canada
C++ For Dummies™	by Stephen R. Davis	1-56884-163-9	$19.95 USA/$26.95 Canada
Mac Programming For Dummies™	by Dan Parks Sydow	1-56884-173-6	$19.95 USA/$26.95 Canada
QBasic Programming For Dummies™	by Douglas Hergert	1-56884-093-4	$19.95 USA/$26.95 Canada
Visual Basic "X" For Dummies™, 2nd Edition	by Wallace Wang	1-56884-230-9	$19.99 USA/$26.99 Canada
Visual Basic 3 For Dummies™	by Wallace Wang	1-56884-076-4	$19.95 USA/$26.95 Canada
SPREADSHEET			
1-2-3 For Dummies™	by Greg Harvey	1-878058-60-6	$16.95 USA/$21.95 Canada
1-2-3 For Windows 5 For Dummies™, 2nd Edition	by John Walkenbach	1-56884-216-3	$16.95 USA/$21.95 Canada
1-2-3 For Windows For Dummies™	by John Walkenbach	1-56884-052-7	$16.95 USA/$21.95 Canada
Excel 5 For Macs For Dummies™	by Greg Harvey	1-56884-186-8	$19.95 USA/$26.95 Canada
Excel For Dummies™, 2nd Edition	by Greg Harvey	1-56884-050-0	$16.95 USA/$21.95 Canada
MORE Excel 5 For Windows For Dummies™	by Greg Harvey	1-56884-207-4	$19.95 USA/$26.95 Canada
Quattro Pro 6 For Windows For Dummies™	by John Walkenbach	1-56884-174-4	$19.95 USA/$26.95 Canada
Quattro Pro For DOS For Dummies™	by John Walkenbach	1-56884-023-3	$16.95 USA/$21.95 Canada
UTILITIES / VCRs & CAMCORDERS			
Norton Utilities 8 For Dummies™	by Beth Slick	1-56884-166-3	$19.95 USA/$26.95 Canada
VCRs & Camcorders For Dummies™	by Andy Rathbone & Gordon McComb	1-56884-229-5	$14.99 USA/$20.99 Canada
WORD PROCESSING			
Ami Pro For Dummies™	by Jim Meade	1-56884-049-7	$19.95 USA/$26.95 Canada
MORE Word For Windows 6 For Dummies™	by Doug Lowe	1-56884-165-5	$19.95 USA/$26.95 Canada
MORE WordPerfect 6 For Windows For Dummies™	by Margaret Levine Young & David C. Kay	1-56884-206-6	$19.95 USA/$26.95 Canada
MORE WordPerfect 6 For DOS For Dummies™	by Wallace Wang, edited by Dan Gookin	1-56884-047-0	$19.95 USA/$26.95 Canada
S.O.S. For WordPerfect™	by Katherine Murray	1-56884-053-5	$12.95 USA/$16.95 Canada
Word 6 For Macs For Dummies™	by Dan Gookin	1-56884-190-6	$19.95 USA/$26.95 Canada
Word For Windows 6 For Dummies™	by Dan Gookin	1-56884-075-6	$16.95 USA/$21.95 Canada
Word For Windows For Dummies™	by Dan Gookin	1-878058-86-X	$16.95 USA/$21.95 Canada
WordPerfect 6 For Dummies™	by Dan Gookin	1-878058-77-0	$16.95 USA/$21.95 Canada
WordPerfect For Dummies™	by Dan Gookin	1-878058-52-5	$16.95 USA/$21.95 Canada
WordPerfect For Windows For Dummies™	by Margaret Levine Young & David C. Kay	1-56884-032-2	$16.95 USA/$21.95 Canada

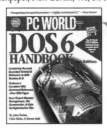

IDG BOOKS

Order Center: **(800) 762-2974** *(8 a.m.–6 p.m., EST, weekdays)*

1 11/94

Quantity	ISBN	Title	Price	Total

Shipping & Handling Charges

	Description	First book	Each additional book	Total
Domestic	Normal	$4.50	$1.50	$
	Two Day Air	$8.50	$2.50	$
	Overnight	$18.00	$3.00	$
International	Surface	$8.00	$8.00	$
	Airmail	$16.00	$16.00	$
	DHL Air	$17.00	$17.00	$

*For large quantities call for shipping & handling charges.
**Prices are subject to change without notice.

Ship to:

Name _____

Company _____

Address _____

City/State/Zip _____

Daytime Phone _____

Payment: ☐ Check to IDG Books (US Funds Only)

    ☐ VISA   ☐ MasterCard   ☐ American Express

Card # _____ Expires _____

Signature _____

Subtotal _____

CA residents add
applicable sales tax _____

IN, MA, and MD
residents add
5% sales tax _____

IL residents add
6.25% sales tax _____

RI residents add
7% sales tax _____

TX residents add
8.25% sales tax _____

Shipping _____

Total _____

Please send this order form to:

IDG Books Worldwide
7260 Shadeland Station, Suite 100
Indianapolis, IN 46256

Allow up to 3 weeks for delivery.
Thank you!

IDG BOOKS WORLDWIDE REGISTRATION CARD

RETURN THIS REGISTRATION CARD FOR FREE CATALOG

Title of this book: AutoCAD For Dummies

My overall rating of this book: ❑ Very good [1] ❑ Good [2] ❑ Satisfactory [3] ❑ Fair [4] ❑ Poor [5]

How I first heard about this book:

❑ Found in bookstore; name: [6] _____

❑ Advertisement: [8]

❑ Word of mouth; heard about book from friend, co-worker, etc.: [10]

❑ Book review: [7]

❑ Catalog: [9]

❑ Other: [11]

What I liked most about this book:

_____

_____

What I would change, add, delete, etc., in future editions of this book:

_____

_____

Other comments:

_____

Number of computer books I purchase in a year: ❑ 1 [12] ❑ 2-5 [13] ❑ 6-10 [14] ❑ More than 10 [15]

I would characterize my computer skills as: ❑ Beginner [16] ❑ Intermediate [17] ❑ Advanced [18] ❑ Professional [19]

I use ❑ DOS [20] ❑ Windows [21] ❑ OS/2 [22] ❑ Unix [23] ❑ Macintosh [24] ❑ Other: [25] _____

(please specify)

I would be interested in new books on the following subjects:

(please check all that apply, and use the spaces provided to identify specific software)

❑ Word processing: [26] _____

❑ Data bases: [28] _____

❑ File Utilities: [30] _____

❑ Networking: [32] _____

❑ Other: [34]

❑ Spreadsheets: [27] _____

❑ Desktop publishing: [29] _____

❑ Money management: [31] _____

❑ Programming languages: [33] _____

I use a PC at (please check all that apply): ❑ home [35] ❑ work [36] ❑ school [37] ❑ other: [38] _____

The disks I prefer to use are ❑ 5.25 [39] ❑ 3.5 [40] ❑ other: [41] _____

I have a CD ROM: ❑ yes [42] ❑ no [43]

I plan to buy or upgrade computer hardware this year: ❑ yes [44] ❑ no [45]

I plan to buy or upgrade computer software this year: ❑ yes [46] ❑ no [47]

Name: _____ Business title: [48] _____ Type of Business: [49] _____

Address (❑ home [50] ❑ work [51]/Company name: _____)

Street/Suite# _____

City [52]/State [53]/Zipcode [54]: _____ Country [55] _____

❑ **I liked this book!** You may quote me by name in future IDG Books Worldwide promotional materials.

My daytime phone number is _____

IDG BOOKS

THE WORLD OF COMPUTER KNOWLEDGE

❏ **YES!**

Please keep me informed about IDG's World of Computer Knowledge.
Send me the latest IDG Books catalog.

BUSINESS REPLY MAIL
FIRST CLASS MAIL   PERMIT NO. 2605   SAN MATEO, CALIFORNIA

IDG Books Worldwide
155 Bovet Road
San Mateo, CA 94402-9833